The Rise of the Right to Know

§552. Public information: agency rules, opinions, orders, records, and proceedings (a) Each agency shall make available to the public information as follows: (1) Each agency shall separately state and currently publish in the Federal Register for the guidance of the public — (A) descriptions of its central and field organization and the established places at which, the employees (and in the case of a uniformed service, the members) from whom, and the methods whereby, the public may obtain information, make submittals or requests, or obtain decisions; (B) statements of the general course and method by which its functions are channeled and determined, including the nature and requirements of all formal and informal procedures available; (C) rules of procedure, descriptions of forms available or the places at which forms may be obtained, and instructions as to the scope and contents of all papers, reports, or examinations; (D) substantive rules of general applicability adopted as authorized by law, and statements of general policy or interpretations of general applicability formulated and adopted by the agency; and (E) each amendment, revision, or repeal of the foregoing. Except to the extent that a person has actual and timely notice of the terms thereof, a person may not in any manner be required to resort to, or be adversely affected by, a matter required to be published in the Federal Register and not so published. For the purpose of this paragraph, matter reasonably available to the class of persons affected thereby is deemed published in the Federal Register when incorporated by reference therein with the approval of the Director of the Federal Register. (2) Each agency, in accordance with published rules, shall make available for public inspection and copying — (A) final opinions, including concurring and dissenting opinions, as well as orders, made in the adjudication of cases; (B) those statements of policy and interpretations which have been adopted by the agency and are not published in the Federal Register; and (C) administrative staff manuals and instructions to staff that affect a member of the public; unless the materials are promptly published and copies offered for sale. For records created on or after November 1, 1996, within one year after such date, each agency shall make such records available, including by computer telecommunications or, if computer telecommunications means have not been established by the agency, by other electronic means. To the extent required to prevent a clearly unwarranted invasion of personal privacy, an agency may delete identifying details when it makes available or publishes an opinion, statement of policy, interpretation, staff manual, instruction, or staff referred to in subparagraph (D). However, in each case the justification for the deletion shall be explained fully in writing, and the extent of such deletion shall be indicated on the portion of the record which is made available or published, unless including that indication would harm an interest protected by the exemption in subsection (b) under which the deletion is made. If technically feasible, the extent of the deletion shall be indicated at the place in the record where the deletion was made. Each agency shall also maintain and make available for public inspection and copying current indexes providing identifying information for the public as to any matter issued, adopted, or promulgated after July 4, 1967, and required by this paragraph to be made available or published. Each agency shall promptly publish, quarterly or more frequently, and distribute (by sale or otherwise) copies of each index or supplements thereto unless it determines by order published in the Federal Register that the publication would be unnecessary and impracticable, in which case the agency shall nonetheless provide copies of an index on request at a cost not to exceed the direct cost of duplication. Each agency shall make available to the public, in subparagraph (E) available by computer telecommunications by December 31, 1999. A final order, opinion, statement of policy, interpretation, or staff manual or instruction that affects a member of the public may be relied on, used, or cited as precedent by an agency against a party other than an agency only if — (i) it has been indexed and either made available or published as provided by this paragraph; or (ii) the party has actual and timely notice of the terms thereof. (3)(A) Except with respect to the records made available under paragraphs (1) and (2) of this subsection, each agency, upon request for records which (A) (i) reasonably describes such records and (B) is made in accordance with published rules stating the time, place, fees (if any), and procedures to be followed, shall make the records promptly available to any person. (B) In making any record available to a person under this paragraph, an agency shall provide the record in any form or format requested by the person if the record is readily reproducible by the agency in that form or format. Each agency shall make reasonable efforts to maintain its records in forms or formats that are reproducible for purposes of this section. (C) In responding under this paragraph to a request for records, an agency shall make reasonable efforts to search for the records in electronic form or format, except when such efforts would significantly interfere with the operation of the agency's automated information system. For purposes of this paragraph, the term "search" means to review, manually or by automated means, agency records for the purpose of locating those records which are responsive to a request. (4)(A)(i) In order to carry out the provisions of this section, each agency shall promulgate regulations, pursuant to notice and receipt of public comment, specifying the schedule of fees applicable to the processing of requests under this section and establishing procedures and guidelines for determining when such fees should be waived or reduced. Such schedule shall conform to the guidelines which shall be promulgated, pursuant to notice and receipt of public comment, by the Director of the Office of Management and Budget and which shall provide for a uniform schedule of fees for all agencies. (ii) Such agency regulations shall provide that — (I) fees shall be limited to reasonable standard charges for document search, duplication, and review, when records are requested for commercial use; (II) fees shall be limited to reasonable standard charges for document duplication when records are not sought for commercial use and the request is made by an educational or noncommercial scientific institution, whose purpose is scholarly or scientific research; or a representative of the news media; and (III) for any request not described in (I) or (II), fees shall be limited to reasonable standard charges for document search and duplication. (iii) Documents shall be furnished without any charge or at a reduced charge below the fees established under clause (ii) if disclosure of the information is in the public interest because it is likely to contribute significantly to public understanding of the operations or activities of the government and is not primarily in the commercial interest of the requester. (iv) Fee schedules shall provide for the recovery of only the direct costs of search, duplication, or review. Review costs shall include only the direct costs incurred during the initial examination of a document for the purposes of determining whether the documents must be disclosed under this section and for the purposes of withholding any portions exempt from disclosure under this section. Review costs may not include any costs incurred in resolving issues of law or policy that may be raised in the course of processing a request under this section. No fee may be charged by any agency under this section — (I) if the costs of routine collection and processing of the fee are likely to equal or exceed the amount of the fee; or (II) for any request described in clause (ii)(II) or (III) of this subparagraph for the first two hours of search time or for the first one hundred pages of duplication. (v) No agency may require advance payment of any fee unless the requester has previously failed to pay fees in a timely fashion, or the agency has determined that the fee will exceed $250. (vi) Nothing in this subparagraph shall supersede fees chargeable under a statute specifically providing for setting the level of fees for particular types of records. (vii) In any action by a requester regarding the waiver of fees under this section, the court shall determine the matter de novo, provided that the court's review of the matter shall be limited to the record before the agency. (B) On complaint, the district court of the United States in the district in which the complainant resides, or has his principal place of business, or in which the agency records are situated, or in the District of Columbia, has jurisdiction to enjoin the agency from withholding agency records and to order the production of any agency records improperly withheld from the complainant. In such a case the court shall determine the matter de novo, and may examine the contents of such agency records in camera to determine whether such records or any part thereof shall be withheld under any of the exemptions set forth in subsection (b) of this section, and the burden is on the agency to sustain its action. In making such determination, the court shall accord substantial weight, and shall accord substantial weight to an affidavit of an agency concerning the agency's determination as to technical feasibility under paragraph (2) (C) and subsection (b) and reproducibility under paragraph (3)(B). Notwithstanding any other provision of law, the defendant shall serve an answer or otherwise plead to any complaint made under this subsection within thirty days after service upon the defendant of the pleading in which such complaint is made, unless the court directs otherwise for good cause shown. [(D) Except as to cases the court considers of greater importance, proceedings before the district court, as authorized by this subsection, and appeals therefrom, take precedence on the docket over all cases and shall be assigned for hearing and trial or for argument at the earliest practicable date and expedited in every way. Repealed by Pub. L. 98-620, Title IV, 402(2), Nov. 8, 1984, 98 Stat. 3335, 3357.] (E) The court may assess against the United States reasonable attorney fees and other litigation costs reasonably incurred in any case under this section in which the complainant has

Rise of the Right to Know

Politics and the Culture of Transparency, 1945–1975

MICHAEL SCHUDSON

The Belknap Press
of Harvard University Press

Cambridge, Massachusetts
London, England
2015

Library of Congress Cataloging-in-Publication Data

Schudson, Michael.

The rise of the right to know : politics and the culture of transparency, 1945–1975 / Michael Schudson.

pages cm

Includes bibliographical references and index.

ISBN 978-0-674-74405-9 (hardcover : alk. paper)   1. Freedom of information—United States—History—20th century.   2. Transparency in government—United States—History—20th century.   3. Consumer protection—United States—History—20th century.   4. Environmental impact statements—United States—History—20th century.   I. Title.

KF4774.S339 2015

342.73'066209045—dc23

2015007935

For Charlie and Karen

Contents

The Rise of the Right to Know

one

A Cultural Right to Know

Thomas Jefferson once wrote that "information is the currency of democracy," or so it is easy to learn online. Fortunately, it is just as easy to learn that he wrote no such thing. The people who run the website for Jefferson's home at Monticello cannot find that quotation anywhere in Jefferson's papers. And there is really no need to spend time searching.[1] The American founders rarely spoke of democracy, and they labeled the American form of government not "democratic" but "republican." They judged democracy to be unstable and undesirable. So we can feel confident that Jefferson never uttered nor wrote these words.

Not Thomas Jefferson but Ralph Nader declared information the currency of democracy.[2] Information and its availability to the public at large became a theme for a wide variety of reforms and reformers in just the years that Nader came to national influence in the mid-1960s and into the 1970s.

Nader might well agree—Jefferson surely would not have—with this assertion by two distinguished historians: "It is a tenet of democracy that citizens should have full access to information so they can make informed decisions about policies that affect their lives."[3] This may seem an unremarkable claim. And yet it is not self-evident. Is it even coherent? What could "full access" possibly mean? Presumably a citizen who is being watched by undercover police officers, operating according to the law, should not be informed of the surveillance—in the interest of public safety. And the public should not have access to personnel records of government employees without good cause—in the interest of personal privacy. Nor should genuine national security information be publicly available. Activists who support transparency in government do not generally advocate *complete* transparency in *all* facets of government. Most democrats accept many limitations to "full access to information"; in the United States, many of these limitations are long established and well institutionalized, including in explicit clauses of the pioneering Freedom of Information Act itself, whose origins in the 1950s are the focus of Chapter 2.

Earlier in North American history, there were many conditions under which subjects, later citizens, did not have full access to relevant information. It troubled the government of Virginia in 1682 that an upstart printed the laws of the colony without a license. He was punished, since printing was forbidden in Virginia until 1729, and from that point until 1765 the only printing press in Virginia was controlled by the governor.[4] In the Commonwealth of Massachusetts, which was a representative democracy (in today's terms) at least with respect to its legislative assembly (though not with respect to its governor, who was answerable only to the king), legislative proceedings were confidential, even including how one's representative voted on particular measures. It is hard to imagine a matter more central to the "tenets of democracy" than the availability to voters of a public record of the votes of their representatives, but apparently this was not something the people of Massachusetts in the 1700s demanded. Nor, as Chapter 4 will show, did the people of the United States demand it until 1970. Only then did the U.S. House of Representatives make members' votes on amendments to bills part of the public record. Only then did a reform coalition in the House sponsor a set of "anti-secrecy" measures that ushered in a major increase in the public visibility of legislative action.

Somehow we have collectively backdated ideas and innovations of the past half century to the country's founding era. I hope to help set this record right.

What I will ponder in this book is not why forms of secrecy endured so long but why they changed when they did. How did information disclosure or transparency come to be identified with self-government, "being informed" with good citizenship, and openness with both public and private virtue? This is not to suggest that Americans today have full access to government information, or that they should, but only to note that there are now laws on the books, practices in executive agencies, a culture in newsrooms, a presupposition in many nonprofit watchdog organizations, and public expectations that give body to an ideal that honesty is (usually) the best policy and that the people have or should have a right to know.

In a rich essay on the cultural changes of the 1960s as a religious "awakening" akin to earlier moments of religious revitalization in U.S. history, Hugh Heclo summarizes his argument as follows: "The Awakening of the Sixties was transformative, for better or worse. It created an unprecedented openness of institutions to critical public view and correction. It established a presumption for an inclusive social union of equals beyond anything ever attempted by a nation-state. It nationalized policy-making on issues touching virtually every aspect of one's daily life. It drove a fundamental pluralism into the very heart of America's understanding of itself."[5]

Most historians would readily agree that the 1960s were a cultural and political watershed, but to focus on openness as one of its key features—in fact, the first characteristic Heclo mentions—is unusual. It is also unusual, amid a general celebration of transparency, particularly concerning government information, to discuss it with the ambivalence of Heclo's "for better or worse" remark. Transparency today seems to be a motherhood-and-apple-pie value. It often links supporters from the left with the libertarian right, and sometimes with moderate and conservative Republicans, too. Various nongovernmental organizations march behind the banner of transparency. Taxpayers for Common Sense (founded 1995) has compiled the most comprehensive database on congressional earmarking; the group's data—publicly available—serve as a starting point for Washington reporters who cover the earmarks.[6] This organization's agenda of keeping a close watch on government spending is usually associated with conservatives, but the group insists on its nonpartisanship and on its commitment to transparency as a fundamental democratic value. Similarly, the Sunlight Foundation (founded in 2006) also provides publicly available databases, but these are focused on the dangers of money influencing and corrupting the legislative process, a theme usually sounded by liberals. For instance, Sunlight teamed up with ProPublica, a leading investigative journalism nonprofit, to create a downloadable database of federal filings for registered foreign lobbyists.

Right, left, and center, there is broad support for the ideal of transparency. At the same time, there are limits to the value of openness. Full transparency in government, in professional-client relations, and in personal life can do great harm. It threatens privacy. It threatens relations of intimacy that invariably are built on closely held confidences. In government or other decision-making groups it inhibits honest conversation. It may expose vulnerable individuals or groups to intimidation by powerful and potentially malevolent authorities.

My mission in this book is not to show that disclosure is good or bad, nor is it to explore what conditions might make secrecy, not transparency, the morally better choice. My aim is to show that openness was a key element in the transformation of politics, society, and culture from the late 1950s through the 1970s. I want to bring this topic close to the center of how we understand the social and political transformations of that era. I believe this is important because I think that American politics and society in this era became more fully democratic than they were before, and that for all the hazards and shortcomings of transparency, its expansion has made our politics more worthy of the name "democracy."

To suggest that openness advanced between 1960 and 1980 is not to say that it originated then. The phrase "right to know," for instance, has been traced to James Wilson, arguing at the Constitutional Convention that the House and the Senate should keep a record of their proceedings. "The people have a right to know what their agents are doing or have done, and it should not be the option of the legislature to conceal their proceedings," he held.[7] Wilson was successful in supporting what became part of Article I, Section 5 of the Constitution: "Each House shall keep a Journal of its Proceedings, and from time to time publish the same, excepting such Parts as may in their Judgment require Secrecy; and the Yeas and Nays of the Members of either House on any question shall, at the Desire of one fifth of those Present, be entered on the Journal."

What, one wonders, did the authors of the Constitution mean by enjoining Congress to publish its journals "from time to time"? They did not say. But we can make a reasonable guess. When the Virginia convention on ratifying the Constitution met in June 1788, it proposed that the Senate and House journals be "published at least once in every Year except such parts thereof relating to Treaties Alliances or Military Operations as in their Judgment require Secrecy."[8] This is much more limited than Wilson's rhetoric might suggest—and, Article I, Section 5 notwithstanding, the Senate proceeded in full secrecy for its first six years. Moreover, what in practice "journals" came to mean was the publication of laws and resolutions enacted and votes taken—but not debates. The *Annals of Congress,* a publication that covers the years 1789 to 1824 and includes debates in the House and Senate, is a set of volumes put together between 1834 and 1856 based primarily on newspaper reports.

At the Virginia ratification convention, even the most outspoken advocates of free inquiry and a free press recognized limits to what the governors should share with the public. Patrick Henry acknowledged that government business concerning military operations "or affairs of great consequence, the immediate promulgation of which might defeat the interests of the community," could legitimately be kept secret. George Mason, who like Patrick Henry was among the most ardent advocates of open government, likewise acknowledged that military operations and diplomatic negotiations sometimes required secrecy. Legal historian David M. O'Brien comments: "Hence, even the two most vociferous advocates of the public's right to know did not entertain the notion that the public's interest in access to governmental information was unconditional or unqualified. Notably there was no claim that individuals have a directly enforceable constitutional right to know."[9] The term "right to know" did not appear in any Supreme Court opinions or even in popular rhetoric until 1945, when Kent Cooper, executive director of the Associated Press, employed it in a speech in which he said, "Citizens are entitled to have access to news, fully and accurately presented. There cannot be political freedom in one country, or in the world, without respect for 'the right to know.'"[10]

The right to know—or, if not the right, the organized passion to know or what we might think of as a cultural right to know—championed by news organizations, various nonprofit reform groups, and many political theorists would seem to be simply what comes with a vibrant democracy, but it has not always been accepted, let alone applauded. In the midst of the frenzy over the Whitewater scandal of the Clinton administration—does anyone remember the Whitewater scandal?—a British journalist lamented the peculiar demands placed on the American president. Addressing an American audience, he wrote, "You demand total financial integrity from your politicians, while agreeing to a system that requires them to raise millions of dollars to have any hope of being elected. You say in effect, 'We will vote for you if you woo us at stupendous expense, but every penny you raise must be unblemished.'"[11] He might have added that Americans expect every penny to be publicly accounted for, created a federal agency to examine the accounting, expect political parties and various specialized public interest groups to keep tabs on the federal agency, and rely on law enforcement and the news media to let citizens know about egregious violations. The institutional apparatus for this particular American mania dates to the Federal Elections Campaign Acts of 1971 and 1974, not to the founders and not to any earlier efforts to clean up campaigning. Prior efforts date back to the early twentieth century, but none before 1971 had nearly so much visibility, so well institutionalized a set of procedures, or so much impact.

Campaign finance disclosure was just one of the newly established or newly expanded domains of institutionalized disclosure that multiplied in the 1960s and 1970s, responding to and helping forge a new direction in culture and politics. This new direction, and some of its constituent parts, is my topic. I focus here on institutional shifts in public life, but "openness" was a theme in private life simultaneously, and in fact, some of the most dramatic changes came in a blurring of the boundaries between public and private. Is choosing to have an abortion a private or public matter? So long as abortion is prohibited or regulated by laws that restrict its use or limit financial support for paying for it, it is a public issue. But so long as having an abortion or having had one is stigmatizing, there is incentive to keep abortions secret. So it was a matter of note and of courage in 1972 when the inaugural issue of *Ms.*, the first mass-market feminist magazine, featured "We Have Had Abortions," an article that listed fifty-three women who acknowledged their own abortions.[12]

People in many countries have come to live in the "society of self-disclosure," as British sociologist John Thompson suggests.[13] Many people seem to no longer have separate public and private spheres but have only a "private/public sphere," as Dominique Mehl, writing of France, has argued.[14] I will not concentrate on disclosure in private life, but so long as people rather than robots run governments, they will seek to protect their spouses, children, bodily intimacies, health, personal relationships, and financial entanglements from the public spotlight that is otherwise so much a part of their professional routines. They will sometimes fail in this, or choose conscientiously to forgo privacy and place the private/public sphere squarely before us.

Sometimes this misfires. In the fall of 1965, President Lyndon Johnson was hospitalized for surgery to remove his gallbladder. President Eisenhower's hospitalization for a heart attack a decade earlier was by no means forgotten. When Johnson met with Eisenhower just before his surgery, Eisenhower urged upon the president complete candor, although this was not something he had practiced himself. Johnson would keep confidential other health issues, but he was open about the gallbladder operation. In fact, what most struck the public at the time was the moment when Johnson pulled up his shirt to expose to the press the surgical scar on his abdomen and the bandages still partially covering it. Reporters were taken aback by the impromptu unveiling, and it seems that many in the public would happily have done without it (one publication dubbed the president "the Abdominal Showman"). The episode came to be seen as an embarrassment.[15]

But consider Betty Ford eight years later. Gerald Ford, president of the United States from August 1974 to January 1977, was a relatively lackluster, caretaker president, while his wife was a culture-symbolizing if not culture-shifting dynamo. When she died in 2011, Rick Perlstein wrote in the *New York Times* that her achievements "may well have been greater than those of her husband, President Gerald R. Ford." He explained, "Though she never was an elected official, industry titan or religious leader, few Americans changed people's lives so dramatically for the better." He mentioned her frankness in discussing her breast cancer and mastectomy, her acknowledgment of her alcohol and drug abuse, and her outspoken views about sexual and reproductive practices, including abortion and premarital sex. She was widely admired for her openness. "No one would have predicted this," Perlstein observed. "America had been a nation of shame-faced secrecy in so many of its intimate domestic affairs. The 1970s was when that began to change. Betty Ford was that transformation's Joan of Arc."[16]

At the end of September 1974, not quite two months into the Ford presidency, doctors found a suspicious lump in Betty Ford's right breast during a routine medical exam. Two days later, Mrs. Ford went into the hospital for a biopsy that, as she knew, would become a radical mastectomy if the biopsy showed a malignant tumor, as it did. Mrs. Ford spoke candidly with the press from the beginning, in part because, as she recalled later, "there had been so much cover-up during Watergate that we wanted to be sure there would be no cover-up in the Ford administration. So rather than continue this traditional silence about breast cancer, we felt we had to be very public."[17]

This remark may seem bizarre: what connection is there between a president's efforts to obstruct justice by authorizing a cover-up of illegal activities he either approved or allowed and a First Lady's entirely conventional decision, if she had so chosen, to maintain privacy about her personal health? President Nixon's cover-up broke the law; Betty Ford's disclosure breached custom, all the more so because it required public mention of two words not then widely circulating in polite public conversation—"breast" and "cancer." The two situations had nothing in common, and yet, in the mood of that public/private moment, much that would have once been veiled seemed to Mrs. Ford important to share.

Betty Ford was a hero of openness, but she was not Joan of Arc; far from being burned at the stake, she was quickly praised and honored in many quarters. By 1974 there was a growing receptiveness to unprecedentedly candid disclosures in public, private, and professional life. As the chapters to follow will show, there was novel legislation to open up government files to the public (the Freedom of Information Act of 1966), to require "truth in packaging" (1966) and "truth in lending" (1968) for consumers, and to open up more of the work of Congress to public view (1970), among other efforts. Supermarkets—sometimes on their own and sometimes spurred by local and state legislation—were by 1970 making extensive use of unit pricing and were beginning to insist on nutritional labeling on packaged goods.

One of the most dramatic shifts—one that, indeed, Mrs. Ford helped encourage—concerned communication between doctors and their patients. Silences surrounding disease and death and dying were breached. As late as 1961, a survey-based study published in the *Journal of the American Medical Association* found that only 12 percent of doctors would tell patients that they had cancer.[18] (In Tennessee Williams's *Cat on a Hot Tin Roof,* first staged in 1955, the character Dr. Baugh does not disclose to Big Daddy that he is dying of an incurable cancer; this would have been typical for that period.) In a follow-up study published in 1979, 98 percent of doctors reported that they spoke frankly with their cancer patients.[19] In 1967 the hospice movement began in Britain and spread quickly to the United States. Elisabeth Kübler-Ross began interviewing dying patients at Chicago hospitals, arriving at her celebrated five-stage model of how people come to accept a terminal diagnosis. In 1969 she popularized this work in *On Death and Dying.*[20]

The relationship between research physicians and their subjects changed, too. In 1966, Henry K. Beecher, a distinguished anesthesiologist and professor of medicine at the Harvard Medical School, published in the *New England Journal of Medicine* an article that detailed the procedures of twenty-two medical research studies that had risked the health or life of their subjects without informing them of the dangers or in any way gaining their permission. The studies had been supported by leading funders, conducted by faculty at major universities, and published in respected medical journals. One study induced hepatitis, another left strep throat untreated and so risked the patients' contracting rheumatic fever, and a third injected subjects with live cancer cells to study immunity to cancer. The hepatitis study was undertaken by the chair of pediatrics at New York University and carried out on a population of children at Willowbrook State School for the Retarded.[21]

In direct response to Beecher's evidence and the publicity it generated, the National Institutes of Health (NIH) and the Public Health Service in 1966 issued guidelines for "all federally funded research involving human experimentation."[22] This was the beginning of the campus institutional review boards that now face any scholar who wants to do biomedical or social research on human subjects, offering some protection to subjects of academic (and particularly medical) research. "Informed consent" was recognized in law as early as 1957, but it became a well-institutionalized directive in hospitals, research laboratories, and universities only after Beecher's publication, the NIH guidelines, the 1972 revelations concerning the Tuskegee syphilis experiment, the 1974 creation of the National Commission for the Protection of Human Subjects of Biomedical and Behavioral Research, and the 1978 release of the commission's Belmont Report, which defined ethical guidelines for medical research.

Meanwhile, in Dayton, Ohio, in 1963, a local broadcaster from a lower-middle-class Irish Catholic family began a radio talk show. In 1967 he took it to television. Phil Donahue began national syndication of the program in 1970 and stayed on the air until 1996. He would be swamped in the last years of his show by the astonishing popularity of Oprah Winfrey, but he pioneered the format that she would later put her own inimitable stamp on. *Donahue,* as the show was called in its later years, brought to television several distinctive new features. It incorporated openness as a practice and as a value, promoting honesty itself as a form of popular therapy.[23] This applied even to taboo topics and taboo practices such as homosexuality; on

Donahue and later programs, "coming out" and telling the truth overrode conventional morality. "Same-sex desire is here simply a personal truth, and *lying* is the problem," as Joshua Gamson observes in a brilliant study.[24] Not only was openness valued, but so was personal or experiential knowledge rather than expert authority. This came out of the feminist movement and generally out of the democratic, anti-expertise sentiments of the 1960s that favored the "storied life" over the "expert guest."[25] *Donahue,* along with other shows in the genre it pioneered, favored tolerance and civility. On television, intolerance and bigotry looked ugly; "acceptance," one television producer told Gamson, is what the programs were about. The sexual minorities and outcasts might be promoted as "freaks" whose unconventional experiences drew in the crowds, but as each show unfolded, "the bigot becomes the freak."[26]

Talk shows offered a fairly conventional morality of tolerance and civility, merely extending it to parties once excluded, but they also proposed a kind of "postmorality" of the spectacle in which discontinuities and incongruities were on carnivalesque display. This was television, after all, not real life, and it could afford to present a "temporary liberation from the prevailing truth and from the established order"—it was not necessarily a set of attitudes that viewers were instructed to bring into their own everyday lives.[27] But neither was it *not* a set of instructions. Television offered a new kind of emotional education and a new location for such education.

This is just to sample some ways that transparency practices have emerged or expanded in the past half century in government, in the mass media, in the marketplace, in popular culture, and in many basic elements of everyday life, including birth, adoption, illness, and death and dying. Visibility and disclosure have become part of our lives, expectations, and instincts; their erosion or retrenchment today would evoke a sense of loss, of injustice, of outrage. Things widely taken for granted since the 1970s, from doctors' willingness to inform dying patients they are dying to unit pricing in the supermarket and nutritional information listed on a package label, are developments of the 1960s and after. They were not born with the First Amendment. They were not dreamed up by Thomas Jefferson or James Madison. And yet today they have become part of both our institutions and our inclinations. There is no right to know in the Constitution, but the expectation that people deserve to be informed has risen to prominence in America's public culture.

Many people would hold that in everyday life, some things should be left unsaid. The daily exercise of "nonacknowledgment," as philosopher Thomas Nagel puts it, or "civil inattention," in the phrase of sociologist Erving Goffman, lubricates social interaction and engenders civility: marriages work better when partners learn to bite their tongues; parenting improves when parents acknowledge threshold ages before which "too much information" shared with children may be incomprehensible, inappropriate, or damaging; confidentiality makes trust possible when people consult with their doctors, lawyers, clergy, best friends, or spouses, and this is recognized in testimonial privilege in law; there is social good when, under some circumstances, government officials, university faculty members, corporate executives, union officials, or nonprofit organizations' board members can talk with one another behind closed doors. Even beneficial disclosure will sometimes rest on a foundation of secrecy, as when journalists raise public alarms based on confidential sources or, at the very heart of democracies, in elections where vote totals are public but, to protect citizens from intimidation, how individual citizens vote is not.[28]

Openness in a democracy is not an absolute value but a kind of secondary or procedural morality. If honesty means not "not lying" but "disclosing everything to everybody," it is not invariably the best policy for individuals, organizations, or governments. What we tell, when, to whom, how much, and under what circumstances—these are matters of policy, judgment, and choices among alternatives. Even First Amendment law recognizes that governmental authorities may acceptably limit the "time, place, and manner" for protected speech. "Let it all hang out" was a slogan in the 1960s, not a practical guide to public policy.

The slogan itself was perhaps original, but the protest it expressed was not. Literary rebels of the 1920s boasted of their "terrible honesty." They were proud to be breaking through the silences and false fronts of a Victorian culture to champion "terrible truthfulness," "terrible sincerity," "fearful honesty," and "brutal honesty." They opposed sentimentality as a form of lying. They loved "facts" and announced their own toughness facing them.[29] But this intellectual bravado did little to shape institutions, laws, and social practices of disclosure (and seems unconnected to the New Deal's required disclosure of financial records of publicly listed securities and the creation of the Securities and Exchange Commission to enforce it). The anti-Victorianism of the artistic avant-garde made a difference as part of a long process of what Dutch sociologists have termed "informalization," which gradually spread across European and North American societies in the twentieth century. But this was not specifically driven by the democratic sense of empowering individuals against the harms that secretive or deceptive government or corporate power might inflict.[30]

My general claim is that in domains public, private, and professional, expanded disclosure practices have become more fully institutionalized in the past half century and the virtue and value of openness more widely accepted, enough so to suggest that both the experience of being human and the experience of constructing a democracy have changed in response to a new transparency imperative and a new embrace of a right to know.

The legislative acts and social and political developments I will discuss here have become part of our everyday experience, as if they had been with us forever, but they have not become a part of the way we tell our own history. Finding them in U.S. history textbooks or other general accounts of our recent past is difficult. Even accounts that focus on the period since 1945, or slices of it, pay them little attention.[31] In few of the general histories I have read is there even passing reference to several of the innovations I attend to in this book, including unit pricing in supermarkets, environmental impact statements, and recorded votes on amendments in the House of Representatives, and only allusive reference to changes in the character of news reporting that I take up in Chapter 5. This is not to criticize other works with other purposes but to note that the path I am taking was not as well marked as I had anticipated.

In suggesting that what opened up between 1960 and 1980 was an insistence on openness, I am calling attention to a change in culture, a shift in what used to be called the "climate of opinion" or the "zeitgeist" or the "spirit of the times." These are embarrassingly vague terms. They have gone out of fashion for good reason, but people nonetheless reach for ways to characterize the mood and motive forces of the day or decade. Is ours the digital age? The information age? The age of globalization? The risk society? The postmodern era? The post-postmodern era? People want to know, not because they naively believe that one or another of these simplifications is the "right" one but because settling on one choice or another for specific purposes helps set a (provisional) framework for discussion.

But how do you write a history of culture? A history of change in beliefs or values or "structures of feeling" that cut across public and private, across economic, political, social, legal, and intellectual arenas? I try to peg my discussion to specific individuals, institutions, and events. I try to detect the shifting sands of opinion or, more precisely, a set of premises and presuppositions that lie just beneath opinion, in specific, identifiable rhetoric, appearing in specific documents and settings and, for that matter, in accidents and coincidences that contributed—through no one's precise intentions—to the advance of disclosure practices and transparency ideals.

The importance of these individuals, institutions, and events is not that they are by themselves the cultural change or its cause, but neither are they merely the designated drivers for forces beyond themselves. The way cultural change works, I believe, is more complicated than that and may even be, to an extent, a self-fulfilling phenomenon based on individuals' beliefs—even mistaken beliefs—that they are working amid and acting in response to irresistible waves of change.

As Chapter 2 will demonstrate, one of the most important openings—the Freedom of Information Act of 1966—began with a modest freedom-of-information movement among journalists in the late 1940s and grew when, in 1955, a dogged congressional effort to open up executive files began. Other developments of the 1940s and 1950s were important, too, from the sensational publication of the two Kinsey reports (in 1948 and 1953) on adult sexual behavior to a matter as mundane as the Automobile Information Disclosure Act of 1958, the legislation responsible for the itemized pricing sticker on the windows of new cars on the dealer's lot or in the showroom. These were at one time known as "Monroney stickers" after the Senate sponsor of the legislation, Mike Monroney (D-Okla.).

The changes I will discuss are not all alike, but they share a family resemblance, and they are all linked to what today is commonly called "transparency," which has become a consensual norm in public life both in the United States, the country that is my specific focus, and in many other parts of the world. In the period at the center of my inquiry, the term "transparency" was not in common use for the phenomena I am examining, and it is somewhat anachronistic to link the changes of the 1960s and 1970s under the umbrella of "transparency." "Disclosure" is the better term for the actual practices mandated by lawmakers. A "right to know" is also invoked to discuss these matters, and I think it is also serviceable as long as it is understood as more of a cultural current rather than a specifically legal claim. The general "opening up" all of these terms refer to is as much what British scholar Raymond Williams called a "structure of feeling" as it is a set of specific laws and policies.

The "right to know," as already indicated, was largely absent from American political rhetoric before 1945, when journalism organizations began to pick it up and promote it. Self-aggrandizing as that may have been, it resonated publicly. Variations on the theme of a "right to know" became a key part of the rhetoric of democratic reform, not only in the effort to pass a Freedom of Information Act but even in the unlikely crusade for truth in packaging of supermarket goods.

The right to know can be distinguished from freedom of speech, the general term for the right to say and especially the right to express dissent. The airing of statements, exclamations, or opinions that criticize or challenge constituted authority or established conventions gained judicial support during the 1960s and 1970s, as when Paul Robert Cohen in 1968 wore a jacket into a Los Angeles courthouse that said across it "Fuck the Draft" and the U.S. Supreme Court in 1971 agreed that he had a First Amendment right to do so, Justice John M. Harlan poetically declaring for the majority of a divided Court that "one man's vulgarity is another's lyric." Generally speaking, freedoms of speech, press, and assembly in practice and in legal principle have been enlarged over the past half century and have enhanced the capacity for public dissent.[32]

The relationship of disclosure to democracy varies according to when in the course of democratic decision making the transparency practice appears. If decision making is publicly visible because everyone is eligible to participate in it (as in direct democracy), be represented in it (as in representative democracy), or be consulted by the decision makers (as in mechanisms in which citizens may advise decision makers in advance of a decision), that may be the most potent form of public visibility. It erases or reduces the divide between governor and governed.

But other forms of transparency appear at a later stage in democratic decision making. Information may be made public after a decision is provisionally made but before action is undertaken, either in the legislature or after a law is enacted but before executive agencies have taken final policy action based on it. We will see a chief case of this in the environmental impact statement, treated in Chapter 6—the requirement that federal agencies prepare statements that detail the expected environmental impact of actions they plan to take, whether building a dam, a road, or a new office building. They must make these statements available to the public in a timely manner. Members of the public may raise objections and may, in fact, sue or threaten to sue the executive agency to prevent the planned action from happening, or to force its modification before it is undertaken. Transparency in this case brings the public into the operation of government not in the original decision making but at a point before execution when the outcome can still be altered.

One step further removed from the original decision making is a form of transparency we might call declarative visibility. When government has passed a law or an agency of government has made a ruling or enacted new guidelines for, say, government contracting, government is generally obliged to post public notice of what it has done. When Congress passes a law, the public is notified. As Chapter 4 will show, since 1971, but not before, the votes of members of the House of Representatives on amendments to a law under consideration have been made public. There is considerable time and energy expended these days on making laws, actions, and rulings not just technically transparent (i.e., publicly available) but also effectively transparent through simple language, easily navigated websites, and other features of design and presentation that enable ordinary people to make real use of public information. This is of special importance to people whose lives are directly affected as consumers of government services, as they draw on veterans' benefits, social security, Medicare, health insurance under the Affordable Care Act, changes in the tax code, information on public transportation operations, and much more.

There is also after-the-fact disclosure. Through the Freedom of Information Act (FOIA), as Chapter 2 shows, any person—citizen or not—may request the disclosure of information identified in the FOIA request. The inspectors general (most of the IG offices have been instituted since the Inspectors General Act of 1978) regularly review and make public their assessments of the efficiency, propriety, and legality of actions taken by the executive agency they review. The Government Accountability Office likewise undertakes and makes public a review of government actions in various domains. Congress frequently reviews actions of the executive and normally makes its reviews and inquiries public. Moreover, there are and have long been disclosures of government information by covertly authorized or unauthorized government employees—the former known as "leakers" and the latter as "whistle-blowers." Because decision makers anticipate that some or all of these after-the-fact disclosures may come into play in relation to the decisions they are currently making, the anticipation itself becomes the vehicle by which after-the-fact disclosure influences the decisions that precede it.

The various changes and reforms in public visibility that emerged in the 1960s and 1970s were not for the most part coordinated. They did not parade under the same banner. In fact, authors of these innovations often focused on objectives that had little to do with making democratic governance more transparent or more participatory. But all of them were touched by and contributed to a profound cultural change. The growing approval for transparency or the cultural expectation of a right to know, and institutional reforms to embrace it, blend together a variety of values. The blend favors the open over the hidden, confidential, or secret; expressiveness over politeness; the grassroots, egalitarian, or democratic over the elitist; the authority of personal experience over the authority of professional expertise; the natural over the adulterated; the accessible and plain-spoken over the recondite; and in general freedom over restraint. These contrasts give favor to a utopian impulse, to the romantic over the classical in style, to a democratic faith in human beings.

I feel the tug of these utopian ideals—and I also resist them. They promise too much, they deliver too little, they slight too often conflicting values of privacy, confidentiality, simple tact, and even paternalism. Paternalism, for all of its distortions and abuses, is a praiseworthy attitude when practiced conscientiously by fathers and mothers toward their children (the word "parentalism" would be better) and, in measured adaptation, when mentors and trustees of various sorts employ them with those they guide and serve.

Information-sharing governmental reforms may be driven by the high value placed on public information in contemporary democracies, but it can be, and sometimes has been, supported because it affords government the least invasive action possible on some social problem—say, not requiring commercial organizations to abide by a minimal standard for chemical emissions but enjoining them to publicly name what chemicals in what quantity their factories emit. In other words, transparency-oriented regulations frequently are market-oriented regulations, created in the belief that putting information in the hands of the public will enable people to make informed choices that will lead to improved social outcomes. Transparency-oriented reforms are also sometimes chosen because they seem to be the least invasive or constraining of state interventions and may even be judged cosmetic, a show of "doing something" when Congress or legislatures see that there is not enough support for more substantial government action. Superficial though this may seem, there is evidence that laws requiring disclosure can have major consequences—requirements that corporations make public their release of toxic chemicals have significantly reduced toxic emissions, for example. Likewise, the use of environmental impact statements and the public participation that has made them effective in modifying significant environment-affecting actions of federal agencies have reduced environmental degradation.[33]

Transparency may be counted as one of a set of values that philosopher Alasdair MacIntyre has called "the secondary virtues." "The secondary virtues," he wrote, "concern the way in which we should go about our projects; their cultivation will not assist us in discovering upon which projects we ought to be engaged."[34] Among its most ardent advocates, transparency attains the status of a primary virtue— an objective worthy for its own sake or perhaps for a presumed intimate or essential connection to a primary value, in this case democratic self-governance. For some of its advocates, transparency is one of the ideals we should dedicate ourselves to and not just a means of reaching something else of primary value.

Disclosure is clearly related to democracy, and I do see democratic self-government as a primary value, but I think transparency is a secondary virtue or perhaps something suspended between primary objectives and secondary virtues. Some of the most thoughtful and careful commentary on secrecy in democracies, to look at the question from the other side, finds secrecy in government suspect on its face but nonetheless justifiable in many circumstances. Dennis Thompson's essay "Democratic Secrecy," for instance, offers criteria for assessing when and to what extent secrecy may be democratically justified. Thompson sees secrets as sometimes necessary but urges that there be open discussion whenever possible in order to define and limit the conditions under which government officials are permitted to keep secrets, and then to minimize the depth of secrecy (how many people may share in the secret; less-deep secrets, with more people privy to them, are better for democracy) and the length of time the information is maintained as a secret (shorter time periods for enforcing secrecy are better for democracy).[35]

The visibility of different features of American society, and particularly the visibility of what we take or once took to be shameful, has grown enormously in the past half century. In fact, this may be one of the most important social changes of our era—but it is the one that unnervingly complicates our capacity to assess how the state of civic and community health today differs from what it used to be. As more and more people have gained a public voice, found ways to speak their doubt and distrust, and seen criticism and skepticism legitimated, they have been emboldened to speak more forthrightly. As more institutions have developed tools for criticism or habits of mind that endorse criticism—higher education, the news media, watchdog lobbies and special interests, and even government agencies themselves—criticism and critics are more visible than ever and the faults of our institutions more loudly proclaimed.

For some people, this popular enlightenment and popular empowerment are entirely to the good. For others, they are troubling because they have made discord, difference, and disillusion more visible. This makes venturing into politics and society a more alarming prospect, and it may generate fear and anxiety disproportionate to the actual conditions of the world. I do not resolve this disagreement here. What I seek to do is to sketch the emergence of a culture of disclosure—that is, a society in which the norms that tend to prevail urge people to be open with spouses and partners and friends; incline medical professionals to preserve patients' confidentiality but recommend high levels of frankness with them; and insist, perhaps sometimes recklessly, that governments should disclose information at every opportunity, that legislative meetings should be open to press and public unless legislature or committee members specifically vote otherwise, and that democracy means keeping the public informed—often while policy is being formulated, not just after the fact.

I will try not only to sketch this developing positive appraisal and institutionalization of civic knowing but also to explain it. There is not any simple or monocausal explanation, as I think the chapters that follow make abundantly clear. Rather, I will lean on three components of a general explanation, tacking informally from one to another as the circumstance of the historical moment I am discussing seems to warrant. The first is the institutional framework within which the developing norms and practices come to make sense. I will discuss this at length in Chapter 7—the emergence after 1945 and especially after 1965 of a form of democracy, not only in the United

States but elsewhere around the world, in which government is held accountable not just at the polling place on election day but continuously. This takes place through the watchfulness of the news media, think tanks, public opinion polling, a variety of nongovernmental organizations that take themselves to be watchdogs of government with respect to specific policy domains, and even watchdog agencies within government itself. Popular and even academic understandings of democracy as a form of government have lagged far behind the changes that now require a reformulation of what democracy has become and what we can and should expect of this new "monitory" democracy.

The second component that enabled the cultural right to know of the 1960s and 1970s is simply the happenstance of everyday politics, everyday events, and the consequences of having one party rather than another in power. Several of the developments chronicled here required making more active use of the powers of the federal government, although several others were efforts of Congress to *constrain* the powers of the executive, notably the Freedom of Information Act and the National Environmental Policy Act, which at once limited executive power and greatly broadened it in committing the government to give consideration to the environment in its planning. Legislative initiatives found support, sometimes active and sometimes only tacit, in the administrations of John F. Kennedy, Lyndon Johnson, and for that matter Richard Nixon, the last of whom sought to cooperate with programs he did not especially care for (environmental legislation) to deprive any Democratic candidate who might face him in 1972 of a good campaign issue. In the case of the environment, environmental advocates in Congress also benefited from several high-profile environmental disasters, happenstances of quite a different but also very potent order.

The third component is a powerful ethos or spirit that made right-to-know or disclosure reforms resonant with a changing culture. A "spirit" is a very spongy kind of causal force. But its elusiveness is no excuse for ignoring it. Besides, I will suggest (especially in Chapter 5) that it can be tacked down, at least in a preliminary way, by attention to the emergence in the 1950s and 1960s of sharply growing enrollments in higher education and, even more important, changes in the content and orientation of the college classroom. Colleges became concerned not so much to pass on well-established traditions but to generate in students a capacity for critical inquiry. This contributed to the constitution of the minds and selves of individuals who became leaders in government, media, universities, business, and elsewhere and also the minds and selves of citizens who might vote, be polled, read newspapers, write letters to their representatives, take notice of or pride in their "rights," join organizations, or (as consumers) be the ones to attend to unit pricing or read nutritional and ingredient labels with care. It is the combination of these elements—the changing institutional framework of democracy, the political alignment and incidents of a particular moment, and an increasingly critical public mind produced by a brew of social change involving everything from the civil rights movement to a mass public with access to a critical culture in higher education and an irreverent culture in the press and popular culture—that kindled and has helped to sustain new practices of openness.

And the Internet? The Internet did not create knowing, the right to know, or transparency, nor introduce it to the human drama. It was not the primary vehicle for intensifying a concern for disclosure in our time; that, I will argue here, was the growing centrality of organized knowledge in the expansion and transformation of higher education in the decades after 1945, the growing critical power of journalism from the 1960s on, and the broad distrust of convention and authority that emerged in the same years. Still, the Internet has radically changed the dimensions of transparency, transformed the speed by which disclosure and revelation circulate, and universalized the reach of information. It is indeed the global information superhighway and it is much more, a development that exceeds our metaphors for it. Its way was paved not only by technical innovation but also by the transformation of culture and politics that gave priority to accounting and accountability, inclusion, and disclosure in general. The Internet has enormously expanded aspirations toward a right to know. Paradoxically, it has also fostered secrecy: What is Google's algorithm? How many passwords do you have, and how do you hide them (and how do you remember them)? But not all studies about contemporary politics and culture are about the Internet. This one is not, although it is a pertinent prologue for understanding the digital age, and one that I think offers a few disclosures itself.

two

Origins of the Freedom of Information Act

James Madison once wrote in a private letter what became a very public and famous line: "A popular Government without popular information or the means of acquiring it is but a Prologue to a Farce or a Tragedy or perhaps both. Knowledge will forever govern ignorance, and a people who mean to be their own Governors must arm themselves with the power knowledge gives."[1] This was cited in an influential treatise on state and federal laws concerning when, how, and by what legal authority documents held by government agencies are made publicly available, Harold Cross's *The People's Right to Know* (1953).[2] Members of Congress quoted this same passage from Madison over and over again in 1965 and 1966 as they advocated what came to be known as the Freedom of Information Act.[3] It continues to be quoted to this day.[4]

Madison was the chief architect of the U.S. Constitution, wrote a third of the Federalist Papers (those brilliant newspaper essays that urged the states to ratify the Constitution), and in the newly established Congress a few years later was the chief advocate for the Bill of Rights. But it was decades later, retired from public life, that he wrote these celebrated lines about popular information in a popular government—referring to the importance of public elementary schools in Kentucky, not to any obligation of government to share information in its possession with inquiring citizens. While the Freedom of Information Act (FOIA, pronounced "foy-a") is not likely to have been born in a country untouched by the eighteenth-century Enlightenment, nothing remotely like it appeared in the early American republic, nor did Madison suggest anything resembling it at any time.

We misunderstand ourselves as a nation and we particularly misunderstand our recent achievements when we get caught up in rhetorical ancestor worship. James Madison was the father of our Constitution, but a California politician named John Moss, a Democratic member of Congress from 1953 to 1978, was the father of the Freedom of Information Act. He was not a profound thinker. He was not much of a legislative craftsman. But Moss, not Madison, holds the secret to how the Freedom of Information Act came to be and how it serves as a beacon of contemporary democracy, whatever James Madison might have thought of it.

It is hard to imagine a way of resisting government secrecy more feeble than a procedure for people to request that the government share its information under a law that affords it all kinds of opportunities to delay or minimize disclosure, or to avoid disclosure altogether if it can claim that the requested information falls under any of nine exemptions itemized in the statute. It is hard to imagine a means more sure to leave physicians and biomedical researchers in control of medical and research judgment than requiring patients or subjects of experiments to fill out incomprehensible papers that testify to their "informed consent." ("Unformed consent" might be more accurate.) And it is hard to believe that a requirement for each government agency to produce a "detailed statement" assessing the environmental impact of proposed actions could not be easily dodged.

And yet when all of these things began, or greatly expanded, between 1966 and 1974, they made a difference. For a variety of reasons and with a variety of consequences, American society in the past half century has adopted more demanding norms and more widespread and enforceable practices of public disclosure in government, in professional relations, and in private life. The Freedom of Information Act, weak as it was when passed in 1966, was a landmark development of a more open society.

Not everyone agrees that the Freedom of Information Act, even after amendments to strengthen it and to streamline its use, lives up to the grandeur of its name. Kate Doyle, an expert on U.S. policy in Latin America at the nonprofit National Security Archive, once declared FOIA to be—but for "a brief heyday" in the 1970s— "profoundly dysfunctional."[5] In June 2007, *New York Times* reporter Nina Bernstein wrote a front-page story about the imprisonment of immigrants who violated conditions of their visitor status, sometimes languishing in detention for months or years, sometimes dying while in custody. Bernstein had learned from her sources that there were some twenty horrifying cases where detainees had died in detention. She filed a FOIA request. Her request was met with a long silence— that is, until November 2007, when a package was delivered to her desk with the information she had asked for, and more: evidence that there had been sixty-six deaths, not twenty. Readers would learn of these deaths in Bernstein's front-page story May 5, 2008 (and of still more deaths in follow-up stories over the next several years).

Bernstein's FOIA request became the topic of a column by the *Times*'s public editor or ombudsman, Clark Hoyt. Hoyt observed that *Times* reporters make aggressive use of FOIA and that in recent weeks the *Times* had published two leading stories based on government information obtained under FOIA, Bernstein's and a story by David Barstow that revealed how the Pentagon influenced TV military analysts to portray the government's position more favorably in the television news. Barstow had filed his FOIA request at the end of April 2006. It was denied. He appealed. The appeal was turned down a few months later. Barstow kept trying—and in the end received 687 pages of documents from the Defense Department. A bit more information trickled in thereafter, but it was far less than Barstow had requested, and the explanations for the denial were not credible. The *Times* took the Pentagon to court—and won. Still the Pentagon moved slowly. Finally the *Times* ran the story with what it had. Several days later Barstow received an additional 2,800 pages.

Barstow judged FOIA "a cruel joke." Hoyt seemed to agree.[6] The phrase "cruel joke" hangs in the air as one finishes reading the column. Nevertheless, early in 2009, Barstow's stories on the Pentagon and TV military analysts won the Pulitzer Prize for investigative reporting, confirming the importance of the work and amplifying its influence.

FOIA helped make these critical stories possible, even as it delayed them while the reporters struggled with the FOIA apparatus and recalcitrant agencies. Would a hundred such stories a year justify all the expense and trouble of FOIA? Ten such stories? One? The question is rhetorical, but it can be tethered to dollars and cents when the actual costs of responding to FOIA requests are examined. In fiscal 2013, the federal government received more than 700,000 FOIA requests and processed 623,186 requests (thus making a dent in the backlog), thanks to the work of 3,691 full-time or full-time-equivalent employees at a total cost of $338 million.[7]

In 2006, in recognition of the fortieth anniversary of FOIA, the National Security Archive published a list of forty notable news stories based largely on information obtained through FOIA. In most cases, a news organization initiated the FOIA request—the Associated Press, the *Baltimore Sun,* the *Chicago Sun-Times,* the *Chicago Tribune,* the *Des Moines Register,* Knight Ridder, the *Los Angeles Times,* the *Minneapolis Star Tribune, Newsday,* the *New York Times,* the *Richmond Times-Dispatch,* the *San Francisco Chronicle, USA Today,* and the *Washington Post.* In other cases, the FOIA request came from nonprofit civic, advocacy, and research organizations—the American Civil Liberties Union, the Electronic Privacy Information Center, Judicial Watch, the Migration Policy Institute at New York University Law School, People for the Ethical Treatment of Animals, Public Employees for Environmental Responsibility, Texans for Public Justice, the Transactional Records Access Clearinghouse, the Union of Concerned Scientists, and in several cases the National Security Archive at George Washington University itself.[8]

In 2011, in testimony before a Senate committee, Sarah Cohen, then Knight Professor of Journalism at Duke University and former prize-winning *Washington Post* reporter, testified that in her own work FOIA was "critical to stories ranging from the quality of drinking water in Washington, D.C. to the use of federal homeland security grants. More recently, the law has been used by journalists reporting on possible Medicare fraud, sex discrimination in the Texas National Guard and human trafficking. . . . These stories and many others could not have been done without access to records locked inside technological and physical file cabinets throughout the government."[9]

The law can be improved. The government's faithfulness to its spirit can be strengthened. Using FOIA is often awkward, difficult, and frustrating. The roughly 4,000 FOIA officers spread across federal agencies are overburdened with requests and undersupported in their labors. Besides, many people who submit FOIA requests are ill prepared to specify the documents they seek—or even to know which department or agency they should contact. According to Cohen, FOIA "simply does not appear to work as intended—and hasn't for the generation in which I've been a reporter. The FOIA process remains exceedingly difficult to navigate and is useful only to the most patient and persistent journalists." She added, "I have never received a final response to a FOIA within the required time frame. Some reporters joke about sending birthday cards to their FOIAs, as the response times are measured in years, not days."[10]

Whatever celebration of FOIA might be warranted, complacency is not in order. The same can be said of the freedom-of-information acts at the state level, and there are numerous complaints as well about freedom-of-information laws in the many countries around the world that have adopted such legislation, frequently modeled on the American example. There are innumerable accounts of both successful and unsuccessful FOIA requests and the many cases that fall in between in which much requested material is released but with heavy redaction that limits the utility of the disclosures. Former CIA agent John Marks received 16,000 pages of CIA documents to help him write a very critical 1979 book—in which, in his acknowledgments, he thanks the congressional sponsors of FOIA. Historian David Garrow waited seventeen years for some of the documents he requested for his biography of Martin Luther King Jr. Nevertheless, Garrow reports that he received "tens of thousands of pages" through FOIA requests, and he thanks by name seven individuals at the FBI and the Department of Justice's Civil Rights Division and Community Relations Service who helped process his requests. In his book *Secrecy Wars,* Philip H. Melanson titles a chapter on FOIA "The User-Unfriendly Law." There he writes that the law is weighted toward the government, not the requester, and even so, its procedures "are often ignored or manipulated by agencies." He follows this immediately by quoting a booklet of the Reporters Committee for Freedom of the Press: "The possibilities of the act are endless. All that is required is that you use it." And Melanson comments: "Both positions are correct."[11]

In a 1998 essay, historian Jon Wiener recounted his effort to use FOIA to obtain John Lennon's FBI files. Wiener first requested the files in 1981. With the American Civil Liberties Union of Southern California, he filed suit in 1983 to see the files the FBI withheld for "national security" reasons. In 1997 a settlement was reached, the FBI paying $204,000 in legal fees while still withholding ten documents. (Those documents were finally released in 2006.) Still, in his essay, Wiener acknowledges that "in many respects the FOIA has been a spectacular success."[12]

What Exactly Is FOIA?

Congress approved the Freedom of Information Act on June 20, 1966, and a reluctant President Lyndon Johnson signed it into law July 4, 1966. It took effect one year later. Technically, FOIA became law as an amendment to the Administrative Procedure Act of 1946 (APA), which identifies norms and procedures for the effective and accountable operation of government administration. But what little the APA had said about the public disclosure of information was vague and easily read to protect agencies from having to disclose information to Congress or the public. FOIA changed that. It declared that fed-

eral agencies shall make public documents regarding their operation, procedures, opinions and orders, staff manuals, and indexes to
these materials, through postings in the *Federal Register* and through
other standard procedures. The governmental bodies subject to FOIA
essentially are all executive agencies; not subject to the act are Congress, the courts, and the president as well as bodies whose sole responsibility is to provide advice to the president, such as the Council
of Economic Advisers.

The requirement to make basic agency documents public is important, but the great originality of the act came in its provision that
executive agencies also make records available "promptly" to "any
person" who "reasonably describes" the information desired and requests it in accord with published rules and fees. Fees will be reduced
or waived when the disclosed information is "in the public interest
because it is likely to contribute significantly to public understanding
of the operations or activities of the government and is not primarily
in the commercial interest of the requester."[13] If the records are denied, the requester may file a complaint with a U.S. district court.
The act, when amended in 1974, would also contain a provision that
agencies must respond to requests within a time limit (the length of
which has altered over the history of FOIA; currently it is twenty
business days).

A key part of the law itemizes nine exemptions. When an executive agency successfully invokes any one of them, it is relieved of the
obligation to disclose the information requested. These exemptions
are (1) information designated by an executive order to remain secret
for the sake of national defense or foreign policy, (2) information related exclusively to internal personnel practices, (3) information
specifically exempt from disclosure by statute, (4) trade secrets, (5)
information that would be available only to an agency in litigation

with the agency in question—information that judicial opinions later refer to as "predecisional deliberation," as in the records of meetings in which agency officials consider alternative courses of action, (6) information, such as personnel and medical files, whose disclosure would invade personal privacy, (7) information compiled for law enforcement purposes that if disclosed might impair law enforcement or the rights or privacy of an individual involved in criminal law enforcement proceedings, (8) information prepared in relationship to an agency regulating financial institutions, and (9) geological and geophysical information.[14]

If an agency does not release some or all of the information that a requester has demanded, the requester may go to court for a ruling that would require the agency to comply. This, of course, can be time-consuming and expensive. Even so, prominent news organizations, among other parties, have been willing to engage in this process. In recent years, free law clinics have been established to help news organizations file FOIA requests and appeal FOIA denials to the courts.[15]

The term "Freedom of Information Act" is an informal usage not attached to the original legislation. What President Johnson signed into law on July 4, 1966, was S. 1160, the Senate version of the bill that, as Johnson noted in signing it, "revises Section 3 of the Administrative Procedure Act to provide guidelines for the public availability of the records of Federal departments and agencies." The *New York Times* ran Johnson's statement in full, with a brief one-sentence preface referring to the signing of "the freedom of information bill" and a headline about "the Information Bill."[16] "Freedom of Information Act" emerged as the standard term for the act sometime after FOIA became law.

The Moss Committee 1955–1966

Picture a kind of Mr. Smith gone to Washington and you will not be far wrong about John Moss. An experienced but provincial California politician when he came to Congress, Moss was a longtime Democratic activist with an indomitable work ethic. Lionel Van Deerlin, a nine-term (1963–1981) congressman from San Diego, remembered him as "one of my early mentors" and took him to be, along with Rep. John Dingell, the "hardest working member of Congress I knew." He recalled Moss conducting some hearings in the 1960s about Vietnam one evening when the electricity went out. It was already ten-thirty at night, and others in the room thought they might as well go to bed, but Moss said, "Let's find some candles." They did, and the hearings continued.[17] Benny Kass, who served as legal counsel to the Moss Subcommittee on Government Information from 1962 into 1965, remembered his work ethic and also his devotion to his constituents. "Moss was the kind of guy who refused to use the automatic signature" to sign routine letters to constituents. Instead, he would call Kass or someone else into the office to talk while he signed a stack of letters. Kass recalled Moss as very serious: "He laughed sometimes. I don't know if I remember him smiling." He also remembers their relationship as being at some remove: "He's a god. I'm twenty-four or twenty-five years old."[18]

Moss served in the House of Representatives from 1953 to his retirement in 1978, well respected in his day as a dedicated legislator and the leading proponent in the House of freedom-of-information legislation for more than a decade.[19] He was not a colorful figure, nor much of a self-promoter. A *New York Times* profile of him in 1956 was headlined "A Quiet Investigator," and the cutline under the photo is "No House-afire legislator." The story describes him as "a grave, quiet, hard-working, humorless, undramatic 42-year-old Democratic Representative from California." The reporter says that Moss is "conceded to be one of the nicest and most diligent persons on the Hill" and at the same time "conceded to be no man to set the prairies blazing in pursuit of a cause."[20] But Moss turned out to be a bulldog about the cause that consumed the first half of his congressional career: the effort to limit the power of the executive to withhold public information from Congress and the people.

If political theorist Nancy Rosenblum is right in holding that the two cardinal virtues of the democratic citizen are treating people in an easy and equable manner and speaking up in the face of everyday injustice, John Moss was a democratic citizen par excellence.[21] He treated his staff as colleagues, not as underlings. For the people on his staff and for more than a few of his colleagues, he was a model of what the elected representative should be. He did not like his Washington staff to visit Sacramento for fear they would be lobbied by local interest groups and would begin to think of serving local interests rather than the public good.[22]

Moss was born in Hiawatha, Utah, in 1913 to Mormon parents; he himself was never a practicing Mormon. Along with his brother and three sisters, he moved as a child to California to be cared for by an aunt and uncle when, after his mother died, his father abandoned the children. His father, as Moss generously put it, "became a free soul." Moss attended public schools and earned a degree from Sacramento Junior College. He made a living in various jobs, working for tire companies, selling cars, joining his brother's real estate and insurance business, and establishing a small appliance store. Meanwhile, he developed a strong interest in government, was active with the Young Democrats, and in 1948 won election to the California

State Assembly, where he served two terms. Perhaps not incidentally, the California legislature passed an open-records statute in 1949 (California would pass a fuller open-records law, the Brown Act, in 1957, named after Ralph Brown, a California legislator Moss knew).[23]

In 1952, Moss won a close election and went to Congress, where he would remain through 1978. He was an ardent Democrat, writing to a California Democratic crony just two months after taking his seat in Washington that President Eisenhower, himself two months in the White House, was "incompetent" and "not big enough" for his office.[24] He was admonished some months later by a Sacramento-area supporter for the language of his newsletter and press releases—he used "I" too often, wrote *Woodland Democrat* editor Paul Leake, who advised him to "hold your fire until the President and the Republicans in Congress have more time to show themselves." After all, Leake advised, Moss might well need some Republican votes in 1954.[25]

Moss became interested in freedom of information during his first term. In a 1965 interview, he offered what seems to be his most detailed account of what led him to his freedom-of-information crusade. When Moss came to Washington, the Democrats were the minority party in the House. Moss recalled that, as a freshman, he was appointed to the lowly Post Office and Civil Service Committee, when "the old 'numbers game'" (of counting up communists or communist sympathizers in the government) began in the newly Republican-controlled House. Republicans sought to determine how aggressive the Truman administration had been in pursuing and dismissing federal employees for security reasons. "This was disturbing to me because I had every confidence that the Truman administration had been diligent in administering the laws and had attempted to hire loyal Americans. I insisted in committee that we get the facts from the Civil Service Commission. Well, the Commission refused to supply the information requested by the committee. This was my first experience with an agency refusing to respond to the legitimate demands of the legislative body."[26]

When the Democrats gained control of the House in 1955, Moss was appointed chair of the new Subcommittee on Government Information of the Government Operations Committee. Committee chairman William Dawson conferred the subcommittee chairmanship on Moss in a letter that declared the topic's importance: "An informed public makes the difference between mob rule and democratic government."[27] In the 1965 interview, Moss was asked if the subcommittee had been formed in response to "a developing pattern of withholding information." Moss replied, "No. It was the case of a freshman member being somewhat outraged over Executive arrogance. A cooperative chairman, Congressman Dawson, agreed that it was time Congress took a look at the problem of information policy in the Executive Branch and in the independent agencies of government."[28] Moss was elevated to the chairmanship because of his personal interest, not because he was any kind of specialist or expert in the area.

The other members of the subcommittee were Florida Democrat Dante Fascell and Michigan Republican Clare Hoffman. Hoffman had aggressively but ineffectually tilted against executive secrecy throughout the Truman administration. He became a more grudging supporter of the freedom-of-information cause with Republican Dwight Eisenhower in the White House. (Moss, Fascell, and Hoffman served on the subcommittee through 1962. In 1963 the subcommittee was expanded to eight members; only Moss continued with it to—and past—the enactment of FOIA in 1966.)[29]

In a number of accounts, Moss took up the subcommittee chairmanship because he was eager to get off the Post Office and Civil

Service Committee and onto something more meaty. In others, not inconsistent with this, he had sniffed out the likelihood that executive restrictions on information might be a growing concern and a fine issue for an ambitious young congressman.[30] George Kennedy, a historian of the freedom-of-information movement, cites his own 1977 interview with Moss as evidence for the congressman's outrage when the Civil Service Commission denied his request for information. Moss told him, "My experience in Washington quickly proved that you had a hell of a time getting any information."[31]

Organized groups in journalism cheered the establishment of the Moss committee.[32] James S. Pope, who led the freedom of information committee for the American Society of Newspaper Editors (ASNE) in the early 1950s, recalled, "We had not really expected to get such political clout so early; it was like gaining a fleet of nuclear subs."[33] Moss Committee staff early on consulted with James Russell Wiggins of the *Washington Post,* then head of that ASNE committee; Lyle C. Wilson, United Press vice president and Washington bureau manager; Bill Beale, Associated Press Washington bureau manager; and "at least a dozen reporters who know of specific instances of news suppression."[34] From the beginning media leaders backed Moss, and Moss encouraged their support. "I hope more of you will bring your complaints to the Subcommittee," he told a meeting of news executives in 1957. "By demanding your right of access to Federal information—and by bringing the case to the attention of the Subcommittee if your right is disregarded—you can help reverse the present Federal attitude of secrecy."[35]

That there were journalists to consult with about government secrecy was new. The American Society of Newspaper Editors, founded in 1923, had taken no interest in the subject until World War II, and then only as a problem in other countries; ASNE took it for granted that Americans could and should instruct the rest of the world in press freedom. Only as the Cold War developed did journalists become concerned about press freedom at home. The loyalty program President Harry S. Truman established in 1947 included a provision that disclosure of "confidential or non-public" information by government employees could be considered evidence of disloyalty. The Veterans Administration codified this directive by defining as "confidential" any information "prejudicial to the interests or prestige of the nation" or any information that "would cause administrative embarrassment or difficulty." That roused the ASNE to protest vehemently—and, in fact, these regulations were modified.[36]

The ASNE created its first committee on freedom of information—the Committee on World Freedom of Information—in 1948. In the same year, Sigma Delta Chi, the national journalism honor society, created a Committee on Advancement of Freedom of Information, which likewise had a global focus, not a national one. The ASNE dropped "World" from the committee's name in 1950, and Sigma Delta Chi's committee moved toward a domestic focus in 1951.[37]

ASNE recruited the retired media lawyer Harold Cross to examine the legal environment for freedom of information in the United States with respect to local, state, and national government. Cross had long served as counsel to the *New York Herald Tribune* and also taught media law at the Columbia Graduate School of Journalism. His ASNE work led to a book, *The People's Right to Know* (1953), which became the much-cited bible of the freedom-of-information movement. The book boldly began: "Public business is the public's business. The people have the right to know. Freedom of information is their just heritage. Without that the citizens of a democracy have but changed their kings."[38]

Cross himself intended the work to be a "manual of arms" for media lawyers and journalists.[39] He met several times with the Moss Committee, testified before it, and corresponded with the committee, writing at least twenty-six times before he died in 1959.[40] On one occasion, on the eve of House passage of the bill that became FOIA, Representative Moss traced the origins of the Freedom of Information Act to a conversation he had with Cross.[41]

A freedom-of-information movement among journalists was taking shape at the state level, where of course it was by no means focused on secrecy related to national security. A 1952 *Indiana Law Journal* article, "Access to Official Information: A Neglected Constitutional Right," opens with three examples, only one of which is about national security—a New Mexico newspaper reporter was denied permission to witness a U.S. Navy rocket test at the White Sands, New Mexico, proving grounds. The other examples are about the confidentiality of federal tax collectors' actions in levying fines on taverns in Albany, New York, for adulterating liquor, and secret meetings of Oregon's state board of education that took up the question of separating the state university's dental school from its medical school.[42] Journalists gained significant victories in the 1950s in the states. By 1959, fifteen states enforced both open meetings and public records disclosure, fifteen others open meetings only, and a handful of others public records disclosure only. Journalism professional groups—Sigma Delta Chi, the Associated Press Managing Editors, ASNE, the National Editorial Association, and state press associations—all promoted these laws.[43]

On the national level, there was some caution among the journalism associations. ASNE saw its freedom of information committee as a study group, not an instrument to propose or criticize specific policy positions. The committee's 1952 annual report declared, "We do not believe that the Committee on Freedom of Information should become a legislative committee."[44] In 1953 the committee reported that national legislation would develop to ensure the right to know, but it identified its own role as "watching all such legislation," not advocating for it.[45] Even so, by the time John Moss came to Congress, a freedom-of-information movement in journalism was a natural ally for the Moss Committee.

The legitimacy of prying information out of the executive may have been weakened by the notoriety of Sen. Joseph McCarthy's efforts to do just that. McCarthy gave a bad name to the practice of pressing the executive to release information. In May 1954, President Eisenhower claimed in a letter to Secretary of Defense Charles Wilson that the president was entitled to withhold executive information whenever disclosure would be "incompatible with the public interest or jeopardize the safety of the nation." This was the modern articulation of what then began to be called "executive privilege." Eisenhower provided a memo that traced the practice all the way back to George Washington. John Adams, counsel to the U.S. Army, cited Eisenhower's letter in refusing to testify before Senator McCarthy's committee about a meeting he had participated in with White House officials. The *New York Times* and the *Washington Post,* among other publications, supported the administration's position in its refusal to cooperate with Senator McCarthy.[46]

The Moss Committee was as good for "right-to-know" leaders in journalism as they were for the committee. Journalists and journalism associations were delighted to work with Moss. Sometimes "the Moss Committee staff wrote the press organizations' freedom-of-information annual reports—which were in turn widely reproduced in the press in terms laudatory of the Moss Committee."[47] The Moss Committee was "a unique political hybrid," an unusual locus of cooperation between Congress and the press.[48] The committee's investigations were organized in consultation with key leaders in the press, and Moss's staff was dominated by former newspaper reporters, including chief of staff Sam Archibald, a former *Sacramento Bee* reporter. In 1959, when Victor "Red" Newton, managing editor of the *Tampa Tribune* and chairman of Sigma Delta Chi's national freedom of information committee, wrote an angry letter of protest to Maj. Gen. Donald N. Yates, who had just announced that the press "will no longer be invited" to Cape Canaveral (later Cape Kennedy) to witness missile tests, he sent copies to Representative Moss and Sen. Thomas C. Hennings, leader of Senate-side efforts to limit executive secrecy. Archibald replied, praising the "blistering letter" and indicating full sympathy with its outrage.[49]

Using Cold War Rhetoric to Pry Information from the Government

Moss fired away at government secrecy not only in subcommittee hearings but also on the lecture circuit. There he could both entertain and grab headlines. In a speech to the Magazine Publishers Association in 1958, he recounted how the Air Force had tested a missile, hoping to get the nose cone back safely through the atmosphere, but the experiment failed. Maj. Gen. Bernard Schriever told the press the next day that there had been nothing living in the nose cone. Several days later the *New York Times* reported that a mouse had been in the nose cone, and the Air Force admitted that this was true. Moss joked that he disagreed with the Washington correspondents who said the Air Force had denied the existence of the mouse passenger until next of kin could be notified. He told the magazine publishers that he had asked General Schriever if the existence of the mouse was classified under Executive Order 10501, and if so, why the information was eventually released. If not, why had the information originally been withheld?[50]

Moss used humor to rhetorical effect in this and other instances, but perhaps the most consistent element in his rhetoric was repeated reference to the Cold War. Transparency or "freedom of information" became a political cause in the midst of the Cold War in part because it was such a strong suit in selling the "free world." There is good evidence that political support in Washington for civil rights in the 1950s and 1960s was strengthened when politicians, with some prodding from the State Department, recognized that the continued denial of civil rights to African Americans (particularly when visible instances of discrimination turned up in or close to Washington, D.C.) was an embarrassment before the world. It thrust U.S. racism in the faces of diplomats from all nations and damaged the United States in its global propaganda struggle against the Soviet Union.[51]

Something both similar and different was at work regarding the accessibility of government information. There was no foreign audience for the efforts to create greater freedom of information in the United States—and not much of a domestic audience, for that matter. But no rhetoric was more salient, more available, or more powerful at the time than Cold War rhetoric, and Moss readily adapted it to his own purposes. Freedom of information became a political issue because of growing secrecy in government that emerged out of World War II, particularly with the development of atomic weapons, but secrecy also grew simply as the bureaucracy took on more tasks and the "administrative state" became more substantial and more permanent. In combating secrecy—on behalf of Congress initially, on behalf of the general public as time went on—Moss appealed to the language of the Cold War.

Moss spoke repeatedly of the "paper curtain" of executive secrecy in Washington, an obvious effort to tar an information-withholding executive with the brush of Soviet tyranny. He probably picked this up from journalists themselves. The term "paper curtain" played off "iron curtain," the phrase Winston Churchill had used in his 1946 speech in Fulton, Missouri, to characterize Soviet domination of the satellite countries of eastern Europe. "Paper curtain" was in circulation at least as early as 1952. Sociologist Edward Shils used it then in the *Bulletin of the Atomic Scientists* to refer to bureaucratic barriers the United States had erected to foreign scientists seeking visas.[52] At the first set of hearings in his subcommittee, when Moss invited a group of leaders in journalism to present their views, Red Newton, then chair of Sigma Delta Chi's freedom-of-information committee, testified that his committee had produced a report that "exposed clearly an alarming picture of a 'paper curtain' draped securely over the release of news in the executive branch of Federal Government; of direct censorship in many departments, agencies, and bureaus; of arrogance on the part of many of our public servants; of much propaganda for political gain and privilege; of utter public confusion as to the facts in the big stories of the day; and, in some cases, of favoritism, intimidation, and revenge in the release of news of government to the people."[53]

Newton did not stop there. "Our public servants tell us that secret government is more efficient and uncluttered with political oratory and side issues. But we ask, which is better for the people, the efficient harmony of secret communistic government in Russia, or the turbulence of free, open government in America?"[54] In the summer of 1955, Moss was asked to make a public report on the work of the subcommittee. His aide J. Lacey Reynolds drafted remarks for him, entitled "Is There a 'Paper Curtain' in Washington?"[55]

Moss used Cold War language to oppose the secrecy that the Cold War itself had promoted. In a 1956 speech to the American Society of Newspaper Editors, he proudly reported, "We feel we have punched a few holes in the 'paper curtain' of secrecy which has been lowered between the people and their Government."[56] In a rhetorical move that Moss perfected, he called attention to instances where the Soviets were more open than the Americans in their information policies. In a 1957 speech to the Associated Press Managing Editors, for instance, he observed that the Russians published much of their research concerning the use of nuclear energy for domestic purposes: "This has been going on in open Russian technological publications for more than a year; but practically all information in the same areas are still classified in the United States."[57] In 1958 he gave credit to journalists themselves in a speech at the Syracuse University Journalism School: "The great majority of Washington correspondents—backed by their editors and by nearly every news organization—have been fighting hard to punch a few more holes in the paper curtain surrounding Washington bureaucracy."[58]

Moss was not above directly accusing the executive of using Soviet tactics. In 1959 he attacked the Pentagon for embarking on "Soviet-style control of the news—giving out the good news and hiding the failures."[59] Also in 1959, when he accepted the University of Arizona's John Peter Zenger Award, Moss compared the Pentagon's management of news of successful satellite launches (which got much publicity) and unsuccessful ones (which got little or no publicity) to Soviet information policy; the *Washington Star* headlined its account of the speech "Moss Accuses Pentagon of Red-Style News Curbs on Missile Launchings."[60] In 1960, Moss cited an Air Force memo advising its public relations officers that "flooding the public with facts is very helpful," especially when they "implant logical conclusions."

How far is this attitude, he asked, from a species of 'thought police' who will tell us what to think under pain of whatever sanction appears to be appropriate to the Administration in power?"[61] In an article for the *Bulletin of the Atomic Scientists* in 1961 titled "The Crisis of Secrecy," he urged the federal bureaucracy to "re-examine the paper curtain being erected between it and the people."[62]

"Paper curtain" seems an obvious metaphor for promoting freedom-of-information legislation, but it is oddly inexact. Churchill's "iron curtain" referred to a psychological, political, and physical barrier that kept people in the Soviet Union and its eastern European satellites from contact with, travel to, and information from the West. An "iron curtain" holds people in a prison; the "paper curtain" that freedom-of-information advocates railed against was a withholding of paper, not a curtain made of it. And yet the "paper curtain" phrase worked because the divide between the "free world" and the Soviet bloc that it referred to encircled the globe and dominated the American repertoire of metaphors. It suggested that the "free world" had its own pockets of unfreedom that needed to be liberated—in this case, an unfreedom at the very heart of democratic government.

With Moss, the Cold War framework survived a change of party in the White House. Moss was no maverick. He had an independent style, but he was a loyal, partisan Democrat. Surely he was more willing to give a Democratic administration the benefit of the doubt. In fact, he praised President Kennedy for his January 1961 statement that "I shall withhold from neither the Congress nor the people any fact or report, past, present or future, which is necessary for an informed judgment of our conduct and hazards." Moss said in November 1961 that "that moment marked the turn in the tide of battle, the handwriting on the wall presaging at long last progress in achieving some important victories for the forces upholding the people's right to know."[63] But in an address to the California Press Association a year later, just a month after the dramatic, frightening, but ultimately successful brinksmanship of the Cuban missile crisis, Moss criticized the Kennedy administration for expanding Eisenhower's secrecy. He objected to Kennedy's centralization of information policy in the White House, and he criticized the president for making information release concerning defense and security more and more a matter of political advantage and less and less justified by actual military matters.[64]

Using Cold War rhetoric in pursuit of freedom of information was clearly not unique to Moss, but he was at the center of a network made up mostly of journalists who were pursuing the same cause. In 1956, Kent Cooper, longtime general manager of the Associated Press, published a book, *The Right to Know*, most of it written years earlier, picking up on a phrase he claimed—with some reason—to have invented.[65] In the book, Cooper calls for a "right to know" constitutional amendment because, he argues, what needs protecting is not the privileges of an industry (the "free press") to write what they please but the rights of citizens to have access to the information they need. In his foreword, Cooper explains the sense of urgency in the book: government treatment of news was "slowly pressing toward the totalitarian pattern." He concludes the foreword by holding, "Our government can more profitably accept the broader principle of the Right to Know and ardently maintain it for the benefit of its citizens than to continue totalitarian methods of news suppression and propaganda. Developing loyal interest in this country of ours should begin at home."[66] Cooper, although more flat-footed than Moss and somber rather than provocative, shares with Moss the tactic of using common sentiments about the evils of the Soviet Union to hold the executive branch of government accountable to Congress and to the people.

The Bill Becomes a Law

Communication scholar Robert Blanchard, while a graduate student, served as an American Political Science Association fellow for four months in 1965, assigned as a staff member to the Moss Committee. He wrote his 1966 doctoral dissertation about the Moss Committee's work. He noted that from 1955 to 1960, the committee documented hundreds of instances of governmental restrictions on information. But in a disillusioned account for *Columbia Journalism Review* in 1966, just as FOIA became law, Blanchard sniffed at the new Federal Public Records Law, as it was initially known. Its basic structure was old, he complained, little changed from what had been drawn up in 1960 by Jacob Scher, a lawyer, a Northwestern University journalism professor, and for a time a consulting legal counsel to the Moss Committee. The legislation, Blanchard argued, was of minor consequence compared to the effective watchdog publicity the committee achieved in its hearings. In Blanchard's view, John Moss's great weapons were the telephone (he would call an agency official concerning the withholding of information, and often that call alone reversed the withholding), the letter to the agency head (and its publication if the agency did not respond positively), and, if worse came to worst, a full subcommittee hearing. This activity worked well, Blanchard held, at shaking information out of the government.

Blanchard had been an undergraduate student of Jacob Scher's at Northwestern. He strongly endorsed the agitational and publicity work of the Moss Committee but judged the effort to seek to embody it in legislation a mistake.[67] He was not alone in jumping on FOIA even before the ink was dry. In April 1967, still months before the law would take effect (in July 1967), the annual report of ASNE's freedom-of-information committee was already sounding querulous and alarmed. Nine exemptions! Untested in the courts! Limited to federal agencies! Leaves executive privilege intact! What kind of freedom-of-information act is that?[68] Also in 1967, Kenneth Culp Davis, a senior legal scholar at the University of Chicago Law School, published a scathing analysis of FOIA in the *University of Chicago Law Review*. He found that the drafting was "slipshod," that the product was overall "so unworkable" that it would become whatever the courts and the executive made of it, that the press would benefit little, and that "the bar and their clients will be the principal beneficiaries." In a particularly damning paragraph, Davis wrote: "That the Congress of the United States, after more than ten years of hearings, questionnaires, studies, reports, drafts, and pulling and hauling, should wind up with such a shabby product seems discouraging. The drafting deficiencies cannot be explained away as the product of extreme complexity, intractable subject matter, or unruly struggles between irreconcilable political philosophies. The failures in this instance are in the nature of inattention and indifference."[69]

Many freedom-of-information advocates found the nine exemptions troubling. Harold Cross had believed that a single exemption—for laws that expressly protected the confidentiality of specific categories of information—could alone be trusted. Jacob Scher's 1960 draft, produced during the month he took leave from Northwestern, proposed three exemptions—for laws expressly protecting confidentiality, for national security, and for personal privacy.[70] In the end, the additional exemptions were added on in the Senate bill as the Johnson administration's resistance to the legislation began to seem adamant and as the threat of a Johnson veto seemed real.[71]

Blanchard charged in his *Columbia Journalism Review* article that the committee's effective publicity seeking had pressured federal agencies to disclose more information to the public but that this publicity work declined after 1960. He attributed this to Moss's partisanship in being more cooperative with the Democrat Kennedy than with the Republican Eisenhower, to his ambitions for greater power in Congress and possibly even the Speakership, and to the retirement of key figures in the freedom-of-information movement in journalism. In the end, he argued, the passage of FOIA "could hardly be termed a victory for freedom of information."[72] Blanchard put more faith in agitation and publicity than in legislation, and he urged journalists to revive the freedom-of-information movement as a way to again begin "acting . . . as interest groups in support of a principle that is in the public interest as well as their own."[73]

Even if Blanchard is right about the fact of declining publicity, what of his explanation for for it? Several letters slammed his account in the next issue of the *Columbia Journalism Review,* including one from Moss himself. Moss insisted that "the Subcommittee's aggressiveness in ferreting out and attacking information problems has not diminished one iota in recent years"; rather, it simply drew less publicity because the Kennedy and Johnson administrations were so much more cooperative than Eisenhower's in repairing errors the subcommittee identified. Moss claimed that this was a natural outcome of the subcommittee's success over the years in establishing its reliability and effectiveness.[74] If Moss is right, it means that he made more headway with his quiet phone calls during the Kennedy and Johnson administrations than he had in the Eisenhower years. Still, evidence from coverage in the *New York Times* suggests that Blanchard and Moss were both wrong since news coverage of Moss and freedom of information declined even in Eisenhower's last year in office.[75]

Still, Blanchard had no comprehension of what laws can do that agitation and publicity cannot: establish a permanent resource for citizens that can endure even when legislators' interest flags; enshrine principles and provide a text for ongoing judicial interpretation; construct an extracongressional constituency of nongovernmental organizations, public interest lawyers, and news organization lawyers empowered and emboldened by the law; and provide for the establishment of an entire corps of information officers inside government who—with greater or lesser skill and greater or lesser enthusiasm—are more loyal to the ideals of the law that created their positions than to the specific agencies that employed them. The other critics, like Kenneth Davis, were more trenchant in pinpointing specific failures in drafting an effective bill, shortcomings that would not be repaired until an important set of amendments in 1974.

The "Right to Know"

Sen. Thomas Hennings (D-Mo.), the Senate sponsor of the bill that became the Freedom of Information Act, asserted that the framers believed in "a right in the people to know what their Government was doing."[76] Good rhetoric, poor history. Did the founders believe that republican government required informed citizens? Yes, but in their own terms, not in ours. They established what was at the time the world's most impressive postal system to enable the circulation of knowledge, and they specifically provided newspapers with favorable postal rates.[77] The Constitution encouraged the advancement of science and invention and established patents and copyrights to do so; the Patent Act of 1790 provided the specifics, including the requirement that documents in a successful patent application be available to the public. But nowhere did the framers say or imply that "being informed" meant that citizens should be able to demand information from those serving in the government. They did not even imagine that citizens should keep up to date with the public issues of the day. One of the founders most inclined to put faith in the public, Thomas Jefferson, advocated public education, sponsoring a bill in his home state of Virginia to that end. His bill (it did not pass) asserted that education could prevent tyranny by giving people enough historical knowledge "that, possessed thereby of the experience of other ages and countries, they may be enabled to know ambition under all its shapes, and prompt to exert their natural powers to defeat its purposes." In other words, Jefferson advocated popular education as a defense against bad leadership, not as a mechanism to make popular debate over public controversies the source of policy choices.[78]

Of course, citizens were expected to have information in order to vote intelligently, but what information would this be? For the founders, it was knowledge of the personal character of the candidates, not opinions about the public policies they might favor. The founders were wary of direct appeals to the people. They were ambivalent about the press, postal subsidies for newspapers notwithstanding. They were suspicious of political parties and even of civic voluntary associations, which President Washington declared arrogant, presumptuous, and dangerous when they recommended particular courses of action to elected officials.[79] Nothing in the founding era led inevitably to FOIA. And nothing in the Constitution ordained a "right to know," even if John Moss believed it did.[80]

So where did FOIA come from? It was not the founding fathers. Obviously, it was not the Internet. Nor was it the spirit of The Sixties, either the libertarianism of sex, drugs, and rock 'n' roll or the more sober essays about participatory democracy that circulated among the antiwar left, civil rights organizers, and the emerging women's movement. Moss began his work in the early 1950s, after all. He came of political age himself in the 1930s and 1940s, not the 1960s.

The key sponsors of a federal public records act on the Senate side were Thomas Hennings of Missouri and his successor Edward Long, born in 1903 and 1908, respectively—neither of them shaped by the sixties. As for the general public, the issue attracted neither powerful support nor strong opposition.

The concern about government information control was shared broadly across both parties in Congress, but it attracted consistent opposition from the executive, whether under Eisenhower, Kennedy, or Johnson. Every single government executive agency that testified in the hearings on the bill in 1966 was against it.

Outside the halls of Congress, the forces supporting an information bill had only one significant ally: the news media, particularly the newspapers and prominent organized groups of journalists, editorial writers, and publishers. They all saw their own interests at stake in the issue, and many journalists, though uncomfortable with actively encouraging a specific piece of legislation, did exactly that. They fed Representative Moss information he could use in promoting the cause. They praised Moss and his efforts in editorial after editorial. They covered his hearings and his other efforts to embarrass the executive.

Their advocacy was unusual in the modern, increasingly professionalized press, and that their organized associations took a stand on freedom of information was a novelty, not yet a decade old, when the Moss Committee began its work. The press, like Congress, worried about the rise of an administrative state, which shifted power from elected officials in the legislature to appointed bureaucrats in a rapidly metastasizing administrative apparatus. They shared a concern about how difficult it was to stay informed given "the increase in Federal business and employes," as James S. Pope, editor of the *Courier-Journal* (Louisville, Kentucky) wrote to John Moss in August

1955. In the face of the growing size of federal agencies, "Congress and the Press alike" needed to reexamine "whether our tools and our manpower have not become dangerously deficient." As Pope added, "There's so damn much news," and he meant not news stories but news events that neither Congress nor the press could keep on top of.[81]

In short, FOIA came out of a battle between the branches of government. It emerged from a long but incomplete and inadequate effort by Congress to control the federal bureaucracy—or, if "control" is too strong a word, to learn to live with a bureaucracy it could not control by monitoring it, keeping it on notice that someone was watching. So damn much news indeed! And it was just not clear what to do about it.

FOIA was not the first attempt. A flag had been planted on the road to freedom of information in 1935 with the Federal Register Act. This was an important first step in making public the rule-making actions of executive agencies. The *Federal Register* is an official gazette of U.S. executive activity, modeled on an 1893 Rules Publication Act in Britain.[82] Another milestone was the Administrative Procedure Act (APA, 1946), which the Moss Committee sought to repair. APA required public disclosure of government records "to persons properly and directly concerned" except when "secrecy in the public interest" is required, when the information relates "solely to the internal management of an agency," or when "otherwise required by statute." Even then, agencies could withhold information "for good cause found." These openings—"persons . . . directly concerned," "the public interest," and "good cause"—were ample cover for any administration to keep just about any information secret.[83] Supporters of the APA had urged that it would be a "bill of rights" for individuals facing a rapidly growing administrative state that the founding fathers had never anticipated, but the historian who has written most extensively about the APA's origins and its evolution concedes that "the APA ultimately worked little change in administrative practice."[84]

The APA nonetheless offered a charter for public access to government information. The Freedom of Information Act became law as an amendment to it. Harold Cross had laid out the terms that an improved APA would require in order to become a federal open-records law comparable to those passed in many states. The law would have to define "public records," declare the right of any citizen to inspect public records (with defined exceptions that Congress judged to be important to national security or otherwise vital to the public interest), and to provide court review of denials of requests for information submitted under the act.[85]

In the years during which Moss's subcommittee challenged government information policies, the executive cited not only the APA as precedent for withholding information but also the 1789 "housekeeping" statute (5 U.S. Code 22) that authorized each executive department head "to prescribe regulations, not inconsistent with law, for the government of his department, the conduct of its officers and clerks, and the custody, use and preservation of the records, paper and property appertaining thereto." It was this statute that the Moss Committee successfully amended in 1958. Other than FOIA itself, this was the only legislation the subcommittee ever sponsored. The amendment was simply a sentence asserting that "this section does not authorize withholding information from the public or limiting availability of records to the public" (H.R. 2767). President Eisenhower, upon signing the bill into law on August 12, 1958, added a signing statement to the effect that this addition to the housekeeping statute did not and could not alter the power of department heads "to keep appropriate information or papers confidential in the public interest."[86] In other words, Eisenhower was saying that the law he had just signed would make no real difference in government policy or practice.

The best Moss himself could say for his amendment (and he did tout it as a significant achievement in speeches in 1958 and 1959) is that it demonstrated that Congress had some backbone on the issue and that it forced the executive branch to invoke "executive privilege" and to stop leaning on "the crutch of the 'housekeeping' law." That at least clarified the problem: "If the people and their elected representatives have the right to find out what their government is planning and doing, we live under a democracy. If the executive has the privilege to determine how much the people shall know, we are following the authoritarian course of government."[87]

In practice, during the 1950s, officials felt free to do what they wished in terms of withholding information. Moss understood this very well. As he put it in a 1959 speech to the Aviation Writers Association, federal officials make information available to the press

—unless the information is restricted on grounds of security;

—unless the information is specifically restricted by law; such as personal income tax returns and trade secrets;

—unless the official decides that the information is merely "preliminary";

—unless the official decides the information is part of an "internal" document;

—unless the official believes the information would cause "controversy";

—unless the official believes release of the information is not "timely";

—unless the official believes that the information might be "misunderstood" or "misinterpreted" by the people of the United States;

—unless the official believes the information might cause a
"publicity build-up";

—or unless he feels merely that release of the information would
not be "in the public interest."[88]

This last item suggests that Moss knew his Administrative Procedure Act, not just his Washington politics.

Although FOIA was a landmark of historic proportion, it was less
of a breakthrough than Moss and his allies in Congress and the press
had hoped. Its shortcomings came to the attention of Sen. Edward
Kennedy's Administrative Practice and Procedure Subcommittee of
the Senate Judiciary Committee some years later. Kennedy took a
second look at the law, and his subcommittee drafted a FOIA reform
bill early in 1973, just as the Watergate inquiries were rattling the
Nixon White House and intensifying interest in government policies
of withholding information. FOIA amendments passed in the fall of
1974—unanimously in the Senate and 349–2 in the House. Nevertheless, they were promptly vetoed by President Gerald Ford. Ford objected to provisions that authorized the courts to examine classified
documents, made law enforcement records more vulnerable to disclosure, instituted penalties for agencies that failed to comply with the
law, and introduced time limits for agencies to respond to FOIA requests. Congress overrode the veto (371–31 in the House and 65–27 in
the Senate). Senator Kennedy declared the override "a visible and concrete repudiation by Congress of both the traditional bureaucratic
secrecy of the federal establishment and the special antimedia, anti-
public, anti-Congress secrecy of the Nixon administration."[89]

The 1974 amendments made FOIA far more effective in achieving
congressional intentions. Coming in the wake of Watergate, they
profited from the temporary weakness of the White House. They pro-

vided for the "segregation" of information so that agencies could not classify whole documents or categories of documents as exempt; they provided for in-camera review by the courts of materials the executive agencies judged to be protected by the national security exemption; they made more concrete what fell under the investigatory law enforcement exemption; they standardized the fees requesters must pay while authorizing fee waivers for requests that were for the benefit of the general public; and they established deadlines for agencies to respond to requests.[90]

When John Moss left Congress in 1978, he told the *Sacramento Bee* that his main disappointment was "that I haven't been able to make government totally effective. You like to see ready evidence of improvement (but) that's very difficult. You work a long time on something and you back away with a feeling that you've punched a balloon and it bounces back again."[91] Moss was disappointed that exemptions to FOIA accumulated over time from what he imagined, in the beginning, would be simply the protection of military and diplomatic secrets from disclosure.[92]

In retrospect, I think, FOIA was sounder than Moss realized. Most of the exemptions in the law demonstrated good sense, not weak compromise. There were good reasons to protect information that might bear on the personal privacy of government employees, influence ongoing law enforcement activity, or constrain internal predecisional discussion in executive agencies, or that protected corporate trade secrets. All of these were necessary and salutary concessions to the executive agencies. An unbounded notion of "the more disclosure, the better" is untenable. Friends and skeptics of FOIA alike can, in principle, agree that when the flag of transparency is unfurled, certain values deserve to be taken into account, including genuine national security, personal privacy, legitimate law enforcement confidentiality, and deliberation inside government unconstrained by the fear that legitimately confidential communications will become public.

Balancing openness and the values it impinges upon was never going to be an easy matter. "It is not an easy task to balance the opposing interests," the Senate Judiciary Committee reported in clarifying its support for the Freedom of Information Act in 1965, "but it is not an impossible one either. It is not necessary to conclude that to protect one of the interests, the other must, of necessity, either be abrogated or substantially subordinated. Success lies in providing a workable formula which encompasses, balances, and protects all interests, yet places emphasis on the fullest responsible disclosure."[93]

The efforts of John Moss to make Congress a more effective watchdog on the burgeoning executive, pursued with the willing collaboration of leaders of the nation's press and with avid support from Republicans as well as Democrats, produced something novel for the United States and—since the only earlier freedom-of-information laws, Sweden (1766) and Finland (1951), had not had global influence—something of a small miracle for the world, as other nations borrowed from the Americans to enact comparable laws of their own. Flawed as the American FOIA was, it proved the modern beginning of what Thomas Blanton, director of the National Security Archive, has dubbed the "Openness Revolution." Blanton sees FOIA's passage and the 1974 amendments that strengthened it as the point of origin for the worldwide spread of that revolution, which in the key decade between the fall of the Soviet Union and 9/11 would reach around the globe.[94]

The English Romantic poet Percy Bysshe Shelley wrote that poets are "the unacknowledged legislators of the world." Occasionally legislators are the unacknowledged poets of the world. And there is some poetry in the Freedom of Information Act. FOIA's poetry is condensed into one phrase, "any person"—the phrase that John Moss himself highlighted as the first of the bill's three distinctive features in speaking on the House floor on behalf of his bill in 1966.[95] (The other two were the specification of the nine categories under which agencies could legitimately withhold information and the provision that those who requested information could take the agency to court if the information request was denied.) "Any person" can initiate a Freedom of Information Act request. The requester thus automatically has standing and need not jump any hurdles to make a request. One need not even be a U.S. citizen to seek information from the U.S. government under FOIA. This relieves the agencies of any need to pass judgment on the requester and thereby saves a great deal of time and expense, clearing the way for a request to be examined on its merits.

The practicality of this seems obvious, but the poetry is evident, too. It is a richer, more universal, and more complete rendering of democratic equality than the founders ever endorsed.[96]

three

The Consumer's Right
to Be Informed

Toward the end of the presidential campaign of 1960, John F. Kennedy addressed the plight of American consumers. Just days before the election, at the Concourse Plaza Hotel in the Bronx, New York, he declared: "The wage earners who pay the rent, the housewives who shop for the families, all have a vital interest in governmental policy, which affects them, and affects their ability to meet their responsibilities. And yet all these great interests, of which all of us have a part, really go unrepresented before the committees of the agencies of our National Government." He promised to appoint a "consumer counsel" in the Office of the President and even suggested that such an appointee—"perhaps a woman familiar with consumer problems"—would help ensure "the public interest in a Government where private interests are well represented." He cited Louis Brandeis's response decades earlier when a congressman challenged his testimony by demanding, "Who, sir, do you represent?" Brandeis replied, "I, sir, am the people's counsel." Kennedy concluded this portion of his speech: "It is my hope and belief that this new officer of the Government will also be the people's counsel and speak for the people."[1] Not Kennedy nor his administration but a young lawyer in Hartford, Connecticut, Ralph Nader, would become the consumers' lobbyist and the people's counsel, but that would be a few years ahead.

After Kennedy took office, he was at first silent about consumers. But fourteen months into his presidency, he sent a special message to Congress that identified four vital consumer rights—"the right to safety" (protection against hazardous products), "the right to be informed" (protection against fraud, deceit, and misleading advertising and packaging), "the right to choose" (freedom of choice among a variety of competing products and services), and "the right to be heard" (a voice in the formation of government policies). He wrote that old programs needed strengthening and new legislation needed enactment to secure these rights. He urged that the Council of Economic Advisers create a Consumers' Advisory Council to advise government on consumer needs and that each federal agency designate a special assistant in the agency head's office to attend to consumer interests. With the "right to be informed" clearly in mind, he specifically recommended legislation on truth in lending and truth in packaging, mentioning by name the work of Sen. Paul Douglas (D-Ill.) on truth in lending practices and Sen. Philip Hart (D-Mich.) and his efforts to rein in deceptive packaging and labeling.[2]

Kennedy's consumer "bill of rights" became a point of departure for consumer advocates both in Congress and also in an increasingly visible consumer movement. But the idea that each agency should have its own consumer adviser went nowhere. Esther Peterson, the labor activist whom Kennedy appointed to head the Women's Bureau in the Department of Labor, remembered that, a short time before he was assassinated, Kennedy asked her to be his White House consumer adviser. But the suggestion that there be a consumer representative in the Office of the President would not be acted upon until Lyndon Johnson became president.[3]

Although Kennedy's support for consumers had been largely rhetorical, the rhetoric mattered. The notable Progressive Era achievements were regulatory "fix-its" for specific health-related industrial abuses, not a general recognition of consumer interests. New Deal efforts under Rexford Tugwell were more broadly based and enlisted labor, the cooperative movement, and muckraking journalistic support. But Kennedy gave consumers their first ringing presidential blessing, and consumer advocates repeatedly cited his consumer bill of rights for years to come.[4]

The Renewal of Consumer Legislation

There were many precedents for federal action on behalf of consumers. Most famous was the Food and Drug Act of 1906. That law, among other things, prohibited false or misleading labeling of food. The 1913 Gould Amendment required that the "net quantity" of packaged food be stated on the package. The McNary-Mapes Amendment of 1930 gave the Food and Drug Administration additional authority to regulate the "fill" of a can or other standard package—specifically, how much "slack" in the fill would be allowed—setting reasonable standards for different classes of canned goods. The Food, Drug, and Cosmetic Act of 1938 strengthened rules regarding slack fill and deceptive packaging and prohibited interstate commerce in containers "so made, formed, or filled as to be misleading." All these laws notwithstanding, by the 1960s there remained plenty of consumer complaints about slack fill and lack of clarity or visibility in net weight labeling on packages. The proliferation of different types of packages, with different contents and weights, made it hard for any consumer who was not a genius at mathematics to calculate the relative cost of different packages of the same or similar products. Package labels would identify how many "servings" a package contained without specifying the size of the "serving." Misleading terms abounded on labels, like "full gallon" or "jumbo pound" or "7 cents off" (off from what?).[5]

President Kennedy's consumer message resonated in part because it was so well attuned to pervasive social and economic changes. By 1960, people experienced themselves as "consumers" more than in the past. That is, more people buying supplies for home and family encountered advertisements, packages, and banks rather than salespeople, storekeepers, and bankers. "Marketing is increasingly impersonal," President Kennedy told Congress. "Consumer choice is influenced by mass advertising utilizing highly developed arts of persuasion. The consumer typically cannot know whether drug preparations meet minimum standards of safety, quality, and efficacy. He usually does not know how much he pays for consumer credit; whether one prepared food has more nutritional value than another; whether the performance of a product will in fact meet his needs; or whether the 'large economy size' is really a bargain."[6] In shopping, people found themselves addressed by packages designed to attract their eye, not by store owners or employees hoping to maintain a relationship with a repeat customer.

The shifts toward packaged and branded goods and toward a mass consumption society had become familiar objects of social criticism in the decade leading up to Kennedy's message. This goes back in the postwar era as far as David Riesman's *The Lonely Crowd* (1950) and the lectures historian David Potter delivered in 1950 that became

his *People of Plenty* (1954). Potter wrote of a shift from an economy of
scarcity to an economy of abundance and a necessary reorientation
"to convert the producer's culture into a consumer's culture."[7] Later
in the 1950s, several works by popular social critic Vance Packard became best sellers, including *The Hidden Persuaders* (1957), *The Status
Seekers* (1959), and *The Waste Makers* (1960). So there was an intellectual or cultural climate that emphasized, with considerable disquiet, the movement toward a consumer-centered society. Special
attention was paid to the growing authority and dubious values of
the advertising industry, which Potter, Packard (in *The Hidden
Persuaders*), and John Kenneth Galbraith (in *The Affluent Society*,
1958) singled out as a powerful new force.

Sen. Philip A. Hart, a first-term Democrat from Michigan elected
in 1958, was the primary sponsor of truth-in-packaging legislation.
His efforts began in 1961, but his Fair Packaging and Labeling Act
was not approved until 1966, taking effect in 1967. Hart was a World
War II veteran, a lawyer, former U.S. attorney for the Eastern District of Michigan, and from 1954 until 1959, when he took office
as U.S. senator, Michigan's lieutenant governor. Hart took an early
interest in consumer affairs and in 1961 convened his first hearings
on consumer protection.

Hart's aide Jerry Cohen drew up a memo for him on April 20,
1961, proposing that the inquiry be "aimed at deceptive, misleading
and fraudulent practices in the merchandising of products to the
extent that such practices *directly* affect the choice of the ultimate
consumer." Cohen listed nine different areas to investigate, from deceptive packaging to medical device quackery to misleading warran-
ties. He advised that the "most feasible" topic for hearings would be
deceptive packaging and labeling: "Such an inquiry would be aimed
at those practices which prevent the consumer from making a ra-

tional comparison of prices in the market place. The basis for it is the concept that a rational choice by the consumer is essential to the proper functioning of a free enterprise economy." Cohen listed essentially all of the items that would be taken up in hearings over the next several years—nonstandard package sizes, oversized packages "so designed only for their attention-attracting ability," slack fill, concealment of net weight by placing the legally required figure inconspicuously on the package label, net weight amounts in fractions of an ounce that made it difficult for consumers to calculate the per-unit price, deceptive quantity and quality designations (such as "king size," "family size," "economy size," "fancy," and "extra fancy") that had "no rational relation to the content of the container," and the use of such designations to imply—often falsely—that the bigger the size of the package, the cheaper the unit price.[8]

In writing for *The Nation* on behalf of his bill in 1963, Senator Hart recalled picking up groceries for his mother thirty-five years earlier at Mr. Edie's market, just a block from his house. His mother's relationship with Mr. Edie "was a very personal one. Mr. Edie provided both sales and service. Most of the packages you took home were ones that Mr. Edie had filled himself out of his bins of sugar, beans and cookies. There was no nonsense about weight or volume, either. Products came in pints, pounds or pecks. There were no fractional ounces, no 'giant half-quarts,' and you could tell at a glance how prices compared with those in the store down the street." He acknowledged this memory to be "nostalgic" but insisted it was not "wistful"—the supermarket was a great improvement over the corner store in many ways. Factory-made packaging "has permitted mass distribution with resultant lowered costs." However, the supermarket made intelligent, price-conscious shopping more difficult for the consumer. The equivalent of Mr. Edie had become the package itself—the package is "the only 'salesman' the shopper encounters"—and Hart added that the manager of the supermarket is essentially a landlord who rents shelf space to different manufacturers.[9] Of course, the disappearance of the world's Mr. Edies did not happen overnight, but the postwar economic expansion, suburbanization, the growth of an automobile-dependent society, and the proliferation of supermarkets proceeded quickly.

Concern about the consumers' plight was not far behind. Monroe Friedman, a young psychologist who did some of the first significant research on consumer knowledge of the relative price per unit value of comparable supermarket products, first became aware of consumers' difficulties in making price comparisons when he and his wife and three children moved in 1964 to Ypsilanti, Michigan, from Los Angeles—and from a private research organization to an academic position at Eastern Michigan University. Having taken a substantial cut in pay, yet needing to support a growing family, Friedman was eager to economize wherever he could. While shopping at the supermarket with his wife, he learned "how difficult it was to make price comparisons," and in buying a car, he discovered "how hard it was to make finance rate comparisons" when many lenders presented their finance rates in ways that hid the true costs to the consumer.[10] Hearing about the Hart truth-in-packaging bill and Sen. Paul Douglas's truth-in-lending proposal, he wanted to see what the field of consumer psychology had to say about price comparison. Not much at all, he found, so he undertook a study himself. For his research subjects, he recruited thirty-three women, each of them having at least a year of college, most of them Eastern Michigan students, and all of them living in married student housing on campus. The women were instructed to stop at twenty preselected product locations in a local supermarket where they regularly shopped and—under strict time limits—to choose the most economical brand and size of packaged product. The results were clear: even this well-educated group was often stumped, unable to consistently select the most economical brands.[11]

Politicians could attest to their own experience in facing the confusions of the marketplace, as Philip Hart did in his first public announcement of hearings on packaging and labeling at the annual meeting of the Council on Consumer Information in St. Louis on April 7, 1961. That Hart spoke to this group at all was something of an accident. The organization had been founded in 1954, a gathering of home economists, economists, and other consumer professionals. The 1961 program chair, Richard Morse, an economist from Kansas State University, tried "like the dickens" to secure a notable banquet speaker for the occasion, but he struck out. Sen. Estes Kefauver declined; Sen. Paul.Douglas declined. An aide to Douglas suggested Senator Hart, telling Morse that he had "put in some kind of Senate resolution" concerning consumers. Morse did not call this unknown senator, deciding instead to go with a new documentary from Consumers Union instead of a guest speaker. Then another leader of the group, Marguerite Burk, reported that "somebody from Senator Hart's office stopped by and asked if it would be alright if Senator Hart came to your meeting." Morse agreed, but as late as four-thirty on the afternoon of the banquet, all he knew was that "maybe" Senator Hart would join them.

Hart did indeed turn up. He pulled from his pocket a seven-page document and asked Morse, "If it's all right with you, I have an announcement I'd like to make; would it be all right? I've timed it. It will only take seven minutes." Hart read his announcement, agreed to take questions, and two hours later the question-and-answer session ended. "He was a beautiful man," Morse recalled, "and he was so low-keyed but so powerful, and he did sneak up on us to speak. He just came—he was just going to take seven minutes—I timed it."[12]

In his brief address, Hart noted that "the new Frontiersmen" of the incoming Kennedy administration were newcomers to Washington:

> For the most part these are men who still have small children; and also for the most part they lack the incomes of the now departed captains of industry and the financial world who so recently occupied the seats of federal power.
>
> Why do I mention these facts? Because I think they suggest that the poor, miserable battered, befuddled consumer is about to come into his own in Washington. He is not on the outside looking in; he is the Chairman of the Federal Trade Commission; he is on top in the Department of Agriculture; he is rampant throughout the whole executive branch of government.
>
> The New Frontiersmen have actually shopped in crowded supermarket aisles; have tried to and despaired of comparing prices; have wrung out diapers by hand when the automatic washer breaks down and the serviceman doesn't come and doesn't come; have struggled with tire guaranties and tire grades; have grown impatient with advertisers screaming that Brand Q in the "Giant Half Quart" size is "10% better"; and have never been convinced that water should be sold by the pound at the price customarily charged for ham.

This new Washington scene, Hart told his listeners, "augurs well for the silent millions and millions of American shoppers who day by day pay more and more for less and less in bigger and bigger containers with smaller and smaller type." And he announced hearings that would be "an in-depth study of the shoddy, the shabby, the meretricious, the deceitful and misleading practices of the marketplace."[13]

With the 1961 hearings and subsequent sessions, Hart became a prominent consumer advocate, and this brought him correspondence from ordinary citizens around the country complaining of misleading packaging and labeling of supermarket products. He wrote his constituents about some of these in a 1965 newsletter. He told of a package of frozen cherry pie that pictured one wedge of the pie with thirty-seven cherries visible along one edge of the slice. But, in fact, the entire pie had only forty cherries "swimming in a thin paste of cornstarch." He wrote of a package of chicken croquettes that had been labeled "12 ounces, serves two" when, inside, most of the twelve ounces was sauce and "the croquettes weren't enough to satisfy one moderately hungry child." A six-ounce jar of instant tea marked "25-cents-off" sold for 95 cents, but later the same jar was on the shelves with a label reading "50-cents-off" and selling for 97 cents. Hart concluded by telling his constituents that the average supermarket at the time had 7,500 different items for sale. "That's 7,500 package 'salesmen' that the housewife must cope with. In ten years, the number of items will probably increase to 20,000. It seems to me we'll all be better off if we keep them honest."[14] In his moderate voice, Hart was linking up with a low-grade discontent, a sense of injustice at being had, a disgust that business would blithely treat consumers as chumps.

By the early 1960s, organizations seeking to represent and lobby for consumer interests were widely established. Consumer activists and advocates had gained experience in the labor movement, in consumer cooperatives, and in academic programs in consumer and home economics. Consumers Union, dating back to the 1930s, was well recognized for its independent consumer product testing and rating services and its widely read magazine, *Consumer Reports*. What was new in the 1960s was a cadre of liberal members of Congress,

primarily from the North and Midwest, who, like Hart, came to
national office in the 1958 elections—with more sympathizers elected
in 1960. These newcomers took on the consumers' interests as
their own.

This was a tall order in several respects. First, the consumers' interest seemed to mean women's interest, and that was regarded as a
relatively trivial matter at a time when Cold War foreign policy and
military policy dominated the national stage. Second, government
regulation of economic activity faced organized opposition from business. Business lobbyists were active and effective in wearing down
consumer advocates and watering down consumer-oriented legislation. Third, although everyone was a consumer, no one took this as
a primary identity, and although everyone received injuries through
misleading and deceptive practices in labeling and packaging, from
auto loans to bank savings accounts to cereal packages, the injuries
were generally small and often went unrecognized. They did not arrive concentrated in dramatic blows.[15]

Fourth, with the economy growing, consumers rode a wave of
affluence. Why rock the boat?[16] British journalist Henry Fairlie recalled that when he first came to Washington, D.C., in 1965, his English hostess enthusiastically spirited him off to a supermarket: "We
had monuments and art galleries and fine buildings at home, but we
did not have these cathedrals of a new civilization." Fairlie was awed,
and walked through the store "as if it were Chartres."[17] Finally, although it is hard to know how much credit to give to this factor, some
thirty-five women's magazines did not write anything about Senator
Hart's hearings, although he sent them background materials for publicity purposes. The president of the Grocery Manufacturers Association boasted in a speech that he had met with representatives from
these magazines and urged them that "the day was here when their

editorial department and business department might better understand their interdependency relationships as they affect the operation results of their company; and as their operations affect the
advertiser—their bread and butter." The magazine executives got the
message and, according to the recollection of Sarah Newman, executive director of the National Consumers League from 1952 to 1972,
"began to run articles to create a 'favorable public attitude' toward
food advertisers."[18]

Even so, there was progress. This included noteworthy legislation
and executive action such as the Hazardous Substances Labeling Act
of 1960, which mandated warnings on dangerous household products, and the Child Protection Act of 1966, which banned potentially
dangerous toys and other products for children. The Surgeon General's 1964 report on smoking and health concluded that overwhelming
medical evidence confirmed that tobacco caused cancer, and this led
the Federal Trade Commission to require warning labels on ciga-
rette packages beginning in 1966. Television and radio commercials
for tobacco products were banned in 1971. Responding in part to
Ralph Nader's 1965 investigative report *Unsafe at Any Speed,* the Automobile Safety Act of 1966 required seat belts to be installed in all
new cars. Senator Hart's Fair Packaging and Labeling Act became
law the same year and helped consumers to comparison-shop for
supermarket goods, as Senator Douglas's Truth in Lending Act (1968)
did for shopping for credit.[19]

Progress was often painfully slow. For example, it was in January
1960 that Senator Douglas first introduced his bill to require financial institutions to adopt a uniform standard for reporting the annual interest costs for money borrowed. It would be eight years before that proposal became law—and by then Douglas no longer held
office. Douglas was the elder statesman of consumer advocates in

Congress. Born in 1892, he completed a Ph.D. in economics at Columbia in 1921 and had a distinguished first career teaching economics at the University of Chicago. He became more and more involved in reform politics in Chicago—which meant that in municipal politics he sometimes sided with the socialists, sometimes with reform Republicans, and sometimes with independent-minded Democrats (when he could find any). In 1942, when he was fifty, his political connections enabled him to enlist in the Marines. He saw active duty and earned a Purple Heart in the Pacific. He proved a skillful statewide campaigner, pulled off an upset victory for a U.S. Senate seat in 1948, and served in the Senate from 1949 to 1967.

Douglas's attention to the topic of consumer borrowing went back to his work on consumer finance for the New Deal's National Recovery Administration. In the 1930s, finance companies typically announced only their monthly interest rates—often around 3.5 percent at that time—and consumers did not understand that that made the annual rate 42 percent. In the 1960 bill, Douglas proposed that lenders publish their annual rates and also that they charge interest only on the unpaid balance of the loan.[20] The Douglas bill would require lenders to identify the total cost of the loan to the consumer and to present the interest charges as an annual interest rate on the unpaid balance. Although the proposed legislation was about disclosure only, Eisenhower's Commerce Department spoke against it, and the bill did not get out of the Committee on Banking and Currency.

Douglas reintroduced the bill in 1962, with the Kennedy administration's support; in his message to Congress on March 14 that year, Kennedy endorsed the bill, but it was again blocked in committee. In the Production and Stabilization Subcommittee of the Banking and Currency Committee, committee chairman A. Willis Robertson (D-Va.) sided with the four Republicans on the subcommittee. In subsequent years, Robertson used a variety of procedural stratagems to keep the bill from being reported to the Senate floor, where it surely would have been approved.

After Douglas was defeated for reelection in 1966, responsibility for his bill passed to Sen. William Proxmire (D-Wisc.). The bill finally passed in 1968 as part of the Consumer Credit Protection Act, eight years after Douglas had started it on its way. Douglas, in retirement, had the pleasure of testifying for the bill in both the House and Senate, and he was present at the White House when President Johnson signed the bill into law.[21]

Esther Peterson, the "Giant Food Lady"

Repeatedly during Philip Hart's efforts for consumer legislation, he was criticized for underestimating the intelligence of the American housewife.[22] Surely women could shop for themselves without federal support! Hart addressed this in a 1963 speech in the Senate. Referring to his wife, Janey Hart, a skilled airplane and helicopter pilot (who sought unsuccessfully to be the first woman astronaut), Hart declared: "I wish to make it perfectly clear that I am married to a brilliant American woman. She is a licensed helicopter pilot and a licensed multiengine airplane pilot with an instrument rating. I have watched her with a calculator and radio communications get me from place A to place B through a fog safely—something I could not dream of doing. My wife tells me that when she goes into a supermarket she has a great deal more trouble landing right than she does when she lands in a fog."[23] In the end, Senator Hart's Fair Packaging and Labeling Act did not land so well. Much weakened along the road to passage, it achieved less than it had set out to. Its main impact was to give authority to the Food and Drug Administration to negotiate with the corporate world a reduction in the proliferating variety of package sizes for many commonly purchased products and to eliminate some of the most egregious of the commonly used misrepresentations in package labeling.

Another consumer advocate would fare better, but not, as it happened, with much help from Congress or the White House. Esther Peterson was adept at navigating through fog herself. The most highly placed woman in the Kennedy administration, Peterson would serve even more visibly in the Johnson administration. A Utah Mormon, the daughter of Danish immigrants, Esther Eggertsen graduated from Brigham Young University in 1927 and went on to Columbia Teachers' College for a master's degree. She met Oliver Peterson, a working-class socialist who introduced her to union leaders Sidney Hillman and David Dubinsky, and they led her toward the labor movement. In the 1930s, she taught physical education and drama at the Bryn Mawr Summer School that Bryn Mawr College, the YWCA, and the union movement ran for working women. She joined the staff of the Amalgamated Clothing Workers of America in 1939, working as an organizer in the South, and in 1945 became the union's first lobbyist in Washington. In that capacity, she came to know John F. Kennedy, a young congressman and member of the House Education and Labor Committee. Later she worked for him in the 1960 presidential campaign, and that led to Kennedy's appointing her as head of the Women's Bureau and assistant secretary of labor.[24] In that position, she championed the Equal Pay Act, which became law in 1963. She opposed the Equal Rights Amendment, as did many others in the labor movement, holding that it would make unconstitutional "protective legislation" statutes that regulated work hours and improved working conditions for women. As executive vice chairman of the President's Commission on the Status of Women—of which

Eleanor Roosevelt was chairman until her death in 1962—Peterson was the commission's driving force.[25]

In the fall of 1963, Kennedy followed up his March 1962 message on consumer rights by asking Peterson to serve in the White House as a special assistant for consumer affairs, probably in early November. Peterson recalled later that she was reluctant to take this on. Her experience and expertise were in the labor movement, not in consumer affairs. Just weeks later, Kennedy was assassinated. After that, Peterson wrote, "I just dropped the whole thing. Forgot it."[26]

If Peterson forgot Kennedy's invitation to become a White House consumer adviser, the idea was not forgotten by Lyndon B. Johnson, the new president. (Senator Hart was proud to have suggested her to Johnson for the post.)[27] In December, presidential assistant Walter Jenkins called Peterson to sound her out on it. He called again on New Year's Day 1964, asking her to be at Andrews Air Force Base the next morning to fly to the Johnson ranch. After lunch at the ranch, Johnson told her that he approved of the plans she and Johnson's economic adviser Walter Heller had drawn up for a consumer adviser post: "I approve it, Esther. Now go out and have a press conference." She recalled, "I could have fallen through the floor. 'I want every consumer to know that I'm in your corner.' I think that's word for word what he said." The press took photos, including one of Lyndon and Lady Bird Johnson with Esther Peterson. Johnson said to the reporters, "Now this is my gal and I want you guys out there to take good care of her."[28]

Peterson was completely unprepared for the press conference, at which, among other things, she encouraged consumers to contact her about their complaints and concerns. Within a few days, there were boxes of letters. "The letters showed a great range of unhappiness and belief that the marketplace was not telling the truth. People didn't know what was in packages. They were deceived by pictures when the contents did not live up to their claims, by half-filled packages, by not being able to compare prices. That's why we started on standard-ization of sizes."[29] In fact, Senator Hart's initiative on standardizing package sizes was already well under way. (Peterson recalled in 1970 that the Kennedy White House had been "cool" about the Hart bill, and added, "It was a rough bill. The food industry, you know, was really furious about it, was very furious about it.")[30]

What Peterson failed to clarify in accepting the consumer advis-er's role President Johnson offered her was that Johnson intended for her to keep her Labor Department position and treat the consumer position as an advisory one. As Peterson recalled, presidential adviser Jack Valenti told her, "Esther, we'll get you an office and a secretary and that's all you'll need." This was a message Peterson did not really want to hear—that the Johnson administration wanted little more than good public relations from her appointment. Peterson recalls: "I'll never forget that as long as I live. 'That's all you'll need.'"[31]

Still, Peterson succeeded in getting the truth-in-packaging bill and the truth-in-lending bill on the president's "list of bills we wanted passed." Both bills gained prominence, not only in extensive hear-ings but through President Johnson's endorsement in his 1966 and 1967 State of the Union speeches. In the 1966 speech, Johnson declared: "We must also act to prevent the deception of the Amer-ican consumer—requiring all packages to state clearly and truthfully their contents—all interest and credit charges to be fully revealed—and keeping harmful drugs and cosmetics away from our stores."[32] Peterson also organized the collection of data on product safety. She repeatedly made use of President Kennedy's "four rights" (the right to safety, to be informed, to choose, to be heard) in speeches calling truth in labeling part of the "right to be informed."[33] But in her sober assessment, "I was a political instrument rather than a real instrument for consumer action." She would see her main achievement as "creating consumer awareness."[34]

Peterson served as special assistant for consumer affairs from 1964 to early 1967, pushed out in the end by close associates of the president; she identifies Jack Valenti and Secretary of Health, Education, and Welfare Joseph Califano as her antagonists, and remembers that they found her public advocacy of consumers irksome.[35] She made enemies—the Advertising Federation of America called her a pernicious threat to advertising because she had declared the incontrovertible truth that "some advertisers peddle respectable humbug."[36] When Peterson indicated that she wanted to give up the consumer post and devote herself to her work in the Department of Labor (work she had never left), no one at the White House tried to dissuade her. Presidential assistant Bill Moyers wrote to Johnson that the consumer position "does little substantively" but satisfied a political need and should not be left unfilled. Secretary Califano, in advising Johnson about a successor to Peterson, wrote, "The job is largely a public relations job and may be important in Congressional and Presidential campaigning in 1968."[37] Peterson was replaced as consumer adviser by Betty Furness, an actress best known as a TV spokeswoman for Westinghouse products. Peterson returned to her Department of Labor post for the remainder of the Johnson administration.

While serving in the White House, Peterson came to know executives of a leading Washington, D.C.–area supermarket chain, Giant Food. Giant Food had begun in 1936 when immigrant Nehemiah Cohen established a butcher shop in Lancaster, Pennsylvania.[38] By the mid-1960s, the single butcher shop had become a chain of some ninety supermarkets in Maryland, Virginia, and the District of Columbia. In January 1965, Peterson received a letter from Paul

Forbes, assistant to Giant's president, Joseph Danzansky, expressing his pleasure in meeting her at the inaugural ball and noting that, along with his wife, "we've been fans for several years, reading about you in *Supermarket News.*" He explained that he had been a loyal Democrat since FDR and that he felt committed to Johnson's Great Society. He volunteered to offer her "an unusual glimpse of the inner workings of the top management of a retail chain," promising that "no aspect of our operating philosophy, and no area of our operations will be concealed."[39] In 1970, with Richard Nixon in the White House and Peterson out of government, Danzansky offered her a job directing consumer policy at Giant: "We are convinced that your consumer philosophy is as close to Giant's as it was to that of the Administrations under which you served, and I am further convinced that once you and Giant Management have had an opportunity to educate each other, any few differences in approach will melt away."[40]

Peterson refused the offer several times, but Danzansky kept insisting she could write her own ticket. Finally she did, insisting on complete freedom to speak out publicly and the right to participate in top decision making in the company. She also won the assurance that the company would try out some of the programs she recommended. Before signing on, she consulted with consumer and labor movement colleagues, including Ralph Nader and AFL-CIO president George Meany, both of whom supported her taking the post.[41]

Forbes remained a friend and associate of Peterson's during her time at Giant. Peterson kept in her papers a Christmas poem he sent her, probably in 1970, borrowing from Poe's "The Raven." Here's a portion of it:[42]

Once upon a noonday bleary
While I shuffled, weak and weary

Through a pile of consumer complaints accumulated since the
days of yore . . .
Suddenly there was a brainstorm
Far more welcome than any rainstorm,
Washing away the woes I know will now return no more
If customers are no more to pester, of course we ought to turn to
Esther
There is no need to even test her, the chief consumer ambassador

Deck the store with open dating,
Unit pricing, consumer relating,
With consumer compliments accumulating as they never have
since days of yore,
With telephone calls from customers happy, with even a chance
for a noon-day nappie,
With a management less apt to slap me than they ever have been
before.

Giant Steps with Peterson

At Giant, Peterson led the way to innovations in unit pricing, open
dating, and nutritional labeling, along with other initiatives in consumer education and consumer advocacy. Giant had a unit pricing
system in preparation, and similar experiments were under way at the
Greenbelt Co-op (a small chain whose twenty-two stores adopted
unit pricing in August 1970) and at Safeway.[43] Peterson holds that
"Giant was the first food retailer in its marketing area to adopt
storewide this now-standard procedure."[44] That may be so, but
certainly Safeway was visibly out in front with unit pricing. While
no law compelled Safeway to take this on, politics played a role. Consumer reformers in Congress, disappointed with Senator Hart's

truth-in-packaging-and-labeling bill as finally enacted, complained that consumers still had little help in calculating which brand and package size would be the most economical buy. Rep. Benjamin Rosenthal (D-N.Y.) wanted to require unit pricing, but he believed such a bill would have a hard time in Congress unless a major chain store came on board. Rosenthal knew not only that Safeway was one of the biggest chains in the country but also that it was more vulnerable than other retailers because it was the dominant supermarket in Washington, D.C., and its suburbs. What Congress thought about consumer affairs was closely related to the experience of members of Congress or that of their spouses shopping at Safeway. And when controversy about consumer issues arose in Washington, "it led to investigations in Safeway stores by the horde of news reporters in the D.C. area."[45] So Safeway listened to Rosenthal and agreed to try out an experiment in several of its stores to test how consumers would respond to unit pricing.

Professor Monroe Friedman directed the study. "After speaking with Safeway officials and being assured that I would be able to implement my study design with their full cooperation, I undertook the study in Safeway stores in the inner-city and the suburbs. After seeing the study results, which found, after an in-store, unit-pricing orientation period for shoppers in the test stores, that many shoppers in the stores used the new labels and found them to be helpful, Safeway decided to implement unit-pricing in all of their 2,000 or so stores."[46]

On October 31, 1970, the *Washington Post* ran a story on the front page of its B section with a photo of Basil Winstead, a Safeway executive, Representative Rosenthal, and Dr. Friedman. The photo came from the news conference that Rosenthal had held the day before at the Rayburn House Office Building, at which Winstead announced that Safeway was rolling out its unit pricing program. The headline—"2 Chains to Start Per-Unit Pricing"—included also Giant Food. Esther Peterson told the paper that Giant would adopt unit pricing after Thanksgiving. She said that Giant had been working on unit pricing since March, and denied that the imminent inception of the program was a response to Safeway's announcement.[47] Representative Rosenthal said, "I would predict that within two years you'll see this in every supermarket in the country."[48]

Supermarkets had long dated many perishable packaged products using codes that only store employees could decipher—the consumer was kept in the dark. "Open dating" was the innovation of printing the "sell by" or "use before" day, month, and year plainly for any shopper to read. As Peterson argued, this allowed consumers to make judgments for themselves, improved employees' practices in rotating items, and reduced spoilage. At Giant it improved sales of store-brand products, where managers had the fullest control of open-dating practices.[49]

On nutritional labeling, Peterson's point of departure was the report of the 1969 White House Conference on Food, Nutrition and Health. This gathering, chaired by Jean Mayer, then professor of nutrition at Harvard's School of Public Health, was a notable event, one that Mayer would identify later as "a watershed in American social history."[50] Giant established the first system of nutritional labeling in supermarkets in the nation.[51] Minutes of a January 13, 1971, meeting of Giant executives report the establishment of a consumer advisory committee to develop the nutrition labeling program, with Dr. Mayer as its chair. The committee included also a variety of consumer representatives, including Jim Turner, a Ralph Nader associate. The minutes suggest that Peterson had learned something about the competitive norms of the business world by then: "Mrs. Peterson noted that it is evident that Safeway is trying to come out with the nation's first nutrition labeling program, so it is important that we move expeditiously."[52] Giant also initiated the disclosure of active ingredients in nonprescription drugs and disclosure of all ingredients in Giant-brand health and beauty products. All of these programs "fulfilled the consumer's right to be informed. When I went to Giant," Peterson recalls, "my plan was to take President Kennedy's four consumer rights and build a consumer corporate program around them."[53] She did exactly that.

Giant capitalized on Peterson's reputation for integrity and consumer advocacy to promote its wares. Its full-page ads in Washington-area newspapers would sometimes include a head shot of Peterson and a letter from her to consumers about one or another of Giant's consumer-oriented policies. In one ad—reprinted in Giant's 1971 annual report under the headline "We're Committed!"— Peterson's letter to consumers said:

> I came to Giant because I believed that the company had demonstrated its concern for the consumer and for the citizen in many ways. Now they have asked me to help them go even further.
>
> We have already introduced comprehensive unit pricing and open dating programs among others. But these are more than just isolated consumer programs. To me, they are tangible symbols of a commitment that Giant Food has made to the consumer—a commitment to apply the principles embodied in the "Consumer Bill of Rights" as it applies to Giant shoppers. This means developing real and meaningful programs.

The ad listed five program areas—"Right to Safety," "Right to Be Informed," "Right to Choose," Right to Be Heard," and a fifth that Giant added to President Kennedy's four, "Right to Redress."[54]

A November 12, 1970, ad in the *Washington Post* was headlined "Now at Your Giant: Unit Pricing!" and announced that unit pricing labels had gone up on more than 7,000 items in every Giant store that week (before Thanksgiving). The copy explained unit pricing. A sidebar, with the familiar head shot of Esther Peterson, had its own headline: "Goodbye to the Slide Rule!" In her letter to consumers beneath the headline, Peterson explains, "I've always believed that real changes in the market-place could be accomplished from within a progressive public-spirited company. The institution of such a comprehensive system of unit pricing is a good indication that indeed it can." Peterson's homey, grandmotherly housewife persona is on display as she notes that she understood the need for unit pricing back in 1964, when she had just become special assistant for consumer affairs. Back then, before going shopping with her daughter, Karen, Karen had said, "I'll get the slide rule, Mother." The copy continues, "I looked startled and she asked, 'How can you shop without one? How do you know the best buy?' "[55] Giant encouraged consumers to send in their complaints and suggestions; they were invited to "Pester Esther."[56]

The impact of these consumer information reforms was not always evident, as Peterson realized from the outset. Writing to Sen. Charles Percy (R-Ill.) in 1971, she observed: "It is my feeling that programs such as nutrition information and unit pricing, do not always have an immediate impact on consumer buying habits. But this is no reason to minimize their importance or abandon them. We are educating for the future, and my heavy mail shows that consumers do care and do want the information they need to make meaningful choices in the marketplace."[57] Later surveys of consumers by the General Accounting Office (GAO; later the Government Accountability Office) and others would bear out both these opinions: the studies found that many consumers made little use of unit pricing, but also that a significant minority did pay attention to unit price labels and that this affected their purchasing decisions. Numbers vary from survey to survey, but the GAO, an auditing and investigative branch of Congress, put the average percentage of shoppers making some use of unit pricing at 34 percent.[58] The relatively modest reliance of consumers on new information for their shopping decisions simply did not impress Peterson as an argument against the new policies. "Industry had a responsibility to provide consumers with information to make intelligent decisions, whether they choose to or not," she wrote. "Many citizens don't vote, but that's no reason to eliminate elections."[59]

The innovations quickly became common practice. The *New York Times* reported in 1972 that unit pricing had spread from two Safeway stores in Washington, D.C., in 1970 to "many thousands of supermarkets—perhaps as many as 10,000—throughout the country."[60] Why such rapid diffusion of the new practice? Some retailers feared government action would require it—laws to that effect were already in force in New York City, Seattle, Massachusetts, Connecticut, Rhode Island, and Maryland. Paul Korody, director of consumer and environmental affairs for the National Association of Food Chains, claimed that consumers made little use of unit pricing. Nonetheless, he announced that "more and more chains are feeling a legitimate if limited consumer demand" for the practice, and he believed unit pricing enhanced consumer confidence whether people actually made use of it or not. According to Korody, more than half of the 200 members of the National Association of Food Chains were using unit pricing. In his opinion, it was just smart merchandising.[61]

In 1971, a national conference on food labeling met in Milwaukee. Conference sessions were organized around unit pricing, open dating, nutrition labeling, and percentage ingredient labeling. At the end, participants agreed on a policy statement that endorsed "a comprehensive national food marketing program, encompassing advertising, which will achieve nutrient labeling, percentage ingredient labeling, open dating, grading and unit pricing of consumer-purchased food products." In detailed comments on each of the conference's main topics, the statement asserted that "the public has a right to know" the age and quality of food products, the unit price of competing items for sale, the nutrient value of food products for sale, and the ingredients in all packaged food products.[62] The "right to know" had been a relatively unfamiliar phrase when journalists promoted a freedom-of-information movement in the early 1950s; twenty years later, it was common coin in the consumer movement. At the closing session of the conference, Esther Peterson gave a speech titled "A Charge to Consumers." She reported that people had told her, "Esther, you are taking the romance out of marketing," but she had countered with, "I know a better place for romance than the supermarket. Besides, it is not romance, it is gambling."[63]

Peterson stayed with Giant until 1977, continuing to develop consumer-friendly reforms. A memo to company president Danzansky at the end of 1973 listed her plans for the next two years— "care labeling" (how to store or clean or prepare a product), complete "percentage of ingredient" labeling (which was only partially developed at that time), meat labeling to correspond to the National Livestock and Meat Board recommendations, labeling of ground beef indicating the percentage of fat, improved "pull date" labeling on meat, expanding open dating to more perishables including produce, and the development of Giant private-label products, such as cold-water detergents and low-sugar cereals, to meet new consumer standards.[64] Peterson could not have accomplished what she did at

Giant without the impressive reputation she had established in government service, but she probably did much more for consumers by working as a public advocate for a sympathetic commercial organization than she ever did in the White House. She was instrumental in putting information relevant to consumer choices in the hands of consumers themselves.

Peterson returned to the White House in the Carter administration, again as special assistant to the president for consumer affairs, and seeking—but failing—to establish a cabinet-level consumer agency. Susan Seliger, a reporter for the *National Observer,* followed her around for a profile in 1977. No one had told her, Seliger wrote, that "the major problem will be keeping up with the consumer Viking," then in her early seventies. Seliger was impressed by the framed pens from presidential bill signings displayed on the wall of Peterson's office—Truman's for the Fair Labor Standards Act of 1949, Kennedy's for the order establishing the President's Commission on the Status of Women and for the Equal Pay Act of 1963, and Johnson's for the Highway Beautification Act and the Fair Packaging and Labeling Act of 1966. On the day Seliger spent with her, the consumer agency bill squeaked through committee in the House and was reported out of committee in the Senate, too. Peterson agreed to celebrate over hot fudge sundaes with her staff, some of Ralph Nader's staffers, and Nader himself. When Nader complained about one senator (unnamed in the story), Peterson replied, "I'd like to help you burn him." Seliger found that this remark had "an uncharacteristic edge of cruelty," and added, "She isn't vicious. But neither is she the sweet-tempered grandmother some imagine. Says one admirer: 'She's grandmotherly like Golda Meir is grandmotherly.' Says another, who has known her since the Johnson days: 'She's no innocent. She knows exactly what she's doing.'"[65]

No one denied Peterson's great warmth and human appeal. "She had a tremendous personal presence with a tall frame, exceptional warmth and a captivating smile with which she greeted everyone," Monroe Friedman recalls. "When my wife and I visited her at her home in Washington, we experienced her love of life, and especially music and storytelling. At one visit her older sister, also a widow at the time, was present, and when we left, my wife and I shook our heads in amazement at the positive energy displayed by these two women."[66]

It is impossible to write about consumer reforms in the 1970s—or at any point since—without acknowledging the central importance of Ralph Nader. Michael Pertschuk, a leading staff member for Sen. Warren Magnuson and the Senate Commerce Committee in the 1960s and the chairman of the Federal Trade Commission under Jimmy Carter, remembers meeting Nader for the first time in 1965, some months before the publication of his landmark work, *Unsafe at Any Speed*. The topic of their discussion was tire safety. Pertschuk remembers Nader's "barely contained fury" with the industries that, as he saw it, had "an economic stake in the continued high level of automobile accidents—and injuries." He pressed for car safety legislation. Pertschuk expressed sympathy but, "with all the sophistication of a three-year Senate staff veteran, proceeded to lecture him on the realities of the legislative process." Pertschuk saw Nader's plans as quixotic; a legislative offensive against the auto industry was just not possible. "He was disappointed in my response, but undeterred. I was, of course, wrong. He was by that next January—and again and again—to extend our horizon of the legislatively possible."[67]

Nader came to his particular view of how democracy works and should work in the 1950s, not the 1960s. Born in 1934 in Winsted, Connecticut, the son of Lebanese immigrants, and nurtured by parental values that included a concern for social justice and a distrust of power, Nader graduated from Princeton in 1955. There he took a number of courses with political scientist H. H. Wilson, a scholar much influenced by C. Wright Mills. Wilson described himself as a "conservative, anarchist and socialist." As historian Daniel Horowitz suggests, these terms could easily apply to Nader, too. While in law school at Harvard, Nader began thinking about automobile safety, stimulated by a 1956 article in the *Harvard Law Review*. He published a paper himself on automobile safety as early as 1958. In 1964, after working in a private law practice in Connecticut and bringing consumer issues including auto safety before the Connecticut legislature, he moved to Washington to work for Daniel Patrick Moynihan, then assistant secretary of labor, on auto safety—a topic Moynihan himself had written on in 1959.[68]

Nader's influence has been extraordinary. As Horowitz writes, I think without exaggerating, "Nader was able to use his critique of consumer culture to launch a social movement."[69] Still, notwithstanding his meteoric rise to national prominence, even at the beginning he did not work in a vacuum. He had friends in an organized consumer movement, partners in the labor movement, an emerging array of public interest lawyers besides himself, and, even in the domain of automobile safety, allies such as Daniel Patrick Moynihan and Sen. Abraham Ribicoff, former governor of Connecticut and a cabinet officer in the Kennedy administration. Even for the loner Ralph Nader, it took a village.[70]

The Rhetoric of Consumer Reform

If the Freedom of Information Act was promoted with Cold War rhetoric, consumer legislation also borrowed from the Cold War lexicon. The "free market" distinguished the West from the Soviet sphere. It had provided Americans and others in the West with an unprecedented cornucopia of consumer goods. In testifying on Senator Hart's bill in 1965 in her capacity as President Johnson's consumer adviser, Esther Peterson stated that the American economy was exceptional—that the American housewife "marvels, as do we all, at our wonderful food distribution system. In general, she knows that she spends a smaller proportion of her husband's take home pay for food than she would in any other country, or at any other time."

That was not enough for Sen. Thruston Morton (R-Ky.), who began his questioning thus: "Mrs. Peterson, I suppose one could say that the best bargain table in the world is the American grocery store. Isn't that true?" She reminded him that that was exactly what she had just said. She added that, having lived abroad for some years, "I do know how splendid it is here." Senator Morton then added, "Fortunately in this country we don't have to stand in line to buy." This remark, without any direct connection to the subject at hand or the testimony Peterson had just provided, was a gratuitous reference to the Soviet Union and its famously faltering consumer economy. A little later he became more explicit: "We are not standing in line. We are not rationed. Go try to buy a basket of groceries in Russia." What Morton meant to suggest by this was that government action was dangerous: "I just wonder if in trying to achieve what you are trying to achieve we won't kill the goose that laid the golden egg." He worried over who would administer regulations of packaging and labeling—"the people who are running the war on poverty, or will the Great Society start running the grocery stores?" And he concluded, "I don't think you are going to convince me, Mrs. Peterson, and I am not going to convince you."[71]

Proponents of disclosure urged that it was a kind of least-objectionable regulating. It did not tell private companies how to do business; it only demanded that they inform consumers accurately about what that business is. This was a more secure argument with truth-in-lending legislation than with Senator Hart's packaging bill. Is the manufacturer's product the contents inside the package, or is the package itself a part of the product? To the extent that the latter is the case, the Hart bill seemed intrusive when it empowered the federal government to negotiate with businesses to reduce the large number of package sizes. In the colloquy between Senator Morton and Esther Peterson, both recalled grocery stores where the products were in large barrels and were scooped out by the storekeeper and placed in a sack or a bag. Morton said he used to work in the food business, and that in his own company "I put 5 pounds of flour in a box." It looked larger in a box than in a bag, he said, and it was more convenient to place on a shelf than bags. "We started this. We didn't have to go to any department of government and ask for permission to start this. We just did it."[72]

Peterson sympathized with nostalgia for the fading days of the independent grocers, as the language of some of her letters to consumers in Giant Food advertisements suggests. In one column she wrote that she and her husband owned an old Vermont farmhouse where they cooked on a wood-burning stove, drank water piped in from a spring, and bought supplies "from a local grocer who calls us each by name." She thought this related to her work at Giant: "Really, we're trying to bridge the gap—the gap of years between the markets of old, where you knew exactly what you were buying, where you could see the freshness, and where you shopped in an aura of friendliness, with the markets of today, where there is great abundance, confusion and cold efficiency." In Giant's consumer programs, "we believe the retailer is the consumer's purchasing agent, just as I am purchasing agent for my family."[73] The rhetoric of nostalgia could be employed for reform as well as against.

A Report Card on Reform

Senator Morton notwithstanding, "just do it" was no longer the order of the day, even as Giant and some other leading retailers initiated food labeling reforms without much more than gentle prodding from state or federal regulatory agencies. But the federal government was looking over industry's shoulder. The GAO in 1975 produced an extensive report to Congress, "Food Labeling: Goals, Shortcomings, and Proposed Changes" specifically designed to evaluate the progress that the Fair Packaging and Labeling Act had made but going well beyond the provisions of that act to examine not only package labeling but unit pricing, open dating, and nutritional labeling, none of which was part of the act.[74] Like Morton and Peterson, the GAO report began by explaining that "the neighborhood grocery store" had been replaced by "the supermarket with its self-service aisles and rows of prepackaged food."[75] The result was a vastly greater variety of products available to consumers, including "prepared or convenience-type food products," but also "more confusion for shoppers who rely on food labels to help them compare and choose." The report justifies its attention to the topic of labeling by quoting the Fair Packaging and Labeling Act's statement of policy—that because "informed consumers are essential to the fair and efficient functioning of a free market economy," and because packages and labels "should enable consumers to obtain accurate information as to the quantity of the contents and should facilitate value comparisons," it is the policy of Congress "to assist consumers and manufacturers in reaching these goals in the marketing of consumer goods."

The GAO report explains that the marketplace remained a long distance from adequate food labeling. The Food, Drug and Cosmetic Act of 1938 defined "standards of identity" for 284 food products, specifying both mandatory ingredients (ice cream must contain milk) and optional ingredients (ice cream may include sugar, salt, eggs, and nuts). By the terms of the 1938 law, foods whose identity was defined as "standard" need not be labeled. This was a problem, the GAO report observed, particularly for individuals who were allergic to certain ingredients or must for health reasons minimize their consumption of, say, salt or sugar. The GAO examined a sample of 1,000 products at two supermarkets and found that 13 percent did not label product ingredients, as the 1938 law permitted. The Food and Drug Administration told the GAO that it was gradually increasing the number of products for which full labeling would be required, although there was no timetable for this effort.[76]

Nutritional labeling was in its infancy, but it was gaining public attention. In May 1971, five George Washington University law students organized the Law Students Association for Buyers' Education and Labeling (LABEL) and petitioned the Food and Drug Administration to require foods on the FDA's "standardized" list to be fully labeled. Replying the next March, FDA commissioner Charles C. Edwards said the FDA had no authority to require ingredient labeling of the standardized foods but that it encouraged manufacturers and distributors to voluntarily make these disclosures. Edwards endorsed legislation to repeal the labeling exemption, he said, but in the meantime, a voluntary program "could provide one of the most fundamental changes in the history of food labeling in this country." The voluntary program he endorsed emphasized not ingredients but "nutrient values," and the FDA proposed a specific format for nutrient information on food package labels based on the National Research Council's Recommended Daily Allowance figures.[77] In 1973, the FDA began requiring nutritional information on the labels of products whose manufacturers made nutritional claims for them. The White

House Conference on Food, Nutrition and Health of 1969 had recommended that manufacturers provide nutritional information on labels, but in the GAO's January 1973 examination of 1,000 randomly selected food products, only 220 of 491 products with significant dietary impact provided nutritional information. In May 1973, after the FDA initiated its nutritional labeling program, the GAO found that 252 of the 491 products were appropriately labeled or plans for labeling were under way and that thirty-six of forty-three major supermarket chains surveyed intended to provide nutrition labeling on their own store brands.[78]

The report endorsed open dating. Citing a 1973 U.S. Department of Agriculture study, it noted that more than sixty supermarket chains—15,000 stores—had introduced open dating, and that ten states and two local governments required it for certain perishable goods. Consumers were generally pleased with this development, but the 1973 study also found considerable confusion among consumers about open dating. Was the date stamped on the product the "packed date," when the product had been packed and shipped to the store? Or the "pull date," after which the product should not be sold? Or the "expiration date," after which the product should not be used?[79]

As for unit pricing, the report concluded that the Fair Packaging and Labeling Act had successfully reduced the number of different package sizes for a given product but still had not made it possible for ordinary consumers to effectively make price comparisons across packages. There were now just six different package sizes for dry laundry detergents, for example, not twenty-two, but the consumer still had to divide different prices by 20, by 49, and by 84 to find the cost per ounce of the three most popular sizes of detergent.[80]

But unit pricing expanded across the country. In a survey conducted by the trade publication *Progressive Grocer* in 1971, 45 percent of 126 supermarket chains and 34 percent of 1,578 independent stores used unit pricing.[81] The GAO surveyed food retailers in 1973 and found that 48 percent of chain stores (7,904 stores) and 20 percent of independent grocers (142 stores) had instituted unit pricing.[82] Most, but not all, of the adoption of unit pricing was voluntary. Some states and localities required unit pricing (usually in stores at or above a certain level of annual sales): Massachusetts and Connecticut (both 1971), Maryland, Vermont, and Rhode Island (1972), and several cities (New York in 1971, Seattle in 1972, and Ann Arbor in 1973).[83] As the GAO noted, the extent of use of unit pricing across product categories varied across stores, and so did the maintenance of the labels—too many labels were missing, not adjacent to the products, or poorly maintained and hard to read.

Reflecting on the "Pre-Sixties"

Historians today are not much better off than politicians in the 1960s in knowing what to make of the consumer movement in America. And for the same reasons: Who is *not* a consumer? Where does the mere fact of consuming place people politically, if anywhere? Erma Angevine, a veteran consumer activist who became the executive director of the newly established Consumer Federation of America when it opened its first office in 1968, recalled how the news media covered the new organization. "Ironically, announcement of the opening appeared on the women's page in the *Washington Post,* the financial page of the *Washington Star,* and the obituary page of the *New York Times.*"[84] There was no obvious place for a story about a new confederation of consumer groups.

In a 1965 television appearance, Senator Hart was asked, "Senator, if your bill is as beneficial to everybody as you claim, why hasn't Congress passed it?" Hart replied by asking the interviewer to repeat her statistic about the number of consumers in the country. The interviewer complied, saying, "190 million, and I understand they are increasing every day." Hart then said: "And they're the most disorganized element in all of our society. The truth is that every one of us is a consumer, but we don't organize as consumers. We organize as renters or veterans or lawyers or product manufacturers or retailers or wholesalers, but the consumer is the lost fellow at the party. And this accounts, in part, for Congress's reluctance to respond thus far."[85]

But, haltingly and halfheartedly, Congress did respond and passed legislation to constrain business in the name of consumers. These efforts picked up momentum in the late 1960s and 1970s, but they began before there was a Students for a Democratic Society or a Port Huron Statement, before Ralph Nader pursued General Motors, before Rachel Carson wrote about the dangers that insecticides posed to the environment, before Betty Friedan's *Feminine Mystique* helped launch a new women's movement, before hundreds of American "advisers" in Vietnam became tens of thousands of ground troops, and before an antiwar movement emerged. It is not that there were no traces of popular movements in this early work—after all, Esther Peterson herself came out of the labor movement. But legislative initiatives on consumer affairs began before a broad and visible consumer movement was renewed.

Why did a consumer movement revive later in the 1960s? In the most important overview of the problem, historian Lizabeth Cohen points to a host of factors. Growing affluence meant that people acquired more goods as well as giant-sized expectations for the satisfactions they would bring; growing complexity in the consumer goods marketplace, with complicated consumer credit, computerized billing, and a wide variety of new materials and new appliances proved dizzying or distressing; pinpointed appeals from savvy marketers raised specific expectations and therefore identifiable disappointments; marketing campaigns, particularly advertising and marketing aimed at children, aroused vigorous opposition from groups that organized to protect children from flammable pajamas or tooth-decaying cereals; the coming to power in the Kennedy and Johnson years of Keynesian Democrats ready to wield "a strong federal hand in the economy" encouraged public hopes for federal action; and a newly powerful cadre of congressional Democrats saw consumer issues as an opportunity to simultaneously do good and win votes.[86] The legislative consequence, as Cohen summarizes it, was the passage of "more than twenty-five major consumer and environmental regulatory laws" between 1967 and 1973.[87]

In this analysis, congressional activism or the promise of it was as much cause as consequence of organized consumer unrest. A great deal goes on in Washington that has little directly to do with public opinion, social movements, or powerful pressure groups. Some of it has to do with the balance of power in Congress, some of it with individual aspirations and ambitions for higher office, and some of it with the ways powerful, charming, and ambitious people who make their way to Washington befriend, maneuver, and impress one another. But for the 1960s, understanding of such factors on the Washington scene has been clouded over by the enduring story of the civil rights movement, then the antiwar movement, and then the other liberation movements that followed. We inevitably write history backward, but we should not attribute results that occurred in the early 1960s to causes that emerged only later in the decade. Historian David Hollinger has called attention to the difference between "The Sixties"—capital "T" and capital "S"—and "the 1960s." For him, "the early sixties"—meaning roughly the period up to John F. Kennedy's assassination at the end of 1963—"is a distinctive point in time."[88] We might even want to label this period the "pre-sixties." It is not The Sixties of legend, but neither is it The Fifties (also of legend).

It was a period of no small amount of arrogance, ambition, and self-righteousness, be it in the mode of John F. Kennedy or Lyndon Johnson or the less globe-straddling Ralph Nader. But it was also to be found in the self-effacing style of Philip Hart. In 1971, his office printed *Senator Philip A. Hart: A Biographical Sketch Written by His Press Secretary.* That cumbersome title is quickly explained—Hart's staff could maneuver around the senator's "prejudice against self-congratulatory political documents" by announcing the source of the publication so that, Hart was quoted as saying, "no one need take it too seriously." It even included Hart's interpolations. After a sentence about how much time Hart spent "enlarging federal feeding programs for needy, underfed children," Hart comments in parentheses: "No need to get maudlin about it."[89] Not all in the liberal coalition in Congress operated in the same style or toward exactly the same ends, but their gathering force made a difference.

Without question, there would come to be a generational divide between students in the streets and the parents, teachers, and clergy who nurtured them. By the mid-sixties, students adopted tactics of direct action they had learned from the civil rights movement—in many cases from their own experience in that movement. There would be a stylistic rupture, too: a new vulgarity ("Fuck the draft!"), a bitter irreverence ("Hey, hey, LBJ, how many kids did you kill today?"), an embrace of participatory democracy, and a growing impatience with the slow drip-drip of legislative activity.

That impatience, at least, was not confined to twenty-year-olds. It took courage from a rebellion within Congress itself against long-settled traditions and operations, some of them so stunningly undemocratic that one can scarcely believe they had survived so long unchallenged. Only when a new liberal majority came to Congress and invented an innovative liberal caucus to sidestep the hobbled and hesitant Democratic Party machinery did ways emerge to weaken conventional legislative culture. That rebellion would ultimately score real victories and, with the Legislative Reorganization Act of 1970, would reduce the power of committee chairmen and open up once secret or secretive legislative procedures. These efforts, led by people who came of age well before the 1960s, helped create a conducive environment for younger rebels and wider rebellion.

four

Opening Up Congress

Veteran Congress-watchers Thomas Mann and Norman Ornstein in 2012 published a critique of Washington politics titled *It's Even Worse Than It Looks,* about the difficulties of making anything move in Washington when one party—the Republicans—is ideologically committed to making sure nothing happens. That analysis may be exactly right for 2012, but for various reasons Congress has been worse than it looks for a long time. Rep. Jerome R. Waldie (D-Calif.), writing to his constituents at the beginning of 1970, judged the House of Representatives "so outmoded in its machinery and its leadership—on the part of both parties—that it has become impotent in a time when effective action is demanded and its absence is crucial." In particular, Waldie found himself rebelling at the way the culture of Congress silenced younger representatives: "I used to believe the role of a relatively 'new' Congressman—anyone with less than ten years' service as time is agonizingly measured in Congress—was to quietly observe and adjust to the system. . . . I no longer believe that to be the case, and I no longer will remain a quiet, cooperative cog in the machine pretending that all is not as bad as it may seem—because, in fact, it is worse than it seems."[1]

The Freedom of Information Act empowers "any person" to request information from the government and to sue for it if the government balks. But "the government" whose response the law compels is not the whole government—the law covers only the executive branch. There is no provision in the act for requesting information from the federal judiciary, Congress, or even the president or people in the Executive Office of the President whose sole responsibility is to advise the president—in contrast to the executive agencies the president oversees. The act, as we have seen, came from congressional efforts to compel disclosure from the executive. In the decade of work that went into FOIA, there was no deviation from this mission. FOIA in no way applies to Congress itself.[2]

Still, the 1960s saw a rising tide of complaint in Congress about its own procedures, including—but not centered on—secrecy. Demands for greater openness were simply one part of a compendious package of reforms, even if the opening of more legislative proceedings to public view turned out to be among the most important of those reforms.

Congress in the 1960s was shielded from the public by informal traditions, by the politics of a one-party South, and by formal procedural rules in both the House and Senate, all to be discussed below. A complacent and compliant journalism and the absence of watchdog public interest groups (they would emerge later to keep an eye on Congress) made the relative confidentiality of congressional proceedings easy to maintain. So did an intimidating system of seniority in which newer, younger, and more energetic members of Congress learned that power would come to them in due time—so long as they were not prematurely loud, aggressive, impatient, or demanding. They might grasp it sooner if, by personality and well-tailored ambition, they apprenticed themselves to their most powerful elders.

This culture in congressional Washington changed in the late 1960s and the 1970s—not completely, by any means, and not all to the benefit of good government, either, but the changes were dramatic. Externally, they were made possible by a more assertive and critical news media and by a shift in public opinion that elected a more liberal Congress and opened new possibilities for reform. New members, both Democratic and Republican, felt both more impelled and more empowered to take initiative early in their careers. Among the changes this produced was the emergence of an organized coalition of House liberals, the Democratic Study Group (DSG), that used research as a tool of political change and played a pivotal role in sponsoring "anti-secrecy" amendments to the Legislative Reorganization Act of 1970. There was no Project on Government Oversight (1981), no National Security Archive (1985), no Center for Public Integrity (1989), no Sunlight Foundation (2006) and not even Common Cause (whose membership campaign began in August 1970, after most of the DSG's work on anti-secrecy was completed and just two months before the Legislative Reorganization Act was signed into law). A broad array of nongovernmental organizations dedicated to opening up government would be established in the decades to follow, but they arrived in the wake of the key reform effort chronicled here.

Congress on the Eve of Reform

As the liberals saw it, the problem was to wrest control of Congress from committee chairmen, in most cases southern Democrats, who could usually bottle up deliberations on civil rights and other liberal legislative efforts. Liberal members of the House, knowing the legislation they supported would win a strong majority if only they could bring it to a floor vote, watched in frustration as their bills died in committee. The Senate, where a small minority of senators could block popular legislation by filibuster, was even more stymied. In both houses, the key issue for the liberals was how to make Congress "responsive to its own majorities."[3]

Why was Congress beholden to its own entrenched minorities? Why did the American government in the 1950s and 1960s operate as a cartel, with essential decision-making activities closed to the American people and even fenced off from many of their elected representatives, too? From early in the twentieth century, committee chairmen in both houses had been selected on the basis of seniority. This favored representatives from "safe" districts who were elected again and again, rarely facing serious opposition. It handed disproportionate power to representatives from the South. In southern states, Republicans never won elections. So while even veteran members of Congress might face serious electoral challenges in the North, Midwest, and West, southern incumbents were routinely returned to Washington. They held top leadership positions and acquired unmatchable familiarity with the arcane ways of both House and Senate. When the Legislative Reorganization Act of 1946 consolidated forty-eight committees to nineteen in the House, extending the range of issues each of them oversaw, it created, as political scientist Nelson Polsby put it, "a House of Representatives not unlike Jurassic Park, filled with very large, threatening, carnivorous committee chairmen who liked to dine on liberal legislation."[4] This was a barrier to most liberal proposals and normally a death sentence to civil rights initiatives. The Senate was even worse.

So much for the formal barriers that blocked efforts in Congress to represent its own majorities; the informal barriers were equally daunting, particularly within the committees. Rep. Tom Foley (D-Wash.), later a committee chairman himself and Speaker of the House, recounted how Agriculture Committee chairman Harold Cooley (D-N.C.) welcomed him and other freshman members to the committee at its first meeting of the 1965–1966 term. Cooley addressed the new members as follows: "I hate and detest, hate and detest, to hear senior members of this committee, of either party, interrupted by junior members of this committee, of either party. You new members in particular will find that you will require some time, some of you months, others of you regrettably probably years, before you develop sufficient knowledge and experience to contribute constructively to our work. In the meantime, silence and attention, silence and attention is the rule for new members of this committee."[5]

These practices in the House became intensely frustrating to liberal and moderate Democrats after the 1958 election, when their number increased substantially even as the committees, including the centrally powerful Rules Committee, were still dominated by conservative southern Democrats. With House Speaker Sam Rayburn unwilling to push the Democratic Party caucus to take an official party position that could constrain the conservatives, the liberals saw opportunities for their favorite legislation slip away.[6]

One committee, although a committee in name only, caused special concern—the "Committee of the Whole House on the State of the Union" or simply the "Committee of the Whole." The Committee of the Whole is a "procedural fiction," as the Democratic Study Group correctly called it in 1970. The House votes to constitute itself as a Committee of the Whole to deliberate on measures before the House and amendments to them. This fiction proves a great convenience, since in the Committee of the Whole, by agreement, a quorum requires only 100 members to be present instead of 218, the Speaker is not required to be the presiding officer, and time-consuming roll call votes can be avoided.[7] In the Committee of the Whole, the House can also establish special rules for the conduct of debate (for instance, concerning how many speakers may speak to a measure and how long they may speak). When bills are approved by a committee for the consideration of the House, they are referred to the Committee of the Whole for discussion and debate. In the Committee of the Whole, amendments are introduced, debated, and voted up or down.

This is all technical and boring—but here's where the technical runs afoul of democratic aspirations (at least, democratic aspirations of the past half century): by a practice dating to the first U.S. Congress, borrowed from the British Parliament, individual votes in the Committee of the Whole normally went unrecorded. Until the Legislative Reorganization Act of 1970, voting in the Committee of the Whole was either by voice vote, by "standing division" in which people voting yea would rise to be counted and then sit and then people voting nay would rise to be counted, or by unrecorded "teller vote."[8] In an unrecorded teller vote, the chair appoints two tellers, one for the affirmative and another for the negative. Members who support the amendment before the Committee of the Whole then walk up the central aisle where the teller tallies their votes. Thereafter, members voting in the negative follow and the "negative" teller tallies their votes. Both tellers report the tallies to the chair, who announces the result. The total count—so many yeas, so many nays—then becomes part of the public record. *What is not public is which representatives voted which way.*

This means that all defeated amendments to bills taken up in the Committee of the Whole were forever shielded from the public eye; constituents would never know if their representatives had supported or opposed a key amendment on critical legislation if the amendment went down to defeat. Amendments that the Committee of the Whole approved would be voted on again when the bill came up for final passage after the House resolved itself back into the House of Representatives—and there the votes could be recorded individually if so requested by one-fifth (44 members) of the House quorum of 218 members.[9]

Forces for Change

In the 1960s, members of Congress became more vocal about the need for procedural reforms, while the news media became more attentive to the flaws in Congress and congressmen. These two constituencies—reformers in Congress and increasingly aggressive reporters—were by no means in perfect alignment. The reformers were interested in procedural changes, while the journalists were interested in good stories, and procedural change did not shout "front page." On the other hand, media attention to congressional scandal increased, helping to whittle away at the prestige of Congress and enhancing a mood ripe for internal reform.[10]

Several factors led members of Congress to be bolder in challenging the congressional leadership. One was a general shift to a more critical culture in a society of growing affluence where college attendance was fast becoming a prerequisite for professional and managerial careers and for social standing. At four-year colleges in the 1960s and 1970s, the large majority of students majored in the liberal arts (an expansion of more vocationally oriented curricula came later), where they were encouraged to develop skills in critical thinking and learned to read against the grain of assigned texts. At college, they encountered a restive faculty culture where career advancement increasingly rewarded originality, at least within limits, more than it did reverential tributes to classic works and authors. What has been called the "educational revolution" was also an openness revolution, as I will argue more extensively in Chapter 5.[11]

Another factor was the dramatic news coverage of the civil rights movement, particularly television coverage, which reduced the credibility and legitimacy of entrenched southern Democrats, at least outside the South. The brutality of southern racism became visible nationally, and even a soft-spoken, gentlemanly advocacy of legislated racial discrimination seemed increasingly horrifying. Southern governors such as Ross Barnett (Mississippi, 1960–1964), Orval Faubus (Arkansas, 1955–1967), Lester Maddox (Georgia, 1967–1971), and George Wallace (Alabama, 1963–1967, 1971–1979) may have been seen locally as heroes resisting a tyrannical federal government, but in the rest of the country they appeared to be thinly disguised racist thugs. In Congress, southerners were found guilty on the basis of their own intransigence on civil rights or because of the similarity of accent, if not style, with the governors of their states. The South seemed a foreign country—why should the U.S. Congress be its colony?

The transformation of Congress was also part of a general modernization of government. Government was vastly larger in 1970 than it had been in, say, 1900, but decision making in Congress remained the responsibility of just 100 senators (after statehood for Alaska and Hawaii in 1959) and 435 representatives in the House, as it had been when the country's population was half as large and the federal budget a small fraction of what it had become with its vast and expensive

Cold War military, New Deal entitlements, and post-1945 assumption of broader regulatory responsibility for the economy. The addition of computer information processing, funding for additional congressional staff, the establishment of the Congressional Budget Office and the Office of Technology Assessment to offer Congress expert advice, and the expansion of the Congressional Research Service and the General Accounting Office were all significant advances for the efficient operation of Congress in the modern world. Increased efficiency was also part of the effort to hold the burgeoning administrative state accountable to the elected representatives of the people, as was the Freedom of Information Act.

But just how accountable was Congress itself? Efforts to democratize Congress internally gained momentum in the 1960s, leading to new laws or new practices in the early 1970s. The majority party caucus acquired the power to choose committee chairmen rather than to strictly follow a rule of seniority, committee chairmen lost power in relationship to individual committee members, and the autonomy of subcommittees increased relative to their parent committees. Along with these changes, and closely related to them, "sunshine" reforms made the operation of Congress more visible to the news media and to the general public. This included recording votes that had often gone unrecorded, requiring the disclosure of campaign contributions, instituting strict and explicit codes of ethics for members, making public a variety of disclosures (for example, sources of income and potential conflicts of interest), and opening up congressional procedures on the floor and in committees to public scrutiny, sometimes even by televising them.[12]

These changes were enacted in a series of separate laws during the 1970s. I focus here on the first of them—the Legislative Reorganization Act of 1970. This act was the culmination of years of effort by a coalition of reform congressmen to democratize congressional proceedings, and especially to weaken the control of committee chairs. Among the provisions of the law, making votes public in the Committee of the Whole is of special relevance for seeing how the topic of transparency became part of the Washington conversation. It may surprise you—it certainly surprised me—that many vitally important House votes had not been public until the Legislative Reorganization Act went into effect in January 1971. Only with the passage of that act in 1970 did the House of Representatives put secret voting (largely) behind it. The act provided that if twenty members of the House requested a "recorded teller vote," members would each sign a card, green for yea and red for nay, and drop the cards in a box (this would be replaced in 1973 by electronic voting). Each member's vote would be made public. The media, the representative's constituents, and the general public could finally know how each representative voted. This increased the incentive for representatives to show up to vote. That is, it increased the chances that representatives could be punished at the polls by an aggressive electoral opponent if they failed to vote regularly. In 1971, there were 108 recorded teller votes. Until that year, all these votes would have been anonymous. There was a huge increase in members' turning up to vote on amendments— from an average of 163 for the unrecorded teller votes of the 91st Congress to a 360 average for the recorded teller votes of the 92nd.[13]

The Legislative Reorganization Act of 1970

The Legislative Reorganization Act was the first major set of procedural reforms for Congress since 1946. It contained a variety of features besides the provision for recorded teller voting, from increasing the allocation for professional staff in both the House and Senate to authorizing the building of a dormitory and classrooms for congressional pages. Several sections, apart from the provision for recorded teller votes in the House, helped to democratize the operation of Congress, notably those that made committee meetings open to the public unless a majority of committee members specifically voted to go into executive session. It also opened committee hearings to radio and television coverage for the House (the Senate already had established this). Broadcasting, the act stated, would be permitted "for the education, enlightenment, and information of the general public" and "for the development of the perspective and understanding of the general public with respect to the role and function of the House under the Constitution."[14]

Pressure for democratic legislative reform had begun in the early 1960s. Since 1964 legislative reorganization had been on the agenda in the Senate, at the initiative of Senator Mike Monroney (D-Okla.), and in the House, too, at the urging of the Democratic Study Group—about which more in a moment. A set of reforms to give committee members more power relative to committee chairmen (for instance, to hold meetings and report out bills over the objections of the chair) passed the Senate in 1967. In the House, Speaker John McCormack referred the bill to the Rules Committee because this "Committee Bill of Rights" seemed too potent—and the bill died in committee. There were efforts to dislodge it, first by a group of thirteen Republicans led by Donald Rumsfeld (R-Ill.), quickly dubbed "Rumsfeld's Raiders," and then by Democratic liberals, but both efforts failed. As Rumsfeld acknowledged, "Congressional reform is an issue without a constituency."[15]

After the 1968 election, House Democrats regathered and sought reform once more. Again they attacked the House leadership. Morris Udall (D-Ariz.) announced that he would seek to unseat Speaker

McCormack. This was more a symbolic gesture than a practical possibility, but it won the rebels some concessions. McCormack agreed to schedule caucus meetings on a regular monthly basis, holding out to reformers the prospect of greater voice in the party caucus. McCormack seemed to concede that some kind of reform legislation would have to be adopted. House Rules Committee chairman William Colmer (D-Miss.) appointed a special subcommittee to draft a reform bill. That bill—H.R. 17654, coming out of the subcommittee that B. F. Sisk (D-Calif.) chaired—was ready for discussion in the spring of 1970. Its fate would rest in large part with the Democratic Study Group, so I must abandon Rep. Sisk's bill for a few pages to give an account of the DSG's lead role in amending it.

A Social Movement in the House

When the Democratic Study Group celebrated its tenth anniversary in December 1969, the cover of the printed program for the banquet featured a symbol of the DSG itself: a red-caped crusader, a knobby-kneed, glasses-wearing young man with a big Superman-style "S" on his T-shirt, holding a legislative bill in one hand and a briefcase in the other. This cartoon figure was introduced in small print as "stronger than dirt . . . More meetings than a PTA . . . Able to study major issues in a single day."[16]

The DSG at that time was still something of a novelty on Capitol Hill, but it had much to celebrate. It had been born in September 1959 as a caucus for House moderate and liberal Democrats to discuss their concerns and to act as an engine for relevant research and sometimes active group agitation. The Democratic Study Group was a surprisingly original social invention. Next to the emergence of political parties in the early nineteenth century and the institutional-ization of the committee system in the early twentieth century, the caucus has been the most important organizational development in the history of Congress, and the DSG was the first enduring caucus. (The first, that is, apart from the Democratic and Republic party cau-cuses, which were more creatures of the parties than of Congress.) Informal, temporary gatherings of legislators with specific common interests had arisen before 1959, but only with the DSG and subse-quent groups did the caucus emerge as a "persistent, highly organized, and active" voluntary association within Congress.[17] The DSG was the only caucus through 1964; two more formed between 1965 and 1969, ten more between 1970 and 1974, and then caucuses of all shapes and sizes, purposes, and durations tumbled out onto the scene—there were 59 by 1980, 116 by 1990, 185 by 2000, and 665 by 2010.[18] In 1995 House administration rules were adopted that prevented the caucuses—at that time known collectively as "legislative service organizations" or LSOs—from using funds allocated to representa-tives for their support.[19] Under the new rules, all of the LSOs were abolished, and new practices introduced a new name, "congressional member organizations," and new rules for governing them.[20]

There are various reasons that the caucus as an organizational form began to take off in the 1970s, but among them, as political scientist Susan Hammond observes, is that the DSG proved itself a notably successful model.[21] Moreover, its success included legislated changes that brought additional staff and resources to members of Congress and so made it possible for members, or their aides, to divide their time and attention in more focused and productive ways. By reducing the power of seniority-based leadership, DSG-sponsored reforms also created leadership opportunities in the various caucuses—or in newly started ones—at just the time that newer, younger, better-educated, more independent-minded, more entrepreneurial members were seeking to make Congress their own.[22]

One attractive feature of the caucus as an organizational mechanism is that it is easy to start.[23] It does not require formal action by the House or Senate. It requires only energy and entrepreneurship, usually on the part of a single member of Congress.[24] Once begun, it is also relatively easy to maintain, although that task is made much easier if the caucus is able to hire a full-time staff member, as the DSG did in hiring William Phillips at the outset, and bringing on Richard Conlon to succeed him in 1968. Conlon, who continued as DSG director until his untimely death in a boating accident in 1988, was a key strategist for the DSG, particularly in the fight against the unrecorded teller vote.

But why should anyone in the House in 1959 have wanted to turn a set of common interests into an "interest group"? This was not an obvious move. Nor was it prompted, as it no doubt is in many other organizations, by a growing number of members in the organization. The number of members of the House of Representatives has not changed, but nonetheless, something one might well call a social movement arose within it.[25]

Informal assemblages of members of Congress had come and gone over generations without any of them seeking, let alone achieving, permanence. The seeds of change in this state of affairs were planted in 1957, just before President Eisenhower delivered his State of the Union message, when a group of members of the House published a document quickly dubbed the "Liberal Manifesto." Rep. (later Sen.) Eugene McCarthy was its chief author and instigator, but Lee Metcalf, Chet Holifield, and John Blatnik wrote parts of it, and Stewart Udall, Frank Thompson, and James Roosevelt were also key members of the group, initially known as "McCarthy's Mavericks" or, alternately, "McCarthy's Marauders," "McCarthy's Mustangs," and "the McCarthy Group."[26] When issued, the manifesto had twenty-eight signers. By the end of January, when the document was placed in the *Congressional Record,* eighty representatives had put their names to it. It was a distinctively urban crowd—all fourteen New York signers were from New York City, all eight Illinois signers from Chicago, all six Michigan signers from Detroit, and six of the eleven Californians from Los Angeles and San Francisco.[27]

But the McCarthy group did not organize formally. "Notices of meetings frequently were passed by word of mouth. While walking down the corridor, a member might be told that they were assembling in McCarthy's office. When enough persons had drifted in, the discussion would begin."[28] Actions were based on a sense of the meeting; no votes were taken. As McCarthy geared up for a Senate race in 1958, he drifted away from the group, and Lee Metcalf and Frank Thompson served as informal leaders.

Like a fine restaurant that loses its spark when it expands into the next storefront and doubles its size and staff, a caucus does not necessarily improve as it grows. It may lose cohesion and direction. Many caucuses do not last long. But they have become sites for ambitious members of Congress to advance themselves and their causes. Still, as late as 1981 the status of these LSOs was vague enough that the DSG sought legal advice about its own tax status. Should the DSG incorporate as a nonprofit corporation? Should it seek an income tax exemption from the Internal Revenue Service? A Washington law firm advised that neither action was required because the DSG is a "service and coordinating organization for Democratic Members of the U.S. House of Representatives." It is "organized and financed in accord with the rules and regulations of the House." It provides services related to the work of the House; as the DSG's by-laws state, its work is directed toward research and analysis of legislative issues, communication and coordination of efforts to enact Democratic policies, and efforts to make the House "a more effective and responsive institution." At that time, members of the House paid $500 to subscribe to DSG services and another $50 in membership dues, both eligible to be covered by the member's authorized expense allowance. The counsel's advice noted that federal income tax does not extend to components of the federal government, including Congress. The DSG qualified as tax exempt because "an organization can be an integral part of another organization and thus acquire the tax status of the other organization"—and the DSG is a part of the tax-exempt U.S. Congress.[29]

The 436th Member of the House of Representatives

In its first years, the DSG served as an information clearinghouse, and it also originated research reports relevant to the policy objectives of its membership. Its focus on research, and even its academic-sounding name, were part of an effort to make a difference without making waves. The DSG leaders did not want to challenge the formal Democratic Party leadership; they believed they could advance the liberal causes that mattered most to them without invoking the wrath of the leadership.[30]

An emphasis on research and fair-minded factuality was well suited to Richard Conlon. Before Conlon came to the DSG, the DSG style, as he observed in a 1974 interview, "aimed at promoting a piece of legislation rather than briefing on it." Conlon insisted on a genuine briefing—what the legislation is, who favors it and who opposes it, arguments pro and con, and what groups stand where on it. If the

DSG takes a position, it is in letters to members, not in the research papers themselves; "the research is the glue that keeps us together."[31] When Conlon was offered the DSG job, friends warned that the DSG was struggling to survive and that it would be a mistake to become its director, as "it was a sinking ship."[32] The DSG was riven by the Vietnam War, with some of its key members strongly antiwar and others strongly committed to supporting the war aims of the White House. In the House, Democrats had lost forty-seven seats in the 1966 elections, and while they still held a majority, they no longer had a powerful liberal majority.

But Conlon accepted the DSG position, seeing an important opening that the DSG could fill. He hired Linda Heller Kamm as research director. Kamm, a lawyer engaged in politics who had come to Washington in 1967, was at the Department of Housing writing legislation. She came on board just weeks after Conlon did; the two of them, plus a secretary, constituted the entire DSG staff. "It was broke when Dick and I got there," Kamm recalls. At that time, members of Congress had scarcely any information about bills that would come before them for a vote, whether in committee or on the floor. Providing information—a function, Kamm holds, that the Democratic Party leadership should have organized but never did—proved the making of the DSG, and Conlon saw this at once. He "seized these opportunities," following his own (and the DSG's) progressive political agenda, but in a style he brought to the job from his background in journalism and with an energy that was hard to match. "He was indefatigable and expected us to be, too."[33]

At the 1968 Democratic National Convention in Chicago, the DSG offered a "Campaign Workshop," with the first topic being "news coverage." *Washington Post* journalist David Broder was to speak on the panel but canceled at the last minute and was replaced by Conlon.

DSG chair John Brademas introduced the new DSG staff director: "He was a reporter for the *Duluth Herald & News Tribune* and the *Minneapolis Tribune* for five years before coming to Washington in 1963. And for the past three years before joining DSG he served as press secretary for Senator Walter Mondale of Minnesota."[34]

He could also have mentioned that Conlon had reported on the courts in Duluth and in 1961 won an American Political Science Association (APSA) award for distinguished reporting on public affairs. This led him to apply for an APSA Congressional Fellowship. In 1962 Conlon left the Duluth paper for the *Minneapolis Tribune* but soon thereafter began his fellowship in Washington, arriving just a few weeks before President Kennedy was assassinated. During the year's fellowship he worked for Rep. Frank Thompson (D-N.J.) and Sen. Lee Metcalf (D-Mont.), both of whom had been leaders in the DSG from its beginning (Metcalf was the DSG chair in 1959–1960 but then moved to the Senate). When Conlon was offered the position of DSG staff director, he was already familiar with the DSG's mission.[35]

Conlon's message to politicians and others in Chicago in 1968 about how to deal with the press was straightforward: treat newsmen as neither allies (even if the publisher or station owner is your friend) nor enemies (even if the publisher or station owner is your opponent). Why? "Most newsmen are more than employes. They are also members of a profession which is dedicated to report the news fairly. They are committed to the principle that a free press is essential to our form of government, and they deeply resent any implication that how they report the news might be influenced by the publisher or editor's beliefs. So unless you know for a fact that a particular reporter is biased against you, assume that they are all fair and non-partisan and you'll get along fine with them."[36]

At every turn, the DSG found its reputation linked to the reliability of its research reports. Conlon later told political scientist Thomas Mann that he supported giving the full story and that this "came out of my journalist background; you don't get anywhere with one side of the story; one-sided slant gets discounted; this is typical procedure in offices where staff provides Members with arguments on both sides; don't try to persuade Members, but to arm them with the facts."[37] Norman C. Miller, a reporter for the *Wall Street Journal* who followed Capitol Hill closely, noticed the changes Conlon instituted: "With an expanded staff, the research information provided for members is probably the best the DSG has ever produced."[38]

I have paged through stacks of DSG weekly "Staff Bulletins" (on blue paper), "Issue Reports" (also blue), "Legislative Reports" (white), and "Fact Sheets" (yellow, and generally ten to twenty pages) from the first few years of Conlon's tenure as staff director. Comparing them to similar stacks from several years earlier (1962), when William Phillips served as staff director, the evenhandedness and arguments for and against particular legislative proposals are notable. Even more striking is that the Conlon-era publications are more readable. The Phillips-era reports combine items on related topics in the form of a schoolchild's outline—they are overwhelmed by Roman numerals, bullet points, and occasional boxed quotations from President Kennedy. These earlier DSG publications are simply much harder to follow. One longs for simple sentences and paragraphs and a less staccato chain of bulletins.

Marti Conlon, Dick Conlon's widow, remembers her husband as a "perfectionist." She sometimes worked in the office with him, doing the accounts and payroll. She remembers that, for him, "sentences had to be written in a certain format. He could drive you nuts!"[39]

According to Roy Dye, who began as an intern at DSG in 1969 and soon was hired as a full-time staff person, succeeding Linda Kamm as research director and working closely with Conlon until 1974 (when he moved on to a long career as staff director for various committees and members on the Hill), Conlon "would agonize over phrasing, he would get carried away with it . . . he would consider option after option and get feedback from everybody—anybody! This would be ten at night!" What he kept looking for, Dye recalls, was "something that people would understand immediately . . . something simple and direct."[40]

A perfectionist and a workaholic, Conlon tended not to arrive at work until 10:00 A.M. but he stayed late at the office many nights. Both his widow and his oldest son, Chuck, now a *Congressional Quarterly* journalist, remember that when he came home he would work at the kitchen table "with a glass of red wine and Ritz crackers." (Boyhood friends complained to Chuck that it was never possible to "T.P." his house since his father—and the dog—seemed to be always awake and able to scotch their would-be prank.) As Conlon's three children grew older, he sometimes recruited them to work at the DSG on the weekends, walking round and round a table where pages of the latest DSG report were laid out in piles, collating and stapling them.[41]

The DSG's work took on a new urgency after the 1968 election as its members considered how to maneuver in a Washington dominated not only by committee chairs hostile to liberal goals but also, come January, by a Republican White House. So the DSG executive committee began meeting to consider how to push their program ahead in the House.

There was no consensus. In early December 1968, DSG chair Don Fraser (D-Minn.) proposed that the Democratic Party caucus reconfirm—or remove—every committee chairman by secret ballot at the start of each new Congress.[42] This was the first proposal to gain general support among DSG leaders. Nothing came of it in the end, but note that a procedure dependent on secrecy (a secret ballot) occurred first to the liberal caucus that, a year and a half later, would help carry the day for anti-secrecy measures. The primary objective of the Democratic Study Group was not to make House proceedings more public or House operations more democratic but to pass liberal legislation that southern Democratic chairmen blocked. Procedural reforms—most of them making the routines of the House more accountable to the public—were means more than ends.[43]

In B. F. Sisk's H.R. 17654, the Democratic Study Group saw a great opportunity. In May 1970, DSG's executive committee began regular discussions about it. Committee members were Donald Fraser of Minnesota, chair; John Brademas of Indiana, vice chair; chief whip James Corman of California, and staff director Conlon, who would come to be known as the 436th member of the House. Conlon suggested that the DSG back a provision for recording votes in the Committee of the Whole, support other anti-secrecy amendments to the bill, seek to gather support for these amendments in the news media, and build for them a bipartisan coalition.

Why did this strategy interest the DSG? The DSG staff had conducted studies that showed that when DSG members voted cohesively, they provided the margin of victory on what they determined to be the key roll call votes in the Ninetieth Congress. But they only had data on votes on the floor of Congress—they could not determine voting records on the many important votes on amendments that were conducted, unrecorded, in the Committee of the Whole. In the first year of the Nixon administration, unrecorded teller votes in the House included votes on appropriations for the controversial anti-ballistic-missile (ABM) program, the B-1 bomber, other military appropriations, the supersonic transport (SST) plane, anti-pollution measures, anti-crime provisions for the District of Columbia, desegregation efforts, and others.

DSG research also indicated that while House conservatives tended to vote in the non-record teller votes, their own liberal members were often absent from the proceedings. The result was devastating for the liberals. In 1969–1970, when the most conservative representatives introduced amendments in the Committee of the Whole, 54.5 percent of the amendments passed; when liberals introduced amendments, only 15.6 percent passed.[44] DSG members voted in 85 percent of roll call votes in the House but under 40 percent of the unrecorded teller votes in the Committee of the Whole. It seemed reasonable to presume that liberals could be brought into line and the liberal agenda advanced if secret proceedings could be curtailed. Conlon recalled, "We couldn't get our members to the floor for teller votes. Even when we knew an important vote was coming up, we would be foiled by the conservatives, who would delay the vote—sometimes for hours—until many of our members would get bored or boxed in by other time commitments, and leave. Many of our losses on amendments were especially galling because we knew, from earlier recorded quorum calls, that we had enough support there to pass the amendment."[45] A House member added, "Conservatives tend to spend more time on the floor than we do. The Southerners swap stories in the cloakroom while the liberals are out making speeches."[46]

In their May 1970 meetings, the DSG Executive Committee concluded that reforming the unrecorded teller vote should be its "top priority, and let everything else slide."[47] During the next months, the DSG produced several brief reports on secrecy and unrecorded teller voting. "Secrecy in the House of Representatives," from June 24, 1970, quickly describes several forms of secrecy: closed committee sessions (nearly half of all committee meetings, with the major committees especially likely to meet in closed session and the Appropriations Committee closing all of its 300-plus meetings), secret committee votes, the belated availability of printed committee reports and hearings for members to review before they voted, the unrecorded teller votes in the Committee of the Whole, and the closed House-Senate conference committees that hashed out differences between legislation passed in the two houses. The impact of secrecy, according to the report, is to reduce the effectiveness of the House, to inhibit the press in its responsibilities, and to deny the public the "information to which it is entitled in a democratic society."[48] Specifically, the report notes that the non-record votes on amendments reduced turnout for the votes—"less than one-third of all house Members generally participate in non-record votes on amendments." Non-record votes also reduce information available for the press. And they injure the public by giving special interests greater leverage in the absence of accountability to public sentiment. "Finally," the report concluded, "the public interest is not served when such major issues as the ABM, the SST, the invasion of Cambodia, school desegregation, civil liberties and air and water pollution are decided anonymously. The poor attendance on many of these votes effectively disfranchised many constituents and in some cases permitted the continuation of programs and policies opposed by the public."[49]

So the DSG sponsored amendments to Representative Sisk's bill. They won the support of Rumsfeld's Raiders (although by that point Rumsfeld himself had left his House seat for a position in the White House).[50] The Republicans had their own reasons to favor reform.

According to one of them (unidentified) whom political scientists Norman Ornstein and David Rohde interviewed, where the Democrats were primarily concerned to champion recorded voting to advance their legislative priorities, the Republicans were interested for three different reasons. First was "openness—I think it is essential. Our constituents ought to know how we vote." Second, they were just as interested as the liberal Democrats to weaken the committee chairmen and so to democratize political life in the House. Third, "the spotting system had begun. It's a lousy, inaccurate system for telling who voted how."[51]

The "spotting system" was a project of antiwar activist groups that posted individuals in the public galleries to try to identify which congressmen voted yea or nay by spotting them on the House floor. These groups could not hold representatives' feet to the fire on the war in Vietnam if they could not determine how individual representatives voted on war-related amendments. But spotting was very uncertain work, and it was not possible to vouch for its accuracy. (There were other, less notorious spotters. Roy Dye recalls that he and other DSG staffers would sit in the gallery during teller votes in the Committee of the Whole, intending to "spot." Because note taking was not allowed in the House galleries, they came equipped with slips of paper, each with the name of a member of Congress. As members they could identify voted, they would put the slips in their pockets—yes votes in the right pocket, no in the left.)[52]

Liberal Democrats and moderate Republicans, each group for its own reasons, agreed that anti-secrecy could win both support inside Congress and public opinion outside. They recruited two senior colleagues who had not been attached to legislative reform efforts as co-sponsors of the amendment to record all teller votes—Democrat Thomas "Tip" O'Neill (later to become Speaker of the House) and

Charles Gubser, a conservative Republican from California. In a letter to congressional colleagues on June 2, 1970, Gubser made the observation that "a number of student groups had raised a very legitimate point regarding meaningful and important 'teller votes' which are not a matter of record." In debate on the amendment later, he observed that not only young people but other groups had lost faith in Congress. "Our press corps, both privately and in print show disdain for this great parliamentary body. The executive branch often considers the Congress as an albatross. The taxpayers are up in arms. The poor, the rich, men of all races, and everyone view the Congress with a minimum of high regard." Congress, he argued, was under attack; "the charge of secrecy is a valid one and we should move forthwith to correct what is wrong."[53]

Could the press come to think better of Congress? Could it at least think well of the efforts at procedural reform? The prior question seemed to be whether the press would take any interest in legislative reorganization at all. Conlon recalled a conversation with UPI correspondent Frank Eleazar in which Eleazar told him that editors did not see congressional reform as an important issue. To them, it was just "internal housekeeping." This sparked in Conlon the idea of packaging DSG amendments as anti-secrecy reforms. "The reason I kind of went into it? I'm a former journalist." He suggested to the DSG and its allies that "we couch all our reforms as anti-secrecy reforms, and they agreed to do it that way."[54]

On Eleazar's retirement in 1979, Conlon reminded him of that conversation. He wrote that "you provided what I believe was one of the keys to the entire reform movement with your suggestion that we ignore the Washington press corps and take our story directly to local news media around the country." Conlon added, "I remember you saying that the only reform which might excite newspaper editors was our proposal to open committee meetings." And so Conlon cast the DSG proposals as anti-secrecy reforms "regardless of whether or not they had anything to do with secrecy" and to take that message to editors around the country. Conlon concluded his letter to Eleazar, "So as you hang up your spurs, old buddy, I thought you might take a bit of pleasure in recalling your role and knowing how vital it was."[55]

The DSG efforts, inspired by the conversation with Eleazar and coordinated by Conlon, produced results in newspaper editorials and opinion columns around the country, whether or not these published endorsements successfully inspired "public pressure." What the newspapers found irresistible, judging from examples collected in the DSG papers at the Library of Congress, was not simply that journalists were sympathetic to anti-secrecy measures; just as important, they were drawn to the irony that the vote to lift the veil on unrecorded teller voting would be taken by an unrecorded vote. One editorial or column after another relished this—Tom Wicker in his *New York Times* column, Carl Rowan in his syndicated column, and editorials in the *Los Angeles Times, Chicago Sun-Times, New York Post, Washington Post,* and *Washington Evening Star.*[56] Irony permitted the press to praise an obscure reform and ridicule Congress at the same time.

It was no accident that so many publications noticed the irony—the Democratic Study Group told them about it. In DSG chair Donald Fraser's "Dear Editor" letter of June 30, 1970, he wrote that the DSG "is involved in a major bi-partisan effort to abolish secrecy in the House. We are concentrating primarily on ending the practice of taking secret or non-record votes on major national issues such as the supersonic transport, funding air and water pollution programs, school desegregation, and the war in Indochina. This latter reform would not only permit the public to better evaluate the performance of their Representative in Congress, it would also significantly improve Member participation in the legislative process." And then he added: "These reforms will be decided (by non-record vote, unfortunately) within the next two weeks when the House considers H.R. 17654, the Legislative Reorganization Act of 1970. Whether they will be approved, however, will depend largely on whether Members, their constituents and the press care about these issues."[57] In this, Fraser borrowed from the June 24 DSG report that held that replacing the non-record vote with recorded voting in the Committee of the Whole was "perhaps the most important reform amendment" to be offered and that "ironically, however, whether such record votes will be permitted will be decided by non-record vote under present procedures."[58] To the extent that there were public "demands" for reform in the summer and fall of 1970, they were demands the DSG actively solicited in its proactive media strategy. And there is no doubt that Representative Fraser's letter was drafted by Dick Conlon, who may have had the news sense to see that highlighting the irony of a non-record vote to abolish non-record voting would appeal to reporters. Conlon masterminded the letter-writing campaign, Roy Dye recalls, and remembers that it was "an organizational nightmare" to get those hundreds of letters in the mail.[59]

The DSG's anti-secrecy measures sought to win support for causes that a large majority of Democratic Party representatives favored. That is what motivated the DSG, not an ideological commitment to the public's right to know. "Secrecy was just a magic button with the press," Conlon recalled in a 1974 interview. "As a trained journalist myself I know what made me salivate when I was reporting and I know that an editorial writer in particular sitting there behind a desk, frustrated as hell and not being able to get out and get at things is always railing against government secrecy and it was just the magic button that turned a shower of things on."[60] In the end, the amendment on recording teller votes passed by voice vote (a non-record vote) and the Legislative Reorganization Act passed the House 326–19. Ornstein and Rohde observe, "This was perhaps the first instance where public pressure has been effectively utilized in an effort to implement institutional change in Congress."[61] It was also one of the most important cases in which Dick Conlon earned his unofficial title as "the 436th Member of the House."

A Summing Up

Did the reform package and the recorded teller vote specifically help liberals achieve their programmatic goals? It seems likely. The percentage of liberal amendments approved in the Committee of the Whole increased after the new rules went into effect, from 25.4 percent in the Ninety-First Congress to 36.8 percent in the Ninety-Second Congress. But, as Ornstein and Rohde observe, it is difficult to define "liberal amendments," and it is still more difficult to disentangle various intertwined strands of causation. More liberals were elected in 1970, and this certainly contributed to passage of liberal initiatives. Moreover, with added numbers, some liberals may have ventured more extreme liberal amendments with no chance of success, and this may have prevented the new percentage of liberal successes from being even higher. In any event, members of Congress believed the recorded teller vote made a big difference in legislative outcomes and obviously made the legislative process more open.[62]

The House hoped that reforms would increase its legitimacy and popularity. This did not happen. The occasional scandal aside, there is nothing to indicate that the public learned to pay more attention to the House (or Congress as a whole) or grew any more informed about it than in the past. There has also been some retreat from the openness the reforms commanded, with business being conducted in "informal" sessions in which members can speak without the public overhearing.[63]

Whatever the outcome, the drive toward reforms in Congress, as in the media, resonated with a generational shift. Political scientist Leroy Rieselbach holds Vietnam to have been "surely the catalyst" for the democratization of legislative process; he sees the congressional reforms of the 1970s linked to a pervasive "new spirit of democracy, of expanded political participation" characteristic of the 1960s.[64] And in Congress specifically, there was "a great infusion of new blood." There were 36 freshman House members in the Ninety-First Congress (1969–1971). The newcomers were "younger, more policy oriented, and more independent."[65] They were less attached, and sometimes decidedly more hostile, to the traditions of Congress.

When Rieselbach presented these views at a 1981 symposium at Boston College in honor of Tip O'Neill, Dick Conlon was one of the respondents. By that time, Conlon was a fixture in Congress, the "436th member" of the House. He took issue with Rieselbach, and none too politely. Rieselbach's paper, he said, "embodies or reflects most of the misunderstandings, misperceptions, and myths which run rampant through much of what has been written about congressional reform over the past eight years."[66] Congressional reforms "were not a product of the new members elected in the 1970s, they were the product of new members elected a decade earlier in the 1960s. In fact, for the most part they were a direct result of the experiences of the 1960s members being shut out of meaningful participation in the legislative process and watching autocratic chairmen of their own party use their positions of power to obstruct party policies and programs."[67]

Although Rieselbach was right to point to an important generational shift in Congress, Conlon was correct to see the roots of reform not in the newcomers but in the frustrations of liberals in the late 1950s and early 1960s. The "Watergate babies" and others who came to Congress in 1975 or 1977 certainly benefited from and extended a "new spirit of democracy," but the origins of reform went back well before the congressional class of 1969 that Rieselbach emphasized. The leaders who pushed for the Legislative Reorganization Act were by 1970 congressional veterans.

No one was more important in this effort than Dick Conlon. David Obey, a liberal member of Congress from Wisconsin for forty years, came to Washington for his first term in 1969 and found that his office was right across the hall from the DSG office. He came to know Conlon from the beginning. "He was a very bright, very canny, very strategic, and very disciplined guy," Obey recalls. "He was good at understanding . . . the guts of an argument. A shrewd observer of human nature. He was absolutely essential to the progressive victories that we had in those days."[68]

The Democratic Study Group was in some ways too successful—not in pursuing a liberal Democratic agenda but in serving as a model for other legislative services organizations. By 1981, the House Administration Committee made a ruling that would require the LSOs to report their income and its sources, their itemized expenses, and their activities on a quarterly basis. These reports began to be filed in 1983. The rules then also required these organizations to limit income to what they received from Congress or members of Congress themselves. This meant the DSG could no longer sell sub-

scriptions to its reports on bills and issues—it had some 300 sub-
scribers beyond Congress at the beginning of the 1980s, and from
1983 on it would have to provide these reports free to outside sub-
scribers or lose them altogether.

The proliferating caucuses fell on even harder times in the 1990s
when Speaker Newt Gingrich barred Congress from subsidizing
them. They persist—but without office space or other subsidy inside
Congress itself. Dick Conlon would not live to see this. But he left a
legacy in the achievements of the DSG. He made the DSG's offices
on the fourth floor of the Longworth Building a virtual Grand Central for liberal Democratic strategizing at a key moment in history.
His package of anti-secrecy amendments made Congress more open
and its voting more transparent. For Conlon, this was a means to an
end. Much later, as political scientist Thomas Mann observed, advocates of transparency such as the Sunlight Foundation would arise
and seek to clean up politics through the disinfectant of sunlight.
Transparency would be a weapon against the day-to-day wheeling
and dealing of politics. For Conlon, the wheeling and dealing fired
his imagination and won his love.[69] Transparency? Not for its own
sake. Former Rep. David Obey remarked, "Every action you have in
Congress has a positive and negative impact." The recorded teller vote,
he recognized, is in principle good for democracy, but even this has
another side. "The amending process became a 'gotcha' process rather
than a legislative process. It enabled all of these single-issue groups
to get a roll call on everything and run a TV ad against you financed
by special interests."[70] Conlon and his DSG colleagues took "anti-
secrecy" as a workable slogan, and they had no trouble wrapping it
in the theory and spirit of democracy. But their aim was not theoretical. It was practical. They wanted to pass progressive legislation,
and anti-secrecy reforms helped them do it. Obey's cogent second

thoughts notwithstanding, the reforms also made Congress more publicly accountable than ever before.

That Dick Conlon should have been thinking about what would play well in the newspapers is understandable. He was a journalist, and in serving Congress, he brought with him the values of the newsroom. He maintained friendly relations with fellow journalists and felt comfortable with them. But his consciousness of the news media emerged as a potent force because he served at a moment when many others inside government grew more attuned to journalism or, as it was increasingly called, "the media." The news media loomed larger in the minds of Washington insiders than ever before.

five

The Media's Presence

"The media": these two words, yoked together, name something new in the world. They turn the many organizations that constitute what was once more commonly called "the press" into a single looming, forbidding entity, implicitly offering it criticism, even disdain. The press had long offended, of course. But something about the media got worse in the 1970s, even in the eyes of journalists. "The media," wrote Washington-based British journalist Henry Fairlie in 1983, was a term whose current meaning could not be found in *Webster's Third New International Dictionary* of 1966. But soon thereafter the term came to be widely used. The media were not, Fairlie argued, "just an extension of journalism."[1] The media were (or "was"—there remains even now complete confusion about whether the term should be treated as a plural noun or not) somehow new and different, and Fairlie was unsparing in his contempt: "The more dangerous insects who infest Washington today are the media: locusts who strip bare all that is green and healthy, as they chomp at it with untiring jaws; those insatiable jaws that are never at a loss for a word, on the screen or on the platform, and occasionally, when they can spare a moment for their old trade, in print."[2] Fairlie returns to his entomological sneer at the end of his piece: "The media settle on the White House and Congress to strip them like locusts, for the purpose of advancing themselves on television and the lecture circuit, and year by year they complain at the debility of the political system."[3]

William Safire, in remembering his time as a White House speechwriter for Richard Nixon, provided a more conspiratorial account of the term "the media." He recalled, "In the Nixon White House, the press became 'the media,' because the word had a manipulative, Madison Avenue, all-encompassing connotation, and the press hated it."[4] For Nixon, journalism was an "enemy" to be defeated; Safire heard Nixon declare "the press is the enemy" a dozen times.[5] So the Nixon White House insistently used "the media" because to refer to journalists as "the press" handed to these miscreants an aura of rectitude and First Amendment privilege that gave them an emotional advantage, while to call them "the media" took it away. We have "the media" not only for the reason Fairlie focuses on—the mutation of (a few) reporters into obnoxious and ever-jabbering TV celebrities—but also because powerful politicians sought to paint journalists as the misleadingly human faces of an impersonal and insatiable monster.

With the rise of the media, Fairlie argued, the primary activity of Washington switched from governing the country through legitimate political institutions to "the sustaining of the illusion of government through the media and in obedience to the media's needs and demands."[6] This position or something like it, shared by many other distinguished figures both inside and outside journalism, is an important clue to a social change that, among other things, decisively promoted a culture of disclosure in American politics. But in the end, the claim that public officials in the 1960s and 1970s shifted from governing to public relations is not credible. It would be convenient if there were a sharp break between the (good) old journalism and the (bad) new media, the (good) old politics of men dedicated to public service and the (bad) new politics of men and women devoted to seeing their own faces on television, but what happened in the 1960s and 1970s was far more subtle than critics of the day acknowledged. One part of Fairlie's observation is surely correct—that the media became more central to the operation of Washington. Only this is not proof of what he assumes to be an unquestionably "debilitating" impact.[7] It is proof of impact. It is proof that journalism was taking a more independent, less deferential stance toward power. Journalists would have to be reckoned with. This has had effects both good and ill.

No specific moment, case, or condition made all the difference. Not the rise of network television news, important as that was for giving the media a unified national identity. Certainly not Watergate; Watergate was a capstone to a journalism that had become increasingly assertive in the Vietnam years. Vietnam is not sufficient explanation, either. Journalists grew disillusioned with the war in Vietnam in the mid- to late 1960s, but a growing critical edge arose at the same time, if less intensely, in European journalism. An increased media presence was not uniquely American. It was a generational change, an educational change, a cultural change. And while the media were very much agents of that change, it is likewise true that they were responding to something in the air, something that, in the American case, began to take shape in the late 1950s, gathered momentum in the early 1960s in the usual sites of political power— Congress, the White House, and the Supreme Court—and was reinforced and extended by popular action in the streets by the late

1960s as well as by a new sophistication, a new capacity, and a new arrogance in journalism.

Consider the following tale: Peter Buxtun, a young employee working for the U.S. Public Health Service in the 1960s, learned about an experiment the service was conducting on the long-term effects of syphilis on African American men if left untreated. This study had begun in the 1930s and more than a generation later was still in operation. One of the mysteries about this is that a cure for syphilis had become available in the interim with the discovery of penicillin and its wide availability after World War II. Buxtun contacted his superiors in the Public Health Service, convinced they would shut the study down if only it was brought to their attention.

But they did no such thing. Instead, they treated Buxtun as a troublemaker and successfully stalled him. Buxtun put the matter aside for several years, but he could not put it out of his mind. He tried again to sound the alarm with the Public Health Service's Communicable Disease Center (later the Centers for Disease Control, or CDC). Again he made no headway. At that point he went to the news media. He contacted an AP reporter in San Francisco, Edie Lederer. Lederer was leaving for a trip to Europe but promised Buxtun she would pass on the materials he provided to another AP reporter. En route to Europe she stopped in Miami, where her colleague Jean Heller was covering the 1972 Republican National Convention. Lederer provided Heller the materials Buxtun had sent to the CDC and the CDC's reply to them. Heller and her husband, Ray, also an AP reporter, thought the CDC response indirectly confirmed Buxtun's charges—or at least did not flatly deny them. She decided this was well worth following up.

Heller had grown up in Ohio and attended the University of Michigan, studying history and English, but transferred in her junior year to Ohio State, where Ray, her high school sweetheart, was studying. There she minored in journalism and fell in love with it. The dean of the School of Journalism, a former AP bureau chief, helped her get a position in New York with AP Radio in 1954. She went to Washington in 1968 when AP created—for the first time in its century-long history—an investigative reporting team, to which she was assigned.

Thanks to Peter Buxtun and Edie Lederer, the story of the Tuskegee syphilis experiment had just fallen into Heller's lap. It did not require her investigative skills. The CDC told her she could see any records she wanted. The story she produced was sensational. She knew it would be. She and her colleagues wanted to be sure that, for maximum impact on Washington policy makers, it would appear on the front page of a Washington newspaper—either the *Post* or the *Star*. They chose the *Star* because at the time the *Post* "was just consumed with Watergate" and they were not confident it would give the story a front-page spot. So they promised the *Star* they would release the story "on the P.M. cycle if they could guarantee page one." Heller herself opposed the deal because "I figured if it was page one in the *Star* it would never be page one the next day in the *Post*." She was wrong about that. The story appeared the next day all over the country, including in a bylined story in the *New York Times*. Heller was on the phone that night with the *Times* because that paper wanted to do its own reporting and rewrote the story, cutting out, among other things, the potent phrase Heller had used to describe the black Alabama men who were the subjects of the study: "human guinea pigs."[8]

It was July 25, 1972, when Heller's story ran in the *Star,* telling the world that some 600 African American residents of Macon County,

Alabama, in a study begun in 1932, had become human guinea pigs. While suffering from syphilis, they were told only that they had "bad blood," and though they were treated for other everyday medical complaints, they were not treated for syphilis. About one hundred people died from this deliberate decision to leave their syphilis untreated.[9]

Heller went to visit her parents in Ohio not long after. "My folks' best friend was a doctor—his response was 'That's not true.' . . . That's how I had felt, too. I had this pedestal the medical and legal fraternity stood on. . . . It was quite a rude awakening for me. The scales fell from my eyes. It's a terrible cliché, but—this was an evil I couldn't comprehend. What were these people thinking? It was the end of naivete." For the next two years, Heller said, "I wrote about nothing else." She followed the lawsuit, dozens of meetings of the National Commission for the Protection of Human Subjects of Biomedical and Behavioral Research and related topics.[10]

One more story. In Wheaton, Illinois, 1961, a top student at the local high school gave a graduation speech largely devoted to attacking the federal government. The high schooler's father was the town's leading attorney, a conventional Republican and a pillar of the community. Inspiration for the speech came from Barry Goldwater, the conservative Republican senator from Arizona, whose *The Conscience of a Conservative* was published in 1960. The young student himself had favored Richard Nixon in the Kennedy-Nixon contest for president in 1960.[11] Eleven years later, this onetime Nixon and then Goldwater fan, Bob Woodward, would start working on a story for the *Washington Post* about a burglary in the Watergate apartment and office complex.

The rest of that tale is the best-known story in the history of American journalism. Watergate did not simply influence journalism; it galvanized the journalistic imagination. Investigative journalism became the definition of great journalism. Of course, reporters prized the "scoop" long before Watergate, but journalists can get scoops with little more than a well-placed and well-timed interview. But at the moment Woodward and Carl Bernstein began to cover Watergate, there was already a lively new interest in investigative work. *Newsday* had put three reporters, an editor, and a researcher on an investigative "team" in 1967. The *Chicago Tribune* began an investigative task force in 1968, and so did the Associated Press with its "special assignment team." The *Boston Globe* began its "spotlight" group in 1970 on the *Newsday* model.[12]

But this was not the beginning of a new mood in journalism, either, not the point when journalism began to be more open, more inquisitive (and even inquisitorial), more aggressive, more negative. There is no definitive point of origin. Even in 1953–1954 and 1960, when Bernard Cohen interviewed foreign correspondents, he found them attached not only to a role of neutral observer but also to a role of "participant." The latter, however, was still a "bootleg" journalism that, "like illicit liquor . . . is found everywhere" without being publicly acknowledged.[13] But disquiet among journalists grew, a sense that the country's leaders were not leveling with them, either on the record or in confidence. The support that reporters and editors provided John Moss for his efforts to pry public information out of the executive branch of government is one indicator. Another was the public scandal over President Eisenhower's initial, embarrassing lies about the downing of Francis Gary Powers's U-2 spy plane over Russia in 1960. Administration spokesmen at first declared that the U-2 was a weather plane and denied Soviet charges that the plane was engaged in espionage. The Soviets, however, were correct. Roger Mudd, later a prominent national correspondent for CBS, was then a reporter for a local television station in Washington. He recalled later that veteran Washington correspondents were shaken that the government had straight-out lied to them. Most journalists in 1960, he said, were "trusting and uncritical of the government; they tended to be unquestioning consumers and purveyors of official information."[14]

Just a few months after the U-2 incident, the first of the televised Kennedy-Nixon debates took place. Although presidential debates would not be repeated until 1976, they were an important symbol of a new media power and at the same time a novel pressure for a new transparency—staged transparency, to be sure, but nonetheless a site available for surprise and spontaneity. As media scholars Daniel Dayan and Elihu Katz have argued, these first TV presidential debates were among those "media events" that "breed the expectation of openness in politics and diplomacy." Media events "turn the lights on social structures that are not always visible, and dramatize processes that typically take place offstage."[15] As people around the world took up television, expectations of openness spread globally, almost as if bundled into the technological package.

A presumption of openness carried on into the Kennedy administration. Kennedy's critics charged, and many of his friends conceded, that this was more style than substance. But, as historian Cynthia Harrison writes about the Kennedy administration, "style and substance are not unrelated phenomena." Most of Lyndon Johnson's impressive success in domestic legislation grew out of Kennedy administration initiatives, including, notably, both civil rights legislation and engagement in Vietnam; in Harrison's words, "in both cases the 'style' was an authentic political event. It encouraged national energies that continued beyond Kennedy's life, through the 1960s, facilitating movements for women's rights, consumer rights, ecology, and mental health services."[16] As indicated in the work of Esther Peterson and Philip Hart, the hand of the Kennedy administration was visible in encouraging consumer reforms and women's rights, and as Chapter 6 will show, it also played a significant role in abetting environmental awareness and environment-centered legislation.

As virtually all accounts by journalists and historians attest, news coverage of government, politics, and society opened up in the 1960s and 1970s. It was not the jousting on Capitol Hill before the Moss Committee, nor the U-2 incident, nor the TV debates; it was not any specific skirmish or even the sum of the confrontations between the press and U.S. military spokesmen in Vietnam as the war there dragged on; and it was not the rise in the 1960s of irreverent underground publications or the growing respect for maverick reporter I. F. Stone, who became a hero for politically committed young reporters of the day. It was all of this and more. There was a generational change, and there was a broad cultural change that made the news media a chief constituent of the opening up of American society and not simply its transcriber (although "transcribing" is never as simple as it sounds). The change in the media's role was the joint product of several closely connected developments: government—especially the federal government—grew larger and more engaged in people's everyday lives; the culture of journalism changed and journalists asserted themselves more aggressively than before; and many governmental institutions became less secretive and more attuned to the news media, eager for media attention and approval. As the federal government expanded its reach (in civil rights, economic regulation, environmental responsibility, and social welfare programs such as food stamps, Medicare, and Medicaid), as the women's movement proclaimed that "the personal is political," and as stylistic innovation in journalism proved a force of its own, the very concept of "covering politics" changed, too.

News coverage became at once more probing, more analytical, and more transgressive of conventional lines between public and private, as I shall show in the pages to follow, but this recognizes only half of the influence of a changing journalism. The other half is perhaps even more important, if harder to document: not only did the news media grow in independence and professionalism and provide more comprehensive and more critical coverage of powerful institutions, but powerful institutions adapted to a world in which journalists had a more formidable presence than ever before. Of course, politicians had resented the press much earlier—President George Washington complained about how he was portrayed in the newspapers; President Thomas Jefferson encouraged libel prosecutions in the state courts against editors who attacked him and his policies; critics in the 1830s bemoaned that the country had become a "press-ocracy"; and President Theodore Roosevelt, one of the great manipulators of journalists, famously castigated the negative tone of reporters he dubbed "muckrakers."[17] Even so, Washington politics remained much more exclusively an insiders' game than it would be later. The Washington press corps was more subservient to the whims and wishes of editors and publishers back home than to official Washington, and in any event, politicians in Washington kept their jobs less by showing themselves in the best light in the newspapers than by maintaining their standing among their party's movers and shakers in their home state. Members of the U.S. Senate were not popularly elected until 1914; before then, a remoteness from popular opinion was a senator's birthright. And while in the early twentieth century a small number of writers at the most influential newspapers and a small number of syndicated political columnists came to be influential power brokers, the press as a corporate force did not have an imposing presence.

Presence is what the media acquired by the late 1960s. Presence meant not a seat at the table but an internalization in the minds of political decision makers that the media were alert, powerful, and by no means sympathetic. In a shift that was partially independent of how journalists covered Washington (and other centers of political power), those who held political power came to orient themselves in office or in seeking office to public opinion and to their belief that the media both reflected and influenced it.[18]

The story of a transformed journalism has been told many times before, but it has generally failed to specify what exactly the transformation looked like in the pages of the newspapers. Much attention has focused on the very important growth of investigative reporting. But the quantitatively more significant change between the 1950s and the early 2000s has been the rise of what I call contextual reporting, following research Katherine Fink and I have conducted.[19] In contextual reporting, the journalist's work is less to record the views of key actors in political events and more to analyze and explain them with a voice of his or her own. More than other concurrent changes, this one altered the front page, putting a premium on the stories behind the story. This shift, like that toward investigative reporting, made the news media a more assertive presence in American public life, and helped make the press implicitly an evangelist for openness, through its own vigor. As previous chapters indicate, the press became an explicit advocate for practices premised on a cultural or philosophical, if not legal, right to know in promoting FOIA and later in editorializing on behalf of "sunshine" rules in Congress. But much more generally, the move from writing down what political leaders said to contextualizing what they said and did, and why, offered a new model of journalism. The new model seeped into the work of journalism with little fanfare, barely even notice. Journalists continued to defend their work as "objective" or "balanced" while, in the newsroom, the new model transformed what they meant by such terms.

Journalism's Coming of Age in the 1960s and 1970s

The years from 1960 to the mid-1970s brought an end of innocence for a great number of Americans, including journalists. As many journalists have recalled, they grew less deferential to politicians and more insistent and probing in these years. Political scientist Michael Robinson, interviewing journalists, members of Congress, and congressional staffers between 1977 and 1980, found near unanimity that a more aggressive and critical news media was the biggest change in Congress-media relations in their experience. "Ask anybody on Capitol Hill about the most basic change in the relationship between Congress and the media since 1960," he wrote, "and the response is practically catechistic—the media have become harder, tougher, more cynical."[20] This development, unwelcome in Congress, was even more unsettling for the White House. A few months after Richard Nixon became the first (and, so far, the only) person in American history to resign the presidency, Supreme Court justice Potter Stewart observed in a speech at Yale Law School that "less than a decade" earlier, Americans had become aware of "the twin phenomena on a national scale of so-called investigative reporting and an adversary press—that is, a press adversary to the Executive Branch of the Federal Government." Only with Watergate, he added, did people realize "the enormous power that an investigative and adversary press can exert."[21]

This erased a lot of recent history, including *New York Times* reporter Harrison Salisbury's controversial stories from Hanoi, North Vietnam, in December 1966 and January 1967 while American jets bombed the city; Seymour Hersh's reporting in 1969 of the hushed-up 1968 My Lai massacre; and the defiance of the *New York Times,* followed by the *Washington Post,* the *Boston Globe,* the *Chicago Tribune,* the *Christian Science Monitor, the St. Louis Post-Dispatch,* and others in publishing the Pentagon papers in 1971, or stories based on them, as the Nixon administration sought legal means to stop publication. Even journalism's failures to be critical contributed to the trends by the controversy they stirred—as when CBS television producer Fred Friendly resigned from CBS News in 1966 when the network refused to cancel regular programming to air Sen. J. William Fulbright's hearings on the conduct of the Vietnam War. Still, Justice Stewart's general point was correct—enormous changes in government-media relations occurred in the space of a decade.

Media coverage of Congress in the 1950s and into the 1960s had been, as one contemporary gently called it, "overcooperative."[22] One reporter on Capitol Hill said (in 1956) that covering the Senate was "a little like being a war correspondent; you really become a part of the outfit you are covering."[23] In the House during the 1940s and 1950s, cooperation was orchestrated by a powerful Speaker, Sam Rayburn (D-Tex.). For Rayburn, politics was about what happened in Congress, not what outsiders said about it. Rayburn was unwilling to participate on television's Sunday news interview programs, and he banned cameras from the House floor and House committee meetings. At the same time, the Speaker invited an inner circle of trusted reporters to off-the-record sessions of drinking and discussion at the end of the working day. His daily five-minute press conferences were almost totally controlled by these insiders, who protected him from any difficult questions.[24]

If Speaker Rayburn represented a model of coerced cooperation between a relatively obliging press and an entrenched political class, Walter Lippmann epitomized an integrated cooperation where the line between elected politician and journalist all but disappeared. In 1945, Lippmann, already the American journalist taken more seriously than any other by both politicians and intellectuals, along with *New York Times* journalist James Reston, still early in his rise to prominence, convinced the ambitious senator Arthur Vandenberg (R-Mich.) that he would have to move beyond his isolationist foreign policy views if he ever wanted to be president. Lippmann and Reston wrote a speech for Vandenberg expressing a change of heart on foreign affairs that he delivered in the Senate to great acclaim. Some of that acclaim came from Lippmann and Reston: Lippmann praised the speech in his widely read syndicated column, and Reston wrote in the *Times* that the speech was "wise" and "statesmanlike."[25]

Such politician-journalist collaboration did not happen every day, but neither was it unusual.[26] As historian Julian Zelizer writes, "Until the mid-1960s, the press was generally respectful of the political establishment."[27] The decline of this respect helped bring more attention to political scandal. Scandal reporting is frequently decried as a lowering of the standards of the press from serious and fair-minded coverage of issues to a frivolous and sensational focus on political sideshows. In this view, scandal reporting encourages citizens' alienation from a politics portrayed as terminally tawdry. But scandal reporting is at the same time a symptom of a system that has become more democratic. As governing became more public (the Legislative Reorganization Act of 1970 was among the milestones in "sunshine" legislation) politicians and government officers were more often held accountable. The character of democracy shifted from one in which voters normally could express disapproval of government incumbents only on election day to one in which, in Zelizer's words, "the nation would no longer have to wait until an election to punish government officials, nor would it have to depend on politicians to decide when an investigation was needed."[28] To some extent, the proliferation of scandals was made possible by the availability of new information (for instance, disclosure of campaign contributions after the reform acts of 1971 and 1974). More broadly, scandal reporting increased with the growing acceptance of values promoted by the women's movement that blurred the line between public and private behavior or, to put it more strongly, demonstrated that the line had been an artificial construction, and a gendered one, all along.

Are personal recollections of a changing political culture in U.S. journalism after the 1950s confirmed by close analysis of news content? Recollection is a tricky business, and the perception that deference to authority is in decline may be in part a consequence of the simple fact that people grow older. Early in their journalism careers, young reporters defer to senior reporters, editors, and the public officials they interview. Later, as they themselves become veterans on the job, they gain parity with important figures in whose shadows they once stood. Voilà—deference has declined! When they look back, they see—correctly—a decline in deference, but can they distinguish between a historic wave of change, one that lowers the threshold for skepticism or criticism of the powerful, and biographical change, which demonstrates only the sophistication, skepticism, and irony that come with age and the time to write memoirs?

Analysis of newspaper content over time both confirms and disconfirms what journalists and politicians themselves recall. As expected, there was an increase in investigative reporting in and after the late 1960s, but that increase is quantitatively modest when measured as a percentage of all front-page news stories. More surprising, because less a part of how journalists discuss their own past, there has been a stunning growth in "contextual reporting." As Kathy Roberts Forde has observed, there is no standard terminology for this kind of journalism. It has been called interpretative reporting, depth reporting, long-form journalism, explanatory reporting, and analytical reporting.[29] In his extensive interviewing of Washington journalists in the late 1970s, Stephen Hess called it "social science journalism," a mode of reporting with "the accent on greater interpretation" and a clear intention to focus on causes, not on events as such.[30] Although contextual reporting is, in quantitative terms, easily the most important change in reporting in the past half century up to the rise of online journalism, it has neither a settled name nor a hallowed place in journalism's understanding of its own past.

The following propositions summarize much of the available evidence that over the past half century there has been a shift in the content of journalism and in the culture of the newsrooms that produce it: news has grown more critical of established power; journalists have come to present themselves publicly as more aggressive; news stories have grown longer (and presumably deeper); and news has grown more contextual. In summarizing the evidence, I draw on the work of others but also, especially on the final point, on research that Katherine Fink and I have undertaken together.

1. News Has Grown More Critical of Established Power.   Looking at ten mainstream metropolitan dailies from 1963–1964 and 1998–1999 (sampling two weeks in each period) from different regions of the country, media analyst and *American Journalism Review* columnist Carl Sessions Stepp wrote, "To read 1963 newspapers is to re-enter a pre-Watergate, pre-Vietnam, pre–Dealey Plaza world. It is to roll back a gigantic cultural loss of idealism." According to Stepp, newspapers in this earlier period "seem naively trusting of government, shamelessly boosterish, unembarrassedly hokey and obliging." He was surprised to find stories "often not attributed at all, simply passing along an unquestioned, quasi-official sense of things. The world view seemed white, male, middle-aged and middle class, a comfortable and confident Optimist Club bonhomie."[31] This was far different from what he found in his 1998–1999 sample. Today journalists sometimes celebrate critical judgment and a watchdog's instinct for the soft underbelly of politicians as if it were part of a long tradition, but Stepp's analysis finds little evidence of these features in the content of 1963–1964 newspapers.

A study of campaign coverage of presidential elections by political scientist Thomas Patterson found that news coverage (in weekly newsmagazines) grew increasingly negative from 1960 to 1992. In 1960, 75 percent of evaluative references to candidates John Kennedy and Richard Nixon were positive; by 1992, only 40 percent of evaluative references praised Bill Clinton or George H. W. Bush.[32] A similar study of news about presidents, not presidential candidates, in *New York Times* stories found that 12 percent of stories were—on balance— negative in the 1950s, 17.5 percent in the 1960s, 32 percent in the 1970s (or 26 percent if the Watergate years of 1973 and 1974 are omitted), and 28 percent in the 1980s.[33] Not only were evaluations more negative than they had been but campaign coverage grew implicitly more cynical in focusing on the "game" of politics rather than the policies proposed by candidates. That means, of course, that coverage was less about what candidates said on the campaign trail and more about the strategy and tactics of campaigning. It was, critics observed, a kind of "inside baseball" reporting. Over the same 1960–1992 period, Patterson found in another study, news accounts in the *New York Times* paid decreasing attention to what candidates said in speeches and increasing attention to the political strategies behind the speeches. In his terms, this was a move from a "policy" framework for reporting to a "game" framework.[34] News shifted from what politicians said to the political context in which they said it, implicitly or explicitly contending that the strategic or political context partially or fully explained politicians' policy pronouncements and other statements.

There is no single author of this shift, but Theodore "Teddy" White, in his day a famous correspondent and independent author of books on China, gets some credit—or blame—for it. Given privileged access in 1960 to the primary campaigns of Sens. John F. Kennedy and Hubert Humphrey and the general election campaigns of Kennedy and Vice President Richard Nixon, White crafted a bestselling book, *The Making of the President 1960,* that set an unprecedented standard for an intimate, behind-the-scenes portrait of American politics. White offered a romance of the American electoral process through his close-ups of the presidential contenders and their inner circles, turning each politician into a hybrid of a Hollywood idol and a candidate for Mount Rushmore. It was as if he had invented a magician's trick of taking down candidates and installing them on pedestals simultaneously. It was not negative coverage, but it was undercutting, as it took readers backstage, making it more difficult to accept the front-stage acts of politicians as if there were no well-orchestrated manipulation behind them.

Others would copy White, and he would copy himself with subsequent *Making of the President* volumes for the elections of 1964, 1968, and 1972. By 1972, the Associated Press advised its staff: "When

Teddy White's book comes out, there shouldn't be one single story in that book that we haven't reported ourselves." White himself told *Rolling Stone* reporter Timothy Crouse about joining other reporters in Sen. George McGovern's suite at the Democratic convention in 1972 just after McGovern had been nominated. At that moment, White recalled, McGovern was writing his acceptance speech and trying to select a vice presidential candidate while "all of us are observing him, taking notes like mad, getting all the little details. Which I think I invented as a method of reporting and which I now sincerely regret. If you write about this, say that I sincerely regret it. Who gives a fuck if the guy had milk and Total for breakfast? . . . I felt, finally, that our being there was a total imposition."[35]

White focused on the campaign. For him, the hotel suite was a stage setting for the campaign, but the bedroom was not. Still, the White model made the explosion of sex scandals of the 1970s and 1980s more acceptable in news coverage, if not inevitable.

2. Journalists Have Come to Present Themselves Publicly as Aggressive. In a rich series of research papers, sociolinguists Steven Clayman and John Heritage and their colleagues analyzed the questions reporters have asked in presidential press conferences from 1953 through 2000. They find significant increases in "initiative" (prefacing a question with statements to construct a particular context, asking multiple questions within a single turn, or asking a follow-up question), in "assertiveness" (inviting a particular answer—"Isn't it true that . . . ?" or "Don't you think that . . . ?"), and in "adversarialness" ("Mr. President, Senator So-and-So has criticized your Policy X as disastrous for the economy, national defense, and American morals—how do you respond?") There was a notable rise on all of these measures of aggressiveness in 1969, and at no point after 1969 did the questions revert to the more deferential style that had prevailed during the Eisenhower, Kennedy, and Johnson administrations. The scholars find that the only plausible explanation for this is a "normative shift" in the practice of journalism. No other contextual variables—the party of the incumbent president, the state of the national economy, the extent of divided government—explain the persistence of aggressive questions that attempt to hold the president accountable.[36]

Transcripts of presidential press conferences are not the newspaper and television stories based on them. They document change in how reporters have presented themselves, not change in how they have crafted their stories. Still, that Washington journalists came to style themselves as tough and assertive, people able to stand their ground face-to-face with the president of the United States, is important in itself. A presidential press conference is nothing if not a public ceremony, and any ceremony, as sociologist Erving Goffman put it, is "an expressive rejuvenation and reaffirmation of the moral values of the community."[37] The moral values expressed and affirmed in the news conferences unmistakably shifted. Did the reporters who performed "critical distance" on the press conference stage then produce stories that mirrored this attitude? The sociolinguistic analysis of how reporters ask questions at presidential news conferences does not directly provide an answer, but is difficult to imagine that less deferential news conference questions did not to some degree yield less deferential news.

3. News Stories Have Grown Longer.   One well-documented study, by Kevin Barnhurst and Diana Mutz, shows that newspaper stories have become longer over time. Sampling the *New York Times,* the *Chicago Tribune,* and the (Portland) *Oregonian* every twentieth year from 1894 through 1994, Barnhurst and Mutz find a consistently increasing mean length of news stories in all three papers in all three categories of stories that they examined (accidents, crimes, and job-related stories) across the whole time span of their study. The three papers showed little change from 1914 to 1934; the *Oregonian* shows a notable increase in length by 1954, and all three papers—the *Times* especially—show growing story length between 1954 and 1974. Stories in the *Times* and the *Oregonian* continued to lengthen through 1994, although the increases are modest; the *Tribune* story length decreased between 1974 and 1994 but remained higher than in any of the years measured from 1894 through 1954.[38]

Barnhurst and Mutz do not certify that the longer stories of 1974 and 1994 offer "better" journalism than the shorter stories of 1954 and earlier, but it is hard not to believe that, in general, they do. Carl Sessions Stepp acknowledges that the 1999 papers he studied struck him as "less flavorful, less surprising, and—distressingly—less imbued with a distinctive sense of place" than those of 1964. Nevertheless, he judges that the 1999 papers were, "by almost any measure, far superior to their 1960s counterparts." They were "better written, better looking, better organized, more responsible, less sensational, less sexist and racist, and more informative and public-spirited."[39] Less idiosyncratic, with less aroma of a particular locale, these papers provided fare that by any measure was more nutritional.

4. News Has Grown More Contextual.   News stories have grown more contextualized over time, less confined to describing the immediately observable here and now. In 1960 more than 90 percent of front-page stories in the *New York Times* concerning electoral campaigns were largely descriptive, but by 1992 less than 20 percent were, according to Thomas Patterson's research.[40] Reporters took a more active part in their own stories, and not to the benefit of candidates for office. Patterson put it this way: "Journalists had been silent skeptics; they became vocal cynics."[41] According to Patterson, this growth of a more interpretive style in the newspapers was the adoption of the "television model."[42] This suggests an explanation for change—that newspapers copied television to keep up with it. That may be a factor, and newspapers had reason for concern about television, particularly those papers that published in the afternoon and so competed more directly with the evening TV news shows than did the morning papers. Still, the threat to newspaper reading came less from television as such than from the way its importance increased with the spectacular growth of suburbs, an automobile-centered culture, the emergence of suburban newspapers, and a literally distanced relationship between traditional newspaper readers and the city-centered coverage of the papers they read.[43]

In his further analysis of the *New York Times, Chicago Tribune,* and *Oregonian,* Barnhurst found small decreases in the percentage of front-page stories that refer to the past rather than only to the temporally immediate context (hours or days) of the event the stories focus on: 25 percent in 1894, 22 percent in 1914, and 21 percent in 1934. Thereafter there are large increases in references to the past in the stories—28 percent in 1954, 39 percent in 1954, and 49 percent in 1994.[44]

This is consistent also with the recollections of journalists. Max Frankel, Washington bureau chief for the *New York Times* from 1968 to 1972 and the paper's executive editor from 1988 to 1994, recalls a growing pressure in the 1960s to offer "something unique" that other news outlets did not provide. This meant more analysis or more "mood" pieces, like "'what France is up to' or 'what Hitler represents' and so on." This had been acceptable even decades earlier for foreign correspondents, but rarely for national or local news reporters. Abe Rosenthal, managing editor of the paper in the 1970s and executive editor for most of the 1980s, liked to encourage good writing and practiced it himself in his days as a foreign correspondent. "He was a brilliant stylist," Frankel has recalled, a master of "the so-called soft but significant lead." As editor, Rosenthal was "very tolerant of well-written, correspondent-like stories even when they came from the Bronx. Not just from India." Frankel recalls that in his own tenure as editor he was "insistent" in his effort "to get analysis into regular news stories."[45]

To all of this evidence, Katherine Fink and I have added an analysis of the content of three newspapers: the *New York Times,* the *Washington Post,* and the *Milwaukee Journal Sentinel.* We selected the *Times* and the *Post* because of their central importance as national leaders of American journalism from the late 1960s to the present; we chose the *Journal Sentinel,* a well-regarded regional daily, to stand in for the many strong papers around the country that dominate news gathering in a region, papers such as the *Miami Herald, Boston Globe, St. Louis Post-Dispatch, Arizona Republic,* and others. We examined articles on the front pages of each newspaper over two constructed weeks (Monday of week one, Tuesday of week two, Wednesday of week three, and so forth) in the years 1955, 1967, 1979, 1991, and 2003. We steered clear of election years so that campaign stories did not overwhelm other news. Based on their content and style, we assigned each of the 1,891 articles in the sample to one of five categories: "conventional," "investigative," "social empathy," "contextual," and "other."

In our analysis, conventional stories often, though not always, focus on the official activities of government. This category includes stories about lawmaking and politics, but also about government actors like the police, firefighters and other emergency workers, prosecutors, judges, public health authorities, and many more. A conventional story, however, is defined not by its subject matter but by its approach. Three features stand out. First, a conventional story identifies its subject clearly and promptly. Commonly, these stories answer the "who-what-when-where" questions in the lead paragraph or even the lead sentence. Also commonly, the stories ignore or only implicitly address the "why" question. They tend to be written in the "inverted pyramid" style, with the most important information coming first.

Second, the conventional story describes activities that have occurred or will occur within twenty-four hours. (In some cases, the activities may have occurred earlier but were not publicly known until very recently.) One giveaway of a conventional story is a lead paragraph with the word "yesterday" or "today."

Third, conventional stories focus on one-time activities or actions—discrete events rather than long-term processes or sequences. This includes planned events such as public meetings as well as unplanned events such as accidents or natural disasters. Also, these activities may be not events in the world but rather statements about them made by a powerful person, either in public or in speaking with a reporter.

The article "Conferees Approve 8.8 Pct. Pay Raise" (*Washington Post*, May 4, 1955) is an example of a conventional story. It fulfills all three criteria of conventionality (government action, discrete event, occurring in the past twenty-four hours) in its lead sentence: "Senate-House conferees yesterday agreed on an 8.8 percent average pay raise for the Nation's 500,000 postal employees, including 15,000 here and nearby."

Contextual stories, in contrast, tend to focus on the big picture, providing context or background for a topic of current interest. Where the conventional story is a well-cropped, tightly focused shot, the contextual story uses a wide-angle lens. It is often explanatory in nature, sometimes appearing beside conventional stories to complement the dry, just-the-facts versions of that day's events. Sometimes newspapers have labeled contextual stories "news analysis," as if to head off anticipated criticism that these stories mix interpretation with facts. Contextual stories are often written in the present tense, since they describe processes and activities that are ongoing rather than events that have been both initiated and completed in the preceding hours or days. Alternatively, they may be written in the past tense, if their purpose is to give historical context.

Obviously, contextual stories are not all alike. They may be explanatory stories that help readers better understand complicated issues. They may be trend stories, using numerical data to show change over time on matters of public interest such as high school graduation rates, population growth, or unemployment. Trend articles often include charts or graphs. There are also descriptive stories that engage the imaginations of readers, transporting them to unfamiliar places. These are not travel pieces—they describe places that are newsworthy, not likely family vacation sites. An Associated Press story printed in the *Milwaukee Journal Sentinel* (the *Milwaukee Journal* at the time) in 1967, for example, is based on a reporter's observations in Communist China:

Canton, China—AP—Though one million Red Guards throng Canton's streets and are in effective control, there are no civil disorders. The opposition to the guards is covert, furtive and virtually underground.

Police are still on duty, most of them wearing armbands to show they are in the Red Guards. But traffic in the streets of south China's biggest city is limited to a handful of trucks, buses and trolley buses.

Descriptive contextual articles are not always about places far from home. A *New York Times* article from 1991 describes two competing images of Newark, New Jersey: "one of gleaming steel and glass towers, the other of 100-year-old railroad shacks and multifamily wood frame houses in neighborhoods with few stores or amenities, not even a movie theater." Descriptive contextual stories may provide a backdrop for breaking news that is under way or anticipated, such as military activity. Newspapers in 1991 featured many accounts by reporters who described what they saw while embedded with the U.S. military in Iraq. There are different ways to offer context; what all contextual stories share is an effort at offering accounts that go behind or beyond the "who-what-when-where" of a recent or unfolding event.

Consider a front-page story on the U.S. economic recovery in the *New York Times* from May 5, 2012. The "news peg"—a specific in-the-past-twenty-four-hours point of reference—was the monthly press release from the U.S. Bureau of Labor Statistics on employment trends. According to the bureau, employment in April rose by 115,000 jobs and the unemployment rate was unchanged. The press release did not say that job creation in April was less than half of what it had been in the first months of the year. It did not say that the proportion of working-age Americans either working or looking for work was lower than at any time since 1981. It did not say the proportion of men in the labor force fell to 70 percent in April, the lowest figure since the government began collecting this information in 1948. Not the government press release but reporter Catherine Rampell provided readers all of this comparative information. She turned a tepid government press release into a front-page story underscoring that the economic situation remained dismal.

Was this too interpretive? Did it offer too much of Rampell's own opinion, all but declaring the press release misleading? How sure was she that she had consulted the right assortment of economists? Was she too critical of the beleaguered Obama administration, which was trying desperately to revive the sinking economy it had inherited from George W. Bush? Different people may assess this differently, but there seems little doubt that Rampell was conscientiously pursuing what from the 1970s on had become the generally accepted obligation of journalists—to not take government statements at face value, to recognize them as tendentious (even if in a narrow sense true), and to work to provide a context that fair-minded and informed observers would regard as appropriate.

Although conventional and contextual stories together accounted for the large majority of the articles Katherine Fink and I examined, we also tabulated two other types of stories: "investigative" and "social empathy" stories. In investigative stories, the newspaper is clearly playing watchdog, investigating corruption or coming to the aid of a person who has been treated unjustly. Investigative stories often require extensive time and research, due in part to resistance from sources who fear the stories will reflect poorly upon them. Reporters may have to compel government sources to provide information via formal requests for public records through the Freedom of Information

Act or state open-records laws. Other information for investigative stories comes from confidential sources. Reporters often call attention to such methods in the ways they attribute their sources, such as "according to documents obtained by [news organization]." Articles that referenced efforts like these—obtaining nonpublic documents, or conducting many or lengthy interviews—we categorized as investigative.

Social empathy stories describe a person or group of people not often covered in news stories. They may answer the question "What does it feel like to be this person or a member of this category of people?" Such stories encourage readers to be interested in, have compassion for, or empathize with the experiences and problems of people who are largely unfamiliar to them. Social empathy stories often use personal experiences to highlight larger social problems, such as the many stories of struggle in the Lower Ninth Ward of New Orleans in the aftermath of Hurricane Katrina in 2005. Social empathy stories often begin with anecdotal leads, use many direct quotes from their main sources, and structure narratives around the observations of sources rather than those of a detached observer. Social empathy and investigative stories are specific brands of contextual journalism, distinctive enough and important enough to be counted separately, but they can be added to the sum of contextual news stories to measure the general shift away from conventional reports.[46]

The line between conventional and contextual stories blurs, especially in the later years of our sample, when stories that use an inverted-pyramid structure also include a heavy dose of analysis. Interpretive clauses may be embedded within the who-what-when-where statements typical of conventional articles, as if the reporters are interrupting their own thoughts to contextualize the story as they go along. Consider this lead paragraph from "Bush Proposes North Korea Security Plan to China," in the October 20, 2003, edition of the *New York Times* (emphasis added)*:*

> BANGKOK, Monday, October 20—President Bush presented President Hu Jintao of China with a new, *if still vague,* American plan here on Sunday that would provide a five-nation security guarantee to North Korea—*but not a formal nonaggression treaty*— if the North dismantles all of its nuclear weapons programs.

The italicized phrases represent the reporter's attempt to contextualize the security guarantee. By describing it as "still vague," the lead paragraph suggests that the new plan is not very different from the last one the United States proposed. And by mentioning that the security guarantee is not a formal nonaggression treaty, the reporter clarifies that the United States has stopped short of giving North Korea what it really wants. How, then, to categorize this story? Fink and I counted it as a conventional story, since its general structure is strictly conventional and the interpretive or contextual elements, though of an analytical bent rarely to be found in conventional news stories of the 1950s and 1960s, are presented as parenthetical rather than central.

Coding news stories is not foolproof, even with these relatively simple, relatively clear, and relatively few categories. Even so, the general trend lines in the data could not be more clear.[47] Figure 5.1 and Table 5.1 summarize the findings for the three newspapers.

Once the dominant style of newspaper writing, conventional stories no longer overwhelm the front page. Meanwhile, the number of contextual stories has grown tremendously. The numbers of investigative

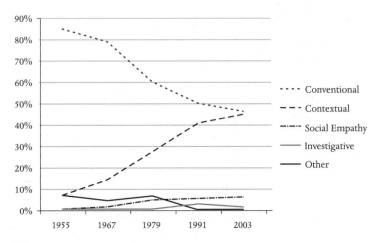

Figure 5.1

and social empathy stories have inched upward over the years, but they remain a small fraction of news stories overall.

The number of investigative stories in our sample is too small to draw any definitive conclusions about their growth over time. More significant is the obvious fact that investigative stories have been a rarity in both past and present. This is not surprising. Investigative work requires considerable time and effort and sometimes does not even lead to a story—if a tip turns out to be wrong, say, or if reporters encounter an insurmountable roadblock in uncovering the information they need. Also worth noting is that contextual stories can perform a function similar to that of investigative stories by shedding light on issues that deserve more public attention, even if there is not a recent event to anchor them. While contextual stories may not require battles over the acquisition of public records or Watergate-style interactions with confidential sources, they often uncover information that is available but unexamined.

Table 5.1 Percentage share of total front-page stories, by genre

	Conventional	Investigative	Social Empathy	Contextual	Other	N:
			New York Times			
1955	89%	0%	0%	10%	1%	181
1967	80%	0%	2%	17%	1%	168
1979	69%	1%	3%	27%	0%	121
1991	54%	3%	6%	37%	0%	95
2003	44%	3%	7%	44%	1%	95
			Milwaukee Journal Sentinel			
1955	77%	0%	1%	6%	16%	212
1967	76%	0%	3%	9%	11%	151
1979	54%	0%	6%	24%	16%	128
1991	52%	3%	5%	41%	0%	64
2003	53%	1%	4%	41%	0%	70
			Washington Post			
1955	90%	0%	1%	6%	3%	177
1967	81%	0%	1%	17%	1%	126
1979	58%	1%	5%	33%	3%	117
1991	47%	2%	6%	45%	0%	89
2003	45%	0%	7%	49%	0%	103

The Context of Contextual Journalism

"Sometime around the late 1960s, the tenor of Washington journalism began to change. A growing body of research converges in its portrayal of a shift toward increasingly vigorous and in some respects adversarial treatment of government officials, political candidates, and their policies."[48] So conclude Clayman and colleagues. Journalists themselves have placed so much emphasis on Watergate

(1972–1974) as a turning point that they sometimes forget that the big change in the news culture became powerful and widely noted several years before Watergate; meanwhile, they rarely acknowledge at all that the rise of contextual journalism represents a much larger change in the character of everyday journalism than does the growth of investigative reporting.

Meg Greenfield, a journalist who became an editorial writer at the *Washington Post* in 1968 and served as editor of the editorial page in 1979 until her death in 1999, said it most simply in her posthumous memoir: "The great change in Washington began in the late 1960s."[49] She recalled pre-sixties journalism as subject to a Washington mystique that "decreed that the people in charge in Washington knew best. They could make things happen if they wanted to. Almost all of them were acting in good faith. And they were entitled to both privacy and discretion to do what they judged necessary for the nation's well-being." She adds that no one believes this any longer and scarcely anyone "admits to ever having believed it—which is a bald-faced lie for hundreds or thousands of people in Washington. So I'll confess: I believed it. My approach to the public people I covered was that they were basically honest, competent, and usually effective."[50]

No one any longer defends the journalism of the 1950s. Paul Duke, a Washington correspondent for the Associated Press, the *Wall Street Journal,* and NBC News from the mid-1950s well into the 1990s, remembered the Washington press corps after World War II as "rather sleepy" and "content to report from handouts and routine news briefings."[51] Reporters and politicians were frequently "pals," as political scientist Larry Sabato observes.[52] And in practice, allegiance to a norm of objectivity was an unconvincing excuse. Veteran journalist Douglass Cater, a writer for the respected *Reporter,* a weekly news-and-analysis magazine in the 1950s, criticized "objective" reporting in his

1959 book on Washington journalism, *The Fourth Branch of Government.* For him, objectivity was a "worn-out concept." And he urged that reporters be free "to contribute an added dimension to reporting which is interpretive not editorial journalism."[53]

In the end, journalism moved exactly in the direction Cater hoped it would. What accounts for the change? Clayman throws his hat in with a change in the culture, norms, and values of journalism. Barnhurst and Mutz offer multiple explanations for their findings: the rise of investigative reporting; a growing availability of social science data and the growing use of computers, leading "journalists to consider the news value of what previously interested only social scientists"; a growing professionalism and higher levels of education among journalists; and perhaps also the growing complexity of everyday life for citizens and their greater need for assistance in seeing "the big picture."[54]

These are not equally compelling possibilities. I discount "investigative reporting" entirely because its rise is part of what needs to be explained, not the cause but the consequence. I discount also the use of computers and social science data because computers in 1968, 1969, or 1970 were mainframes, not desktop personal computers. Look at the 1976 film *All the President's Men* and you will see a replica of the *Washington Post* newsroom of 1972, with a typewriter on each desk and no computer in sight. The first computer of any sort in the U.S. Congress was requisitioned by the Senate Watergate Committee in 1973.[55] "Growing complexity" has been an explanation every time journalism has changed, and while it has always had a grain of truth, it does nothing to pinpoint a specific historical shift. The Barnhurst and Mutz suggestion that seems most persuasive is the one about professionalization and college education. Let me rephrase it in more general terms: it is not only that journalists increasingly had college degrees but also that *Americans* increasingly had college degrees—the audience as well as the authors changed. What a college degree stood for changed, too, as its aims moved from instilling mental discipline to fostering critical thinking, a change consonant with the shift from conventional to contextual journalism.

There are no reliable data before 1971 for the percentage of U.S. journalists with college degrees. But in the first good national survey of journalists, in 1971, 42 percent of journalists did not have college degrees, while in a 2002 survey, only 11 percent had not graduated from college. Of journalists fifty-five years or older in 1971, 55 percent did not have a college degree; of those fifty-five and older in 2002, 22 percent were not college graduates. (Of those between twenty-five and thirty-four years old in 2002, only 7 percent were not college graduates.)[56]

Not only did more journalists have college degrees, but college education was different and, I think it is fair to say, better than it had been. Academic culture itself, like journalism, adopted more "adversarial" habits in the 1960s. This means not politically adversarial but intellectually adversarial. Faculty came to expect students to learn to "read against the text" in courses in the humanities, not simply to learn to revere accepted canons of high culture. In the social sciences, students were increasingly encouraged not to memorize textbooks but to imagine themselves fledgling scholars, moving on to a next level of insight by criticizing the assumptions, methods, or reasoning of the exemplars whose work they were assigned to read.

Rather than a specific focus on investigative and even "adversarial" reporting from the Vietnam-to-Watergate era, general cultural explanations—growing professionalism, growing skepticism, and a growing pride in independence—are consistent with the explosion of contextual journalism. Although journalists have not been consistently aggressive in the past fifty years and arguably have not been sufficiently tough, there is no sign of a retreat to the complaisant journalism of the 1950s and early 1960s. That overcooperative journalistic world is gone.

The journalism that succeeded the deferential journalism of the 1950s and early 1960s is more intellectually ambitious. It is more "featurized," with front-page stories of a contextual cast. It shows, as Barnhurst has observed, "dramatic increases in analysis, and interpretation, if not explanation."[57] Consistent with this trend, the Pulitzer Prizes added an award for "explanatory reporting" in 1985; by the 1990s, the category attracted so many entries that one of the administrators of the prizes said things were getting "out of hand."[58]

Contextual reporting, a rarity in the 1950s, represented by the 1990s roughly half of newspaper front-page stories—and probably more today. The frequent complaint that the news media today are dominated by "he-said-she-said" stories that write themselves is not valid as a general critique of leading U.S. newspapers, nor has it been for several decades.

Explaining the changes in American journalism grows more complicated (and more interesting) when we recognize that European journalism moved simultaneously in the same direction, even without Vietnam and Watergate. This is recounted in a careful content analysis of Swedish public broadcasting from 1925 to 2005, in a study of German campaign coverage from 1949 to 2005, and in an account of changes toward more critical and more journalist-centered reporting in the Netherlands in the 1990s and in France from the 1960s to the 1990s.[59] A recent comparative study of newspapers in the United States, Britain, Germany, Switzerland, France, and Italy in 1960–1961 and 2006–2007 shows a decrease in "news items" (what I call "conventional" news reports) in five of the six countries (not France) and an increase in "information mixed with interpretation" in all six countries.[60] A study of Norway's largest morning newspaper from 1950 to 2008 likewise finds fewer "reports" of events, less dependence on "the diaries and schedules of public institutions," and more coverage of broader topics, including background conditions and trends in public affairs.[61] Whatever explanation one arrives at, it has to account for changes that affected European as well as American journalism, public broadcasting as well as commercial news output, and broadcast news as well as print.

A "Critical Culture" Hypothesis:
The Public Presence of Critique and Dissent

The expansion and shifting character of college education is a relevant causal factor that helps explain not only the changing culture of the newsroom but also the growing public acceptance of all the developments this book takes up, including efforts to keep a more watchful eye on government and sometimes also on corporate enterprise that touches consumers directly and visibly, such as food marketing or the disposal of hazardous waste.

The growth and transformation of higher education and its increasingly central role in everything from personal identity to scientific achievement to professional training to economic development is rarely discussed as a major force of social change. This needs reconsideration. I cannot fully make the case—this is an area where, as scholars routinely opine, "more research is needed." But it is possible to sketch in the outlines of the argument.

The first point is the simplest: after 1945 there was a rapid increase in the number of students and the percentage of young people going to college and a rapid growth in national investment in higher education. In 1940 1.1 million students were enrolled in U.S. higher education; this rose to 3.2 million by 1960 and to 12.1 million by 1980. Federal research dollars granted to universities rose (in constant dollars) from $310 million in 1940 to $2.5 billion in 1963 and $4.5 billion in 1973.[62]

Second, as more Americans started attending college, there was more diversity in the college population, particularly by class, as veterans came to college on the GI Bill. Stimulated in part by the growing diversity of the student body but equally by developments internal to the disciplines of academic research, colleges began to provide instruction in a proliferating array of topics and fields. At the University of Wisconsin, for instance, there were more than 150 different majors by the end of the twentieth century, compared to the six fields of study Wisconsin provided in the late nineteenth century.[63] This reflected a rapidly growing world of research and research funding. It also reflected a growing effort by colleges to please their constituents, new college students (and their parents) looking for a return on their investment. They wanted less Greek and Latin and more study of "relevant" languages such as Russian or Spanish; less emphasis on learning the canon and more contemporary and critical theorizing about what canon formation is in the first place; less training in the classics and more vocationally relevant studies. Even vocationalism, often anti-intellectual, might be packaged in a way that incorporated more critical thinking than in the past.

Third, along with the widening of course offerings, there was a narrowing of the variety of institutional missions in higher education, subsuming historically black colleges, Catholic colleges, small liberal arts colleges, regional comprehensive colleges, community colleges, women's colleges, seriously religious Protestant denominational colleges, and others within a single national system of "higher education," with research universities at the top, setting the standards and setting the pace for the several thousand other institutions.[64] The multiplicity of institutions of higher education became increasingly a "system" of higher education. Previously, different colleges had had distinct, parochial, and often local purposes. Some were finishing schools for the children of wealthy families expected to go on to leadership in business and the professions; others were "normal schools" or teacher training colleges for students who would then be certified to teach in elementary and secondary schools. There were also Catholic colleges that in part shared general secular ambitions but in part insisted on the central importance of moral education, whose faculty were disproportionately Catholic, and whose administrative leadership was almost exclusively Catholic clergy; agricultural and technical colleges located in and serving rural parts of the country; colleges for women; colleges for African Americans; and others.

Most of these schools came to be measured on a single gradient, with all of them deferring to the small set of Ph.D.-granting institutions where a large and growing majority of college faculty received the doctoral degrees that certified them for teaching positions in higher education. These Ph.D.-granting institutions—the research universities—increased in number and prestige as research rather than teaching became the defining feature of the higher education system. All of this developed in the hands of university faculty, much more than in the offices of university presidents or the governing boards they were responsible to. This was the overarching theme of an important 1968 study by Christopher Jencks and David Riesman, *The Academic Revolution*.[65]

A fourth feature of the changes in higher education was the increasingly central place for science, rather than the humanities, and for lessons in critical inquiry rather than the handing down of tradition. After 1945 it was much harder to imagine higher education in which contemporary science could be treated, as it long had been, as peripheral to the arts and letters.[66] There was not only greater investment in the sciences but a subtle incorporation of a scientific ethos in other fields, too. As historian Thomas Bender has written, "The increasingly professionalized disciplines were embarrassed by moralism and sentiment; they were openly or implicitly drawn to the model of science as a vision of professional maturity."[67] This included a shift from the historical to the contemporary in what subjects were taught as well as a shift from a focus on the European cultural heritage to the legitimacy of the study of the United States itself. In these respects, the new academic orientation led the universities to identify themselves with American society—"an association implausible during the interwar years," as Bender puts it, when colleges and universities were fewer, smaller, and less tightly linked to central national institutions.[68]

Historian Jamie Cohen-Cole has gone further to argue that the "open-minded self" became the model person in academic society. Open-mindedness came to be seen as a core attribute of citizens in free and democratic societies generally, a belief reinforced by the Cold War.[69] As the Cold War and the Soviet success in space exploration with the launch of Sputnik in 1957 stimulated increases in federal funding of higher education, so did rivalry with the "closed" society of the Soviet Union accelerate a strong rhetorical commitment to openness as the defining feature of the cast of mind appropriate to democratic citizenship.

Fifth, consonant with the new emphasis on science and, outside the natural sciences themselves, identification with the idea of science, educators came to organize their ambitions for higher education around "shared skills of effective thinking, judgment, communication and the ability 'to discriminate among values,'" as Cohen-Cole put it, rather than around common knowledge. Cohen-Cole sees this emerging particularly in the influential "Red Book" of 1945 (formally titled *General Education in a Free Society*), a report of the Harvard faculty that prescribed a new model of general education for Harvard undergraduates. The faculty committee charged with the reform discovered, after repeated attempts, that they could not agree on a common set of texts all students should be acquainted with. They therefore arrived at a consensus that common knowledge was *not* required in general education.[70] With the rapid expansion of knowledge, the growing diversity of student populations (by religion, by class, and—through the GI Bill—by age, but not in the 1950s by race), and the secularization of schools that had once taken training in Christian ethics as the obvious capstone to a college degree, the Red Book's conclusion that students need not share a common knowledge was all but inevitable. A new self-understanding of the tasks of higher education had to be accepted.

These changes were hammered out on the campuses of colleges and universities but had a close connection to national pressures and national objectives. Not only did the government turn toward university research for military purposes beginning in World War II, but as the Cold War developed, Washington's interest in the universities grew and federal dollars poured into the universities. Particularly after the passage of the National Defense Education Act in 1958, this meant federal support not only for science labs but also for language labs, and the development of programs in "area studies" to develop more specialists in potential "trouble spots" across the globe. The social sciences as well as the natural sciences were of great interest to the National Science Foundation and other federal funding agencies, including those at the Pentagon. The Cold War meant not only greater focus on and support for research but also greater prestige for the research-oriented mind and greater glory for the cast of mind judged to be appropriate to research.

The transformation of higher education from religious to secular, from recitation and drill to critical inquiry, from the cultivation of knowledge of specific classical texts to the promotion of "the power of independent inquiry," and from Latin, Greek, mathematics, and moral philosophy to a greatly enlarged array of subjects that included laboratory sciences, social sciences, and contemporary languages and literatures had begun as early as the late nineteenth century. It is clear, however, that this transformation accelerated greatly after 1945. And it makes sense to me, even though I cannot demonstrate it, that the changes in higher education undergird every postwar development in greater openness, greater criticism, freer dissent, and a presumption that there is a right to know in democratic culture, if not in the U.S. Constitution. In the specific case of the news media, a role for college education seems especially clear. Journalists increasingly had college degrees, as already indicated. So did their target audiences, particularly as newspaper circulation drifted downward, less-educated citizens shifted away from newspapers to television, and cities that had formerly had two or three newspapers became one-newspaper cities. Newspaper reading became more class-marked than it had been since the rise of mass-based newspapers in the late nineteenth century. Meanwhile, and perhaps most important of all, what a college degree had come to stand for by the 1960s was experience in and a belief in critical thinking. Academic culture itself, like journalism, adopted "adversarial" habits.

There was a related growth in publishing. College graduates did not all become lifelong readers, but many did, enough to lead publishers to develop lines of "quality" paperbacks, which fueled book clubs—the most famous of which, the Book-of-the-Month Club, chose as one of its selections Rachel Carson's *Silent Spring* in 1962 and James Watson's *The Double Helix* in 1968, the former closely associated with a growing interest in environmentalism, the latter gaining a popularity that played off the broad public interest in the sciences. *The Double Helix* recounted the race to find the basic genetic code of life, convincing readers that scientists are ordinary people (just a little more vain and a lot more competitive), with bodies, jealousies, prejudices, and so forth, not brains disinterestedly floating in aspic. Science, in other words, is a human social process and a set of human institutions—and as such perhaps within the grasp of a broad public.

The news media have contributed to a culture of openness by learning not to defer to government officials in covering the news of the day (a lesson that they never fully mastered, as certified by media *mea culpas* about failures in covering the run-up to the war in Iraq), but also by several other routes. The media, fundamentally dedicated to observing politics and commenting on it rather than acting as politicians, behaved as political advocates to aid John Moss and others in Congress in efforts to craft a Freedom of Information Act. This is not something that, past or present, journalists proclaim loudly out of school, but in this instance journalists individually and through their organized professional societies judged that they—and democracy itself—had a stake in legislation that would provide access to government information otherwise unobtainable.

All societies organize systems for the storage and retrieval of relevant knowledge, whether in the names they assign to plants and animals, the lists they make in their heads, or the written genealogies, marriage settlements, property divisions, and business agreements that constitute a society's knowledge foundations. These knowledge foundations—not just the contents of the knowledge but the attitudes about knowledge that attend them—change over time. In the United States, they have changed dramatically since 1945, and whether one judges this an "educational revolution" or not, these are surely changes that influence other aspects of society, seeping into the expectations and assumptions of various institutions and the people who have been exposed to them. Attitudes about knowledge are changing again under the remarkable and radical impact of digital technology, but that should not lead anyone to imagine that they were stationary until then.

Changes in education were certainly not the only factor affecting the mainstream news media. Another influence, more directly political but in some respects as much an adversarialism of style as of politics, was the expansion of an "underground" press in the 1960s and the emergence of a very flashy "new journalism" in prominent national magazines, both in established periodicals such as *Esquire* and in new magazines such as *Rolling Stone,* which was launched in 1967. While the highly personalistic, openly subjective elements of "new journalism" had relatively little direct impact on the style of the daily newspapers, its brash outlook and its bold attack on the stodginess of "objectivity" in news was inspiring to many young journalists then and in the decades since.

Contextual journalism has settled in as conventional reporting's significant other. The news media have become a power to reckon with as never before, not because news organizations have political agendas of their own—although sometimes they do, and some more than others—but because they have collectively attained a preeminent role in civil society as a monitor of power. They are the cardinals of accountability for American democracy.

Another way in which journalism played a role in the growing culture of disclosure is that journalists have held positions inside government in which their professional background, which attuned them to how the public reads Washington, enabled them to make a difference in various legislative advances. John Moss hired journalists as key staffers. Former newspaperman Dick Conlon crafted the strategies of the Democratic Study Group and insisted on serious and fair-minded research in the regular reports the DSG published for members of Congress. Conlon's campaign against the unrecorded teller vote, as we have seen, was stimulated by his conversation with a wire service colleague. That friend's suggestion that legislative reforms, generally ignored by the press as too boring to bother with, might get news coverage if Conlon could package them as anti-secrecy measures played a role in their eventual success.

Moreover, the media, by being a business that demands constant efforts to curry favor with the general public or certain large subsectors of the public, helped establish a presumption of populism in the political culture. Television, in particular, helped inscribe on a national scale norms of inclusion, of tolerance, of participation, and thereby of disclosure. Sometimes this was in news programming, as in the televised presidential debates. Sometimes it came in talk shows that existed at the blurred edge between pure entertainment and news, as in *Donahue,* a show that pioneered discussion of contemporary issues in an informal, and sometimes even raucous or raunchy, manner.[71]

The eternal difficulty in assessing the media's role in politics, culture, and society is that the media are everywhere and nowhere at once. Historians have given them too much credit in a few instances (the Spanish-American War or Watergate) or, more often, no credit at all. But journalism increasingly has come to be the playing field of politics, the chief monitor of political democracy, the interpreter and sometimes even orchestrator of public opinion. Individual journalists have a knack for catching the mood of a moment in a word or a phrase or "meme" that then becomes the background assumption about what attitudes or trends are irresistible forces that a politician, university president, manufacturing titan, or start-up entrepreneur ignores only at great peril.

The last third of the twentieth century saw the media become, more than ever before, the water that political fish, big and small, swam in, and many other fish, too. This happened so profoundly and with such speed that it is no wonder we do not have a very good grasp of it. We are all fish in this same pond or same set of networked ponds. It is usually very hard to pinpoint exact media influence, but it is impossible to ignore the pervasive media presence.[72]

six

"To Let People Know in Time"

The National Environmental Policy Act (NEPA) is one of the most important pieces of legislation in U.S. history that you may never have heard of. In late December 1969 both houses of Congress approved it with little debate. Originally proposed in a radically different form in December 1967 by Sen. Henry "Scoop" Jackson (D-Wash.), it gained the support of leading Democrats in the Senate and in the House, where Rep. John Dingell (D-Mich.) was the chief sponsor of a companion measure. President Richard Nixon signed it into law on January 1, 1970. Nixon objected to some of the specifics of the bill, but in the end he bowed to a growing sense that the public demanded the government "do something" about environmental quality. Nixon thus affirmed NEPA's objective that government adopt the mission of protecting and enhancing the environment. That objective was boldly stated in the act's preamble: "To declare a national policy which will encourage productive and enjoyable harmony between man and his environment; to promote efforts which will prevent or eliminate damage to the environment and biosphere and stimulate the health and welfare of man; to enrich the understanding of the ecological systems and natural resources important to the Nation; and to establish a Council on Environmental Quality." In a rambling set of remarks on signing, President Nixon held that a serious effort to stem the degradation of the environment was a "now or never" challenge.[1]

NEPA specifically declares that it is the role of the federal government, in collaboration with other governments and private organizations, "to use all practicable means and measures, including financial and technical assistance, in a manner calculated to foster and promote the general welfare, to create and maintain conditions under which man and nature can exist in productive harmony, and fulfill the social, economic, and other requirements of present and future generations of Americans." This language may sound like empty rhetoric, prefatory remarks fit to adorn any environmental law. But although this section was not part of the original 1967 version of the bill, its addition as a declaration of a newly comprehensive federal obligation toward environmental protection came to be seen as central.

Rhetoric may be empty, but it does not have to be; sometimes rhetoric is exactly the force that moves hearts and minds. Even so, it turned out that the most potent element in the National Environmental Policy Act was not its soaring statement of purpose but a brief clause whose significance was hidden in the plain sight of bureaucratic language. It would come to be known as the environmental impact statement (EIS), although that phrase, as such, does not appear in the law. The flourish of NEPA's preamble was important, but it was the hidden steel in the requirement that federal agencies prepare "detailed statements" about the environmental consequences of proposed actions that made it so. And what would give the "detailed statements" their force was an almost incidental feature of the legislation that was introduced late in the day and whose author-ship is in dispute—that environmental impact statements should be public documents and, as the new Council on Environmental Quality (CEQ) established months after NEPA became law, be made available in both "draft" and "final" form.[2]

The newly mandated disclosure of environmental impact was not disclosure of something that had happened in the past, as with FOIA, nor disclosure of something as it was happening, as in voting in the House in the Committee of the Whole. Instead, NEPA demanded disclosure related to actions that government agencies planned to un-dertake in the future—actions that might be modified or entirely prevented because of the disclosure. One authority on environmental impact assessment terms this element in NEPA "an action-forcing procedure of revolutionary potential," and others agree that it initi-ated a "legal revolution."[3]

For the reader's future reference, the specific language that in-vented the environmental impact statement is the following:

All agencies of the Federal Government shall—
. . . (C) Include in every recommendation or report on pro-posals for legislation and other major Federal actions significantly affecting the quality of the human environ-ment, a detailed statement by the responsible official on—
   (i) The environmental impact of the proposed action,
   (ii) Any adverse environmental effects which cannot be avoided should the proposal be implemented,
   (iii) Alternatives to the proposed action,
   (iv) The relationship between local short-term uses of man's environment and the maintenance and en-hancement of long-term productivity, and

(v) Any irreversible and irretrievable commitments of resources which would be involved in the proposed action should it be implemented.

Prior to making any detailed statement, the responsible Federal official shall consult with and obtain the comments of any Federal agency which has jurisdiction by law or special expertise with respect to any environmental impact involved. Copies of such statement and the comments and views of the appropriate Federal, State, and local agencies, which are authorized to develop and enforce environmental standards, shall be made available to the President, the Council on Environmental Quality and to the public as provided by Section 552 of title 5, United States Code, and shall accompany the proposal through the existing agency review processes.[4]

It took time for federal bureaucrats to recognize just how much this language would change their lives. The courts very quickly took this section of NEPA seriously, but many executive agencies were begrudging about preparing environmental impact statements. At the Bureau of Reclamation, engineers assumed responsibility for the environmental impact statement, but as sociologist Wendy Espeland discovered in her detailed study of the bureau's work on the Central Arizona Water Project, "environmental groups, public citizens, and eventually courts began to insist that the new expertise now required by EISes was best provided by people with some training in different fields. Slowly, federal agencies began hiring 'environmental specialists,' people trained in biology, geology, archaeology, sociology, social psychology, and recreation" to help prepare EISes, and more lawyers and economists, too. One "old guard" engineer at the Bureau of Reclamation referred to the newcomers as "all the 'ologists' we had to hire after NEPA."[5] Norms, values, external constraints, public visibility, and agency personnel all changed in the direction of opening up governmental decision making to public review and public participation because the courts insisted that an agency had to make its draft EIS and its final EIS available to other relevant agencies, to the president, to the Council on Environmental Quality that NEPA established, and to the public. How did this come to be?

The environmental impact statement was not part of Senator Jackson's 1967 bill, which called primarily for government support of ecological research. Even in 1969 in the months before NEPA's passage, by which time the EIS was part of the bill, when Jackson spoke publicly about his initiative, he listed its main purposes without mentioning the EIS. This was so in speeches in Seattle on April 8 and September 1 and in San Francisco November 18. In a speech to the annual meeting of the National Audubon Society in St. Louis on April 26, 1969, he called attention to the requirement in the draft bill for each agency to declare a "finding" (later revised to "detailed statement") about environmental impact, but even in that speech he said that the three goals of the bill were to establish a national policy statement on the environment, to authorize expanded research on environmental matters, and to establish a Council on Environmental Quality in the Office of the President.[6] Only after passage of NEPA would Jackson recognize that one of the important objectives NEPA achieved was that "it requires Federal agencies to perform their assignments giving full weight to environmental factors," as he told the American Association for Health, Physical Education, and Recreation.[7]

NEPA, according to a leading historical overview of U.S. environmental policy, "marked the beginning of the 'environmental era' in U.S. governance and policy."[8] Nonetheless, at the outset its importance was judged to be more symbolic than substantive. At first the requirement that federal agencies provide a "detailed statement" assessing the environmental impact of all "proposals for legislation and other major Federal actions significantly affecting the quality of the human environment" attracted little public notice. Among the federal executive agencies themselves, however, controversy erupted quickly. Russell Train, first chair of the Council on Environmental Quality, which NEPA created as a body advisory to the president, issued instructions requiring agency heads to develop procedures for preparing environmental impact statements. These procedures had to comply with NEPA's requirement that agencies should consult with and obtain comments from other federal agencies with jurisdiction or expertise in the proposed area; that the statement and comments on it should circulate among relevant federal, state, and local agencies; and that the statement should also be transmitted to the president, the Council on Environmental Quality, and the public.

Clearly, what makes NEPA relevant to this study of public disclosure and the right to know is the environmental impact statement process that makes environmental decisions in government open to public review, comment, and potentially litigation. What makes NEPA an especially puzzling topic is that this public-participation element of the law was not part of its original 1967 language, nor was it even in the bill reported out to the Senate from Senator Jackson's Committee on the Interior in July 1969. The key phrase in Section 102(C)(v) that commanded that the "detailed statement" be available "to the public" emerged in October 1969. How and why that happened is my subject here.

Those in Congress who crafted a national environmental policy in 1969 did not think of it as related to freedom of information or public disclosure. The public as a participant in environment-preserving action, as opposed to the public as a beneficiary of such action, was not a core consideration. They intended an ambitious and historic document—and they had a clear precedent in mind as they proceeded, a precedent twenty-five years old and from an entirely different policy domain. What they arrived at, however, was both what they intended and something more. The "something more"—described at the time as an "action-forcing" mechanism—soon became both lauded and reviled as the environmental impact statement. What the EIS would become, in practice, was not clearly defined in the law and would only become a powerful tool for environmental protection through environmental leadership in the Nixon administration and through judicial action, neither clearly foreseen at the time of passage.

Background to NEPA

The origins of the environmental impact statement are not widely known. It is easy to get the story wrong, and even distinguished historians have done so. The most common error is to confuse the Environmental Protection Agency with the National Environmental Policy Act of 1969, as if the EPA, established in late 1970, ordained environmental impact statements, written into law on January 1 of that year.[9] This is an innocent but not trivial mistake: NEPA, like FOIA, was an effort by Congress to assert its authority over the executive branch. The environmental impact statement arose from a congressional effort to make executive agencies take the environment seriously as an objective of federal responsibility.[10] It was NEPA that, as environmental law scholar Bradley C. Karkkainen has put it, "launched the most widely emulated environmental policy innovation of the twentieth century: environmental impact assessment (EIA)."[11]

Like FOIA, NEPA proved itself to be of global significance, largely because of the few simple clauses that launched environment impact assessment. The origins of the EIS lie not in administrative action in the White House nor in a new executive agency but in congressional efforts to hold executive agencies accountable. In this regard, it is a close cousin to FOIA.

Like FOIA, NEPA is surely among those relatively rare laws that some legal scholars call "super-statutes," laws that not only address relatively narrow policy objectives but also "successfully penetrate public normative and institutional culture in a deep way."[12] With NEPA, Senator Jackson clearly intended a statute of broad, near-constitutional reach, even if it attained that influence on normative and institutional culture in ways he did not anticipate. But the ambition of the act was visible early on. Legal analysts Eva H. Hanks and John L. Hanks crisply observed in 1970, "In form, the National Environmental Policy Act is a statute; in spirit a constitution."[13]

NEPA resembled FOIA also in emerging without significant public pressure or public interest. This, too, has been misreported by historians.[14] Just how much was NEPA a response to public pressure or to public opinion? While the environmental movement was growing when Senator Jackson began work on his bill, its heyday was yet to come. The leading advocates of NEPA and other environmental protection policies had been at work on these issues for years. And NEPA became law with little public input or media attention. Only one environmental organization, the Conservation Foundation, played a role in shaping NEPA, as I will show, but that was behind the scenes. Only one environmental organization, the Sierra Club, testified in favor of the bill in 1969 hearings. And by the time the bill came to President Nixon's desk, he judged it politically astute to support it. There was a sense, which grew practically feverish in the

White House, that it could be politically damaging to let the Democrats run away with the environmental issue. But Congress was not merely reactive to perceived public concerns; inside-the-Beltway politics operated with great autonomy in advancing this legislation. In fact, as I will suggest, the passage of NEPA had more to do with creating a vital environmental movement than the other way around.

Still, even when the details have been reported fairly and skillfully, as in the study by J. Brooks Flippen, *Nixon and the Environment* (2000), the author may organize the narrative so that a popular impulse for environmental protection implicitly becomes the hero of progressive social change. Flippen opens his book with a paragraph about the first Earth Day on April 22, 1970, "one of the largest demonstrations in American history." Its "amazing turnout" brought together people from "every strata of American society," including many who were divided over other issues but united on this one.[15] This is all true—although the term "demonstration" does not quite cover a collection of 20 million people in sites all over the country, including some 1,500 colleges and universities, in a show of concern organized by a sitting U.S. senator.[16] But why should a book about Nixon and the environment begin with an event that took place fifteen months after Nixon took office, and 112 days after he signed into law what was arguably the most important environmental legislation of his presidency?

This chapter is not an account of the environmental movement or the vicissitudes of environmental protection, although I will need to say a few words about these topics. My aim, rather, is to unearth the history of the environmental impact statement because it became the chief mechanism whereby environmental policy fostered transparency in federal agency initiatives. It was that transparency that opened executive decision making to citizen interventions in ways that advanced environmental protection. The publicness of the environment impact statement process broke open the federal bureaucracy to legal challenge from environmental groups and environmentally minded individuals.

The Environment as a Flash-in-the-Pan Issue

There was no assurance in 1969 that the environment would become a potent issue or that environmental organizations would become formidable in membership and influence. Richard Lazarus, a lawyer and litigator on behalf of government agencies and environmental organizations, former assistant to the U.S. solicitor general, and later a professor at Harvard Law School, recalled how in 1975, as a college senior planning to go to law school to become an environmental lawyer, he had a conversation with a corporate executive who urged him to find a different path. This friendly adviser cautioned him that environmental law was a "flash in the pan" that would not lead to a lifelong career.[17]

The environment is in fact the *defining* flash in the pan in the public policy literature. The distinguished public policy analyst Anthony Downs took it as his chief example in a famous 1972 paper that named the "issue-attention cycle" in public affairs, noting the short attention span of both the news media and the general public.[18] But Downs realized almost at once that he had chosen a poor example; the last third of the article is devoted to explaining why, although he believed the environmental issue would eventually fade from public view and although "we should not underestimate the American public's capacity to be bored," interest in environmental problems would dissipate "at a much slower rate" than other domestic issues.[19]

For his part, the young Richard Lazarus dismissed out of hand the advice the executive offered him, although, looking back, he saw that "there was far more force to his intuition than my own youthful self-assuredness allowed me to perceive." Even so, Lazarus concludes, "what is even more remarkable than my youthful impertinence was that my intuition, notwithstanding its thin basis, turned out to be correct. Environmental law in the United States has been surprisingly persistent—almost stubbornly so." It has thereby contributed to remarkable changes. EPA data show that under the Clean Air Act there has been a 60 percent decrease in controlled air pollutants in the United States from 1970 to 2008 despite a doubling in the size of the economy, a 44 percent growth in population, and 49 percent more energy consumption.[20] Lazarus provides a list of consequences that includes a $190 billion pollution control industry employing more than 1.4 million workers, a 25 percent decrease since 1970 in the six leading measured air pollutants despite sharp increases in energy consumption and automobile use, and a doubling of the number of waterways safe for fishing and swimming (bodies of water that were "no better than open sewers once again support healthy aquatic ecosystems suitable for recreation").[21] By 1990 there were some 20,000 attorneys specializing in environmental law.[22] From 1970 to 2012, federal agencies have produced approximately 34,000 draft and final environmental impact statements that have "successfully prevented at least hundreds, and likely thousands, of actions from causing unnecessary damage to the nation's environment."[23]

A study of a large sample of environmental law cases in federal courts in the decade of the 1970s (1,900 cases were coded) shows that by far the largest number were generated by NEPA (765). Runners-up were the Water Pollution Control Act of 1948 as amended in the 1970s (313) and the Air Pollution Control Act of 1955 also as amended in the 1970s (208).[24] Throughout the decade, even as public opinion grew relatively less concerned about environmental protection and relatively more concerned about the "energy crisis," pro-environment litigants in the courts continued to win about 50 percent of the cases.[25]

Of all the topics in this book, the development of a mechanism for comprehensive governmental attention to the environment is the only one fervently linked to a blend of utopian and apocalyptic visions. Few friends of freedom of information, for example, actively expected the United States to become a police state without vigilant enforcement of FOIA, and no one pictures consumer product packages that daze and deceive shoppers in supermarket aisles to be the first step toward Armageddon. But failure to stave off environmental deterioration has been conceived as potentially catastrophic to the continued human habitation of North America or even of the planet. Proponents of environmentalism past and present have consistently urged that the stewardship of the earth is a task the U.S. government must shoulder as its own. At the dawn of the twentieth century, President Teddy Roosevelt and his chief forester, Gifford Pinchot, worked tirelessly to establish a system of national parks and national forests to conserve fish and game and to ensure environmental sustainability. Modern prophets of nature from Aldo Leopold to Rachel Carson to Barry Commoner, along with modern apostles of the environment as a focal point of public policy—notably Lynton Keith Caldwell, the public policy professor whose ideas helped bring the environmental impact statement into being—spoke of nature's spiritual splendor but spoke also in tones of apocalyptic dread of its loss. In the 1960s, their anxieties were readily reinforced by a series of well-publicized environmental disasters. The burning of Ohio's badly polluted Cuyahoga River, a major oil well blowout that contaminated miles of beaches along California's Santa Barbara coast, the "death" of Lake Erie from pollution, and a rapid decline in the number of songbirds ("silent spring") caused by DDT ingestion all provided evidence that human actions could prompt uncontrollable damage to the natural world.

The rhetorical fuel for FOIA was the Cold War and a mythologized understanding of the founding fathers' faith in an open society. For advocates of consumer information reform, it was a nostalgia for a world in which commercial relations were embedded in face-to-face communities, mixed with growing anxieties about the underside of affluence. The rhetoric of the more strident voices within the environmental movement was one of impending doom, the "end of days" brought on not by nuclear bombs but by our collective carelessness about tending the planet. If John Moss was a scold and Philip Hart and Esther Peterson reproachful but kindly grandparents, the champions of ecological reform mixed Old Testament prophecy, New Deal ambition, spiritual inspiration, and a future-environment-based orientation that called out not only to policy-makers and voters but also to young people and children.

The orientation toward the young was most famously enacted in Earth Day. The first Earth Day took place on April 22, 1970 (although other local or regional environmental teach-ins preceded it).[26] It was the brainchild of Sen. Gaylord Nelson (D-Wisc.), who took his inspiration from the Vietnam teach-ins that had begun on college campuses in 1965. Some who participated in Vietnam teach-ins judged Earth Day to be an insufficiently radical follow-up. Just before the first Earth Day, the editors of the prominent left-wing magazine *Ramparts* issued *Eco-Catastrophe,* a book of articles they had published on environmental themes. They introduced it with an editorial that declared their distaste for Senator Nelson's project: "We think that any analogy between what is supposed to happen around April 22 and the organization of the Vietnam teach-ins is obscene," they wrote. "We think that the Environmental Teach-In apparatus is the first step in a con game that will do little more than abuse the environment even further. We do not think it will succeed."[27] For the *Ramparts* editors, ecological problems were caused by capitalism, and unless capitalism was overthrown, there was no hope for a human future.

Ramparts notwithstanding, Earth Day was a resounding success. It drew attention to environmentalism and launched a new tradition that more than forty years later is still recognized around the country by families, schools, and civic events that mark the day as one on which to ponder ecological problems and even do something about them. On that first Earth Day, it was not apparent what practical effect the four-month-old National Environmental Policy Act would have. Nor was it appreciated that the new environmental impact statement, open to public comment and review, would increase the public accountability of executive action.

Scoop Jackson Takes an Interest in the Environment

Environmental activists had long been concerned about the lack of adequate public information about the environment. This is poignantly memorialized in the short introduction that David Brower, the longtime president of the Sierra Club, penned to Eliot Porter's 1963 book of photographs of Glen Canyon, a beautiful natural area destroyed to make way for the Glen Canyon Dam and the development of the Colorado River. Brower had tried to block the building of the dam, but with legislation on the ten-dam Colorado River Storage Project making its way through Congress in 1956 after years of conflict, the Sierra Club board gave in, agreeing to support the construction of nine dams, including Glen Canyon, on the assurance that a planned dam at Dinosaur National Monument would never be built. Brower, to his regret, did not press the board to change its position. The dam went forward, and Glen Canyon was no more. From this story Brower urged the following lesson: "Progress need not deny to the people their inalienable right to be informed and to choose. In Glen Canyon the people never knew what the choices were. Next time, in other stretches of the Colorado, on other rivers that are still free, and wherever there is wildness that can be part of our civilization instead of victim to it, the people need to know before a bureau's elite decide to wipe out what no one can replace. The Sierra Club has no better purpose than to try to let people know in time."[28]

"To let people know in time" is a good definition of what, in the end, legislators accomplished in NEPA. Trying to let people know in time was also the objective of the most famous document of the environmental movement, Rachel Carson's *Silent Spring* (1962). *Silent Spring* became the wake-up call that helped catalyze the environmental movement—in part by drawing attention to the absence of wake-up calls. For Carson, as she wrote in her famous book, if the public was to decide questions about chemical pollutants, people would need to be "in full possession of the facts." And then she quoted Jean Rostand, a French biologist and philosopher: "The obligation to endure gives us the right to know."[29] Carson pointed out that "if a huge skull and crossbones were suspended above the insecticide department" in stores, "the customer might at least enter it with the respect normally accorded death-dealing materials." Instead, she observed, "the display is homey and cheerful, and, with the pickles and olives across the aisle and the bath and laundry soaps adjoining, the rows upon rows of insecticides are displayed."[30] Moreover, household insecticides were displayed next to poisonous chemicals for lawn and garden use. In the suburbs, Carson explained, weed killers had become status symbols, yet "to learn that they contain chlordane or dieldrin one must read exceedingly fine print placed on the least conspicuous part of the sack."[31] Three years later, President Johnson cited Carson by name when he signed the Clean Air and Solid Waste Disposal Act and, quoting her, declared: "'In biological history, no organism has survived long if its environment became in some way unfit for it, but no organism before man has deliberately polluted its own environment.' We intend to rewrite that chapter of history. Today we begin."[32]

There were multiple beginnings to the new environmentalism. By the 1960s there had been conservation laws in place for nearly a century, and in the 1950s and 1960s there was a proliferation of environment-related law in the states.[33] But Senator Jackson had a bold new beginning in mind. Jackson, a Democrat from Washington, an environmental progressive, a notable hawk in foreign policy, and a likely presidential aspirant for the 1972 election, observed in a Senate speech in 1969 that eighty major federal agencies were engaged in programs or projects with environmental ramifications. "If environmental policy is to become more than rhetoric," he held, "each of these agencies must be enabled and directed to participate in active and objective-oriented environmental management. Concern for environmental quality must be made part of every Federal action."[34] This idea—the acceptance of improved environmental quality as an explicit goal for the federal government and its agencies—became the main thrust of Jackson's thinking about environmental policy.

While members of Congress were quietly working on what would become NEPA, environmental organizations far beyond Washington were growing. The total membership of seven leading old-line conservation organizations grew from 124,000 in 1960 to 819,000 by

1969.[35] But these organizations were not focused on directly influencing public policy. Bill Van Ness, Jackson's chief legislative aide, later recalled, "There was little or no interest at all in NEPA among any national environmental organizations and practically no interest in the Congress."[36] Despite growing public interest in environmental problems, neither candidate for president in 1968 paid more than lip service to the topic. At the beginning of his administration, President Richard Nixon's only apparent interest in the environment was to do enough or say enough to keep it from being a Democratic Party rallying cry when he would run for reelection in 1972.

Professor Caldwell's Vision

Lynton Keith Caldwell, sometimes judged the author of the environmental impact statement, was at the least a co-author and a spiritual father. Caldwell was a political scientist and professor of public policy at Indiana University who had worked since the early 1960s to establish and develop environmental policy studies as an academic subfield. In 1962, about the same time that the *New Yorker* was running a serialization of *Silent Spring,* which Houghton Mifflin would publish in the fall, Keith Caldwell wrote an essay, "Environment: A New Focus for Public Policy?," that *Public Administration Review* published in 1963.[37] It would be the most celebrated article he wrote in a long and productive academic career. It offers a vision of a comprehensive study of and administrative attention to the human relationship with nature. It is an essay in search of a concrete embodiment for remedying government's episodic and piecemeal attention to environmental issues.

More than fifty years after its publication, Caldwell's essay seems to me vaporous—it never breaks out of a very general level of diction, offering no stories, no cases, nothing a reader can really latch on to. When it contemplates a name to cover the territory that Caldwell held must be studied all together in all of its interrelations, it briefly takes up the "ecological perspective" but settles on "ekistics," a term introduced by C. A. Doxiadis that quickly died. The essay is a conscientious musing out loud, but its eight pages add little to the provocative and influential rhetorical question of its title. There were "conservationists" when the essay was published, but there were no "environmentalists," and "the environment" was not yet the recognizable topic it would soon become. It was certainly not a topic in political science. Caldwell probed for a way to turn broad ecological concern into practical consequence-producing policy. The essay advocates for finding an operational mechanism for turning theory into practice, but it does not bring this wish down to earth. What the paper achieved was to bring the word "environment" to the world of public policy studies. Simple and obvious as that may sound half a century later, it was no small feat. "Conservation" identified a policy position, a human activity, a set of good deeds; "environment" named an independent entity with a relationship to us and with a character of its own that humans would have to understand and adapt to—or die.

Whatever Caldwell's limitations as a prose stylist, he proved himself a determined champion of introducing the environment into policy studies. In that work, he had become a member of an advisory board to the Conservation Foundation, a Washington-based organization founded in 1961 (and merged into the World Wildlife Federation in 1990). The Conservation Foundation was headed from 1965 to 1969 by Russell Train, a former federal judge who would soon join the Nixon administration as Under Secretary of the Department of the Interior and the first chair of the Council on Environmental

Quality that NEPA created. In late 1967 Senator Jackson sought out Train to get recommendations for a consultant who combined expertise in both environmental affairs and public administration. Train suggested that Caldwell might be just right. Jackson's Committee on Interior and Insular Affairs wanted to hire Caldwell but lacked the funds to pay for a consultant; they asked if the foundation would be willing to pay Caldwell's fees, and Train agreed to this. "As it turned out," Train recalled in his memoirs, "Caldwell was responsible for developing the environmental impact statement process, which became central to the NEPA legislation and an integral part of decision making by all federal agencies."[38]

This overstates Caldwell's role. As I read the record—and, for that matter, as I think Caldwell himself understood it—Caldwell was responsible for keeping Senator Jackson and his staff focused on developing some unidentified environment-regarding procedure that executive agencies would feel compelled to follow. Specifying what that procedure might be was the work of Jackson's aides, Dan Dreyfus and Bill Van Ness; forcing it into a practically viable form came with the aggressive intervention of Sen. Edmund Muskie; making sure that form was publicly visible was the somewhat casually invented outcome of a conversation of Senators Jackson, Muskie, and Nelson; giving that procedure a set of operating rules and regulations was the work of the Council on Environmental Quality (which NEPA created) in the Nixon administration, acting very quickly in its first months of operation; and ensuring that the process would be taken seriously was the work of the federal courts, especially in an opinion issued July 23, 1971, by District of Columbia (10th Circuit) appeals court Judge J. Skelly Wright in *Calvert Cliffs' Coordinating Committee v. Atomic Energy Commission.*

Without Caldwell's vision, Jackson's political prowess, Muskie's insistence on interagency review of environmental impact statements, Nelson's concern for public participation, Dreyfus's bureaucratic know-how, Van Ness's legislative and legal draftsmanship, the CEQ's assertiveness, and Judge Wright's insistence that he could plainly read the intent of Congress, the environmental impact statement process would not have been devised, enacted, and enforced.

Caldwell is a good place to begin the whole story. Caldwell was born in Montezuma, Iowa, in 1913. His political views and political style, as is true of many of the important figures in the emergence of a cultural right to know, were formed long before "the sixties," but they contributed to the emerging environmental movement that embodied a sixties spirit. Caldwell had not always focused his work on the environment. Since the 1940s he had been principally involved in national and international efforts to develop public administration studies in political science. In 1962–1963 the focus of his work shifted to the environment. When Dan Tarlock arrived at Indiana in 1968, a young law professor interested in environmental law, Caldwell was already a central figure in environmental studies on campus. Tarlock remembers him as "a model academic always impeccably dressed, earnest but not pompous at all." Unusual among academics, even in policy-oriented fields, Caldwell developed an "outwardly-focused" career with audiences and colleagues outside the university and became, in that respect, "a model for me."[39] At the same time, Caldwell struck Tarlock as "a lone wolf" who seemed to feel almost "ostracized." Tarlock remembers that Caldwell resented some of his colleagues in political science who, jealous of his growing public recognition, as Caldwell saw it, criticized him for not having published a sufficient number of standard academic articles. Caldwell proudly quipped that, yes, he had been publishing lately: "I now publish in the *Congressional Record!*"[40]

Although Caldwell had long been interested in the natural world and was a member of the Izaak Walton League and the Audubon Society as well as a supporter in the 1950s of efforts to save the Indiana Dunes, the environment was not a subject of his academic work. This changed in 1962 when, on one of his many international trips, after several weeks of consulting in Thailand and Indonesia, he flew to Hong Kong for a brief stop before continuing on to Taiwan, Japan, and Korea. He arrived in Hong Kong on February 5, 1962, Chinese New Year, the start of the Year of the Tiger—a sign, as Caldwell noted later, considered "favorable to bold adventures."[41] He decided to take a tram to the top of Victoria Peak to have tea, rest, and enjoy the famous views.[42]

Caldwell explained in an interview years later: "Looking over the harbor of Hong Kong and the numerous flashes of light from firecrackers below I reflected on my past and future. I there decided to make a major change in my life. . . . I was not yet quite clear what direction to take, except I believed that policy for the environment was the most important subject that I was prepared to investigate."[43] By the time Caldwell returned home, he was "full of a new purpose and ready to take the first steps down his proposed new path in life."[44]

Flashes of inspiration like Caldwell's moment in Hong Kong seem to be an autobiographical tradition among environmental activists. For John Muir, it was an afternoon in 1864 in a Canadian swamp when he was transfixed by two white orchids in a bank of moss: "I never before saw a plant so full of life; so perfectly spiritual, it seemed pure enough for the throne of the Creator. I felt as if I were in the presence of superior beings who loved me and beckoned me to come. I sat down beside them and wept for joy," Muir later wrote. Gifford

Pinchot, appointed by Theodore Roosevelt as the first chief forester of the United States (1905–1910), was riding a horse in Washington's Rock Creek Park when he realized that many of the separate questions he had pondered were all part of "the one great central problem of the use of the earth for the good of man."[45] For the ecologist Aldo Leopold, who worked as a forest ranger when Pinchot headed the Forest Service, the moment came in 1909 when he and others, hunting in the Apache National Forest, shot a female wolf as her cubs, one badly injured by the hunters, ran off. Leopold and a companion approached the dying wolf: "We reached the old wolf in time to watch a fierce green fire dying in her eyes. I realized then, and have known ever since, that there was something new to me in those eyes— something known only to her and to the mountain. I was young then, and full of trigger-itch; I thought that because fewer wolves meant more deer, no wolves would mean a hunters' paradise. But after seeing the green fire die, I sensed that neither the wolf nor the mountain agreed with such a view."[46]

Caldwell's vision came to him seated in a teahouse on a touristic urban hilltop, but it shares with these other moments the sense of transcendence, the union with nature, and the personal dedication or rededication. Caldwell's contribution to NEPA would emerge from this deeply felt sense of ethical responsibility toward the environment combined with long experience thinking about public policy. Caldwell proposed to Senator Jackson what he had been suggesting for several years in various papers and discussions—the need for action-forcing provisions to give "teeth" to legislative proposals. He did not, however, write the actual language for NEPA. The environmental impact statement clauses were drafted by Jackson's senior staff members, William Van Ness and Dan Dreyfus, and then significantly altered during intense negotiations with Jackson's chief environmental sparring partner in the Senate, Edmund Muskie, and expanded by a telling suggestion from yet another Senate environmentalist, Gaylord Nelson.

Nothing Comes from Nothing

In the early 1950s, Washington showed little interest in the environment. Congressional efforts began in the late 1950s to allocate funds for research and study of the environment, but as late as 1960 President Eisenhower had made clear his lack of interest. "Water pollution is a uniquely local blight," he asserted as he vetoed a bill to increase federal aid for local sewage treatment plants.[47] Not until 1963 did a U.S. president assert environmental protection as part of a national agenda: "We must expand the concept of conservation to meet the imperious problems of the new age," John F. Kennedy wrote in the introduction to Interior Secretary Stewart Udall's important book *The Quiet Crisis*. "We must develop new instruments of foresight and protection and nurture in order to recover the relationship between man and nature and to make sure that the national estate we pass on to our multiplying descendants is green and flourishing."[48] In 1965 Lyndon Johnson would declare, "A prime national goal must be an environment that is pleasing to the senses and healthy to live in."[49] By that time the government had started to consider a number of environmental measures concerned with clean water, clean air, the preservation of wilderness areas, the establishment of urban recreational areas, and highway "beautification." In those years, as one contemporary observer put it, the national public consciousness about environmental problems "changed from apathy to awareness, and then to alarm."[50] But though Udall saw a crisis, he dubbed it a quiet one, and there is little alarm in Kennedy's tone, still less in Johnson's.

Efforts in Congress to articulate a broad national conservation policy began as early as 1959 with a bill sponsored by Sen. James Murray (D-Mont.) and reintroduced by Sen. Clair Engle (D-Calif.), and then a similar bill proposed in 1961 by Sen. Gale McGee (D-Mont.). Senators McGee and George McGovern (D-S.D.) introduced related bills in 1963 and 1965, though these bills were primarily centered on developing a federal capacity for gathering environmentally relevant scientific data. Sen. Gaylord Nelson (D-Wisc.) proposed a further bill in 1965 to establish a council of environmental advisers. None of these bills passed. Nor did any of them have the uniquely comprehensive character that would set NEPA apart.

The politicians who promoted these early bills were policy entrepreneurs, not spokesmen for a movement or even for a mood. Caldwell himself would observe, "NEPA was not a product of activist environmental groups or 'blue-ribbon' presidential commissions; its genesis occurred within the Congress, responding in a statesman-like manner to a perception of national interest."[51]

But what shaped that perception? There was an intellectual, political, and social context for the National Environmental Policy Act. The intellectual context included Rachel Carson's *Silent Spring* and the work of emerging advocates of ecological consciousness, including Barry Commoner, Paul and Anne Ehrlich, Garrett Hardin, and Ian McHarg. It involved a piecemeal, gradually accumulating concern about the environment—laws had been enacted regarding insecticides (1947), water pollution control (1948), authorization for federal research on clean air (1955), the Clean Water Act (1960), Clean Air Act amendments (1963), the Wilderness Act (1964), the Water Quality

Act (1965), and the Solid Waste Disposal Act (1965). Environmental organizations grew with the creation of the World Wildlife Fund in 1961, the Environmental Defense Fund in 1967, and the Natural Resources Defense Council in 1969.

The news media took little notice of environmental issues in the 1950s or early 1960s. Sen. Gaylord Nelson, the former governor of Wisconsin elected to the Senate in 1962, proposed to President Kennedy that he lead "a national tour on the environment" to focus public attention on the issue.[52] Kennedy liked the idea and went on a five-day tour along with several senators, including Hubert Humphrey and Eugene McCarthy of Minnesota, Joseph Clark of Pennsylvania, and Nelson. But, Nelson recalled many years later, this failed to put the environment on the national agenda. "Most editors, most reporters didn't know a damn thing about the environment and didn't care. It wasn't an issue."[53]

Ecological disaster, however, produced headlines. On January 28, 1969, a week after Richard Nixon became president, an oil slick formed off the coast of Santa Barbara, California, from a leaking oil rig. The huge slick killed hundreds of sea lions, dolphins, and sea otters as it floated toward the Santa Barbara beaches, where it trapped thousands of sea birds, killing many of them. In the account of John Whitaker, the White House aide who would be the chief draftsman of President Nixon's first message on the environment (February 10, 1970), the Santa Barbara disaster provided "some of the most pathetic sights ever beamed to the antennae of 80 million television sets. People were sickened by the sight of a lone bird floundering in the glop on the beach—terrified, helpless, and doomed." Whitaker wrote that it was like "tossing a match into a gasoline tank: it exploded into the environmental revolution, and the press fanned the flames to keep the issue burning brightly."[54]

No doubt that is what it looked like from the White House. But while Santa Barbara attracted the news media and thereby alarmed the public, and media attention to environmental issues grew during the 1960s, coverage was intermittent at best, and dragged behind, rather than barreling ahead of, environmental awareness in Congress. When NEPA was approved by both House and Senate on December 20, 1969, there was no mention of it in the *New York Times*. While environmental coverage was growing rapidly by 1969, with NEPA itself there was what A. Clay Schoenfeld, the only scholar to study the question closely, termed "a virtual news 'blackout.'"[55] Lynton Caldwell received no mention in the *Times,* despite his prominent public testimony. Senator Jackson was mentioned twenty-seven times during 1969 but in no case in connection with NEPA.[56] When *New York Times* foreign correspondent Philip Shabecoff joined the paper's Washington bureau in 1970, hoping to write about the environment, he was told that the subject was not important enough to merit a full-time Washington reporter.[57]

Bill Van Ness tried to make journalists aware of the importance of Senator Jackson's bill, but as he told Terence Finn in 1971, "you just couldn't get the press geared up."[58] Finn's judgment was that "the communications media simply did not believe that the environmental agenda, however important, was newsworthy."[59] This would change, to be sure. The Society of Environmental Journalists, founded in 1990, would have more than 1,000 members by 2000. But in the 1970s Shabecoff remembers that his editors' "prevailing response" was something like, "What, another story about the end of the world, Shabecoff? We carried a story about the end of the world a month ago."[60]

Given the slow dawning of the ecological age of Aquarius, it may not be surprising that NEPA's authors did not have an environmental precedent in mind as they formulated their bill. What they were

thinking about as a model, thanks to Professor Caldwell, was an earlier legislative expansion of federal authority, the Employment Act
of 1946. In 1965, Caldwell presented a paper at an Airlie House conference (published in 1966) that proposed the Employment Act as a
model for what the government might do to take responsibility for
the environment. "A generation ago the idea of public responsibility
for the state of the economy was utopian," he wrote. "Is it less con-
ceivable that public responsibility for the quality of the biophysical
environment may be generally accepted . . . within the generation
ahead?"[61] In introducing NEPA for a vote on the Senate floor on
July 10, 1969, Senator Jackson called the Employment Act "the only
precedent and parallel to what is proposed in S. 1075." The Employment Act declared it to be the policy of the federal government to
promote "maximum employment, production, and purchasing
power," and it established the Council of Economic Advisers in the
White House to keep the president informed on economic matters
relevant to these objectives. As the Employment Act made it the government's explicit task to manage the economy, Jackson held that
NEPA would ensure "an equally important national policy" for managing the environment.[62]

On introducing the bill in the Senate, Jackson declared—in a
speech written by Bill Van Ness that clearly borrowed from Caldwell's
writings—that the environment was emerging as a new focus of
public policy. Only recently, he said, had government become responsible for public health, housing, and consumer protection: "Today
we have come to take these responsibilities for granted. We must
now proceed to make the concept of a government responsible for
the quality of our surroundings an accepted tenet of our political
philosophy."[63]

Jackson, Caldwell, and others had participated in an unusual joint House-Senate colloquium on a "National Policy for the Environment" July 17, 1968. At that meeting, Senator Jackson urged the group "to provide thoughts on the possible 'action-forcing' processes that could be put into operation" in new ways for government to care for the environment.[64] Just what these action-forcing mechanisms might be was not clear. Secretary of the Interior Udall may have come closest to the notion that Jackson's S. 1075 would eventually echo. He said that there would be no easy way to reorganize the executive branch to provide environmental oversight. Combining all relevant programs into one would be impossible. Instead, each agency "should designate responsible officials and establish environmental checkpoints to be sure they have properly assessed this impact."[65]

Caldwell had been thinking about an action-forcing mechanism for several years. He had broached the topic in an unpublished paper in 1964 where he looked favorably on the idea of a "checklist of criteria for environmental planning."[66] In 1966 he published a short article that suggested the "drawing up of a balance sheet of ecological accounts by which the probable costs and benefits of alternative environmental decisions might be compared."[67] With "checkpoints," "checklists," and "balance sheets," serious people were fumbling for a metaphor to guide them toward a format, procedure, or regulation that could hold agencies to account in relation to the environment.

A solution would not come easily. In fact, the first version of the bill that became NEPA—as introduced by Senator Jackson in 1967 and reintroduced in the new Congress in February 1969—centered on establishing a Council on Environmental Quality to advise the president and on authorizing the Secretary of the Interior to conduct ecological research. But nowhere was there a general statement of federal responsibility for the environment nor any hint of a specific policy mechanism for making environmental responsibility operational.

The itch in the Interior Committee to find a way to turn environmental anxiety into practical policy would not go away. On March 24, 1969, Jackson asked Caldwell for a further brief report, and Caldwell responded with the suggestion that a broad statement of national policy be included in the legislation. Meanwhile, he was in discussion with Van Ness and Dreyfus about an action-forcing mechanism. Van Ness suggested that Caldwell introduce the idea of an action-forcing provision in his scheduled April 16 public testimony. Caldwell did so, proposing that "a statement of policy by the Congress should at least consider measures to require the Federal agencies, in submitting proposals, to contain within the proposals an evaluation of the effect of these proposals upon the state of the environment."[68] He suggested that the Bureau of the Budget should scrutinize agency actions and plans with respect to their impact on the environment before approving them. "Now," he added, "these are what I mean by action-forcing or operational measures. It would not be enough, it seems to me, when we speak of policy, to think that a mere statement of desirable outcomes would be sufficient to give us the foundation that we need for a vigorous program of what I would call national defense against environmental degradation. We need something that is firm, clear, and operational."[69]

The moment was ripe. By the fall, as White House environmental adviser Whitaker remembers it, the mood in Washington was one of "hysteria." "The words pollution and environment were on every politician's lips. The press gave the issue extraordinary coverage, Congress responded by producing environment-related bills by the bushel, and the President was in danger of being left behind."[70] This all seems much overdrawn. Whitaker may have projected White House hysteria out onto the general public. The mass public participation in the first Earth Day in April 1970 came as a surprise, even to the event's organizers. Although membership in environmental organizations had steadily grown in the 1960s, in 1970 the Sierra Club remained a small, California-centered organization, and it would not endorse candidates for political office until 1980. It was during the 1970s that environmental groups turned to direct efforts to influence public policy.[71] Environmental legislation, to that point, including NEPA, was primarily inside-Washington business.

Moreover, beginning with NEPA and the Clean Air Act, and a few years later with the Toxic Substances Control Act, laws did not respond to public pressure so much as open up the roadways along which public pressure could travel.[72] Government initiatives did not simply react to social change, public opinion, street demonstrations, and strategically applied pressure from powerful lobbyists. Instead, they constructed new opportunities for civic engagement.[73] NEPA, by opening new opportunities for environmental groups to sue the government, directly fostered the emergence of litigation-oriented environmental organizations. Political scientists Helen Ingram, David Colnic, and Dean Mann hold that NEPA, the Clean Air Act (1970), and the Toxic Substances Control Act (1976) have been "particularly important in generating interest group formation and maintenance."[74] As they observe, several forces converged to make this happen—not only the legislation that opened an opportunity for nonprofit organizations to litigate, but an easing of what was required for an individual or group to gain standing to sue the federal government, the relaxation of Internal Revenue Service rules for environmental law

groups to qualify for nonprofit status, and the rapid professionalization of membership organizations that had been largely amateur
operations.[75]

Professor Caldwell's earlier statements about an action-forcing
mechanism and even his April 1969 testimony that generated the
clause enjoining executive agencies to prepare a "finding" (later
changed to a "detailed statement") about the anticipated environmental impact of proposed initiatives show that his thinking and
the Committee on the Interior's thinking, while pressing forward,
remained vague. There was no specification of who was to review the
findings; there was nothing to indicate that findings were to be made
public.

The story of NEPA's passage, including how public disclosure came
to be incorporated in the law, is told in a remarkably clear and thorough doctoral dissertation by the late Terence Finn, completed in
1972 at Georgetown University on the basis of extensive interviews
with many of the principals. Finn interviewed forty-eight members
of Congress and their staff assistants for this work and drew also on
his firsthand acquaintance with Congress as a legislative assistant to
Sen. Millard Tydings (D-Md.) from 1968 to 1970. The narrative goes
something like this: Senator Jackson came to believe that NEPA
could succeed only by making all agencies of the federal government
actively consider how their projects affected the environment. Finn
wrote that Jackson took federal agencies to be run by "reasonable men
who would respond to a mandate or a procedure requiring consideration of environmental values."[76] This may sound naive, but no one
associated naivete with Scoop Jackson. What was this practical politician thinking? He seems to have believed that since the government
could exercise its ability to protect environmental quality "only with
the cooperation of the Federal agencies," as Finn observes, agencies

would have to be induced to "internalize" environmental values. Jackson did not want to add to the federal bureaucracy "an environmental overlord, review board, or regulatory council."[77] Aware that bureaucrats were not Boy Scouts and that federal agencies would at least initially resist outside direction, he took the view that a commitment to the environment somehow had to be instilled inside the bureaucracy.

Jackson's strategy, or philosophy, if you will, proved unacceptable to Senator Muskie. Muskie was angry that Jackson's Interior Committee had already voted out and brought to the Senate floor a bill at odds with the standard-setting and outside review approach Muskie championed in his clean-air and clean-water legislation. From Muskie's vantage, Jackson had ignored his Public Works Committee and run roughshod over the strategy of environmental protection that had made Muskie the most widely recognized environmental advocate on Capitol Hill. It made no sense to allow federal agencies to evaluate for themselves the impact of their own activities on the environment. In Muskie's words: "The concept of self-policing by Federal agencies which pollute or license pollution is contrary to the philosophy and intent of existing environmental quality legislation."[78] He argued that agencies, over and over again, placed their own primary objectives—navigable waterways or the licensing of nuclear power plants or any other project—above environmental considerations.[79] For Muskie, it was just plain bad policy to allow the agencies themselves to assess their own environmental impact.

Finn argues that there was a much greater problem than who would undertake the evaluations of environmental impact: who would review them? Jackson's draft was silent about what would happen to the required reports the agencies would prepare. Dan Dreyfus, the Jackson staffer who drafted the original language, believed that the environmental impact statements would be appended to proposed actions as they went through normal review processes and that in the end they would be reviewed by the Bureau of the Budget (BOB). He saw the statements as "but another input for the BOB examiners to consider in evaluating the proposal."[80] Caldwell also believed that the impact statements would be reviewed at the Bureau of the Budget "though he doubted the wisdom of such procedure," according to Finn.[81] Charles Cook, the minority counsel for the Senate Interior Committee, believed that "the very process of preparing the environmental statement would resolve most of the problems."[82] Meanwhile, Van Ness and Senator Jackson himself worried that the Bureau of the Budget was too oriented toward strictly fiscal considerations to give environmental matters their due.[83]

"Who then was to review the environmental statements?" Finn asks. "What in fact were they to do with them? Were the statements to be made public? How extreme were they to be? Neither Jackson, Van Ness, nor Dreyfus ever explicitly said." He adds, "These logical questions . . . were never answered if indeed they were asked. The concept of internalizing environmental values itself suggested that no one was to examine the statements."[84]

Dreyfus had previously worked in the Bureau of Reclamation, where, he said, "we had to write a form of feasibility study for proposals that were circulated among the federal agencies for comments. Then, with comments attached, these studies went to the Bureau of Management and Budget for funding." In his view, these studies did not stop highways or dams from being built, but they did identify their environmental consequences. This "enabled the people involved to fight it out and make a decision. Adverse comments were a handicap to getting the required money. . . . So the first draft wording of the impact statement was based on this."[85] Dreyfus's recollections appear to support Cook's view that the mere process of writing an environmental impact statement and making it available to other relevant agencies for comment could pull off a magic trick of self-regulation. Still, this model of interagency review was not reflected in the wording of the bill that Jackson presented to the Senate in the summer of 1969.

In an undated memo to Jackson, Van Ness defended the Section 102 (EIS) provision. As he saw it, the next level of authority beyond the agency would be empowered to evaluate the environmental impact of proposed actions and alternatives to them. That "next level" Van Ness described as "the Cabinet Officer, the Bureau of the Budget, the President, the Congress, the Judiciary, and the American people." This catchall list (although it omits mention of the Council on Environmental Quality that NEPA was establishing) interestingly includes "the American people." The Van Ness memo is explicit that the impact statements should be made public "so that they may be reviewed, scrutinized, and, if necessary, challenged."[86] Again, this is not in the language of the bill as it stood in July 1969. It did not become part of the bill until an angry Ed Muskie forced changes in NEPA in intense negotiations with Jackson.

After a protracted struggle, Jackson and Muskie reached a compromise on October 8, 1969. This was not easy. Senate majority leader Mike Mansfield brought the two warring senators to his office and told them they had to work out their differences. The language Jackson had brought to the Senate in July required agencies to provide a "finding" of environmental impact. In the October compromise, "finding" was changed to "detailed statement." Richard N. L. Andrews, an early academic analyst of NEPA, writing in 1976, thought this rewording was designed "to *weaken* the legal force of the required document."[87] A "finding" seemed to suggest a conclusory document that could be reviewed, if at all, only by a court; the "detailed statement" was open to interagency review. The language of the law was revised to declare that the detailed statement "shall be made available to the President, the Council of Environmental Quality and to the public." The point, I think, was not to weaken the impact of the "finding" but to make it subject to interagency review. This would not water down the legal force of the document an agency produced but would keep any individual agency from taking autonomous actions unreviewable by other parts of the executive branch. In other words, this was precisely a concession to Senator Muskie's insistence that no agency could be trusted to police its own environmental house.

Before reaching this compromise, Muskie had urged the creation of an environmental oversight agency to review and approve or disapprove the environmental impact statements, but Jackson "objected strenuously," Finn reports.[88] Jackson stuck to his position that only the internalization of environmental values in the agencies could ensure environmental protection. In the compromise, Muskie accepted as a meaningful gesture in his direction the requirement that every agency preparing an environmental statement must seek the comments of other agencies, including agencies with a specific mission to protect the environment. From Muskie's viewpoint, a "detailed statement" subject to interagency review empowered these other agencies in ways that the implicit finality of "finding" did not.

But the compromise went further. In a conversation with Jackson and Muskie, Sen. Gaylord Nelson (D-Wisc.) proposed that these various independent views and the environmental impact statement itself should be made public—and both Jackson and Muskie agreed to this.[89] According to Finn, "Nelson believed that public opinion could be used effectively to halt activity damaging to the environment." Finn concludes, "Senator Muskie with Nelson's assistance thereby achieved a significant change in S. 1075."[90] The language that was then added to Section 102 was as follows:

> Prior to making any detailed statement, the responsible Federal official shall consult with and obtain the comments of any established agency which has jurisdiction by law or special expertise with respect to any environmental impact involved. Copies of such statement and the comments and views of the appropriate Federal, state, and local agencies, including those authorized to develop and enforce environmental standards, shall be made available to the President, the Board of Environmental Advisers and to the public as provided by 5 U.S.C. 552 [the Freedom of Information Act] and shall accompany the proposal through the existing agency review processes.

So far as I have been able to determine, that is the story of how the environmental impact statement became open to interagency review and available to the interested public. Finn's account gives Senator Nelson the role of unsung hero. That the suggestion to make the environmental impact statements public documents came from Nelson is consistent with Nelson's focus on mobilizing public opinion, from his initiative on President Kennedy's "environmental tour" to Earth Day. Historians suggest that Nelson's first notions about an Earth Day came to him in early fall 1969, and he first spoke of what he thought of as a national teach-in on the environment in a speech in Seattle on September 20.[91] So while Finn's report of the colloquy among Nelson, Muskie, and Jackson sometime in the next several weeks has no corroboration that I know of, it is consistent with Nelson's general policy orientation and it is attested to by Finn's dissertation, much admired by both participants in NEPA's history and scholars.[92]

However, Leon Billings, chief aide to Senator Muskie on the Public Works Committee, declared to me that this Jackson-Muskie-Nelson conversation "never took place."[93] Billings was deeply involved in the negotiations between Muskie and Jackson to arrive at the compromise between their two approaches to environmental protection. He often represented Muskie in meetings with Jackson (because, Billings recalled, Muskie loathed Jackson). Billings has undying admiration for Muskie and all he achieved as a public servant, including his dogged determination to improve Jackson's S. 1075. Muskie's efforts brought NEPA's Section 102 to final form. Jackson's July draft had no language to require agency "findings" to be open to review by other agencies, notably agencies with specific environmental expertise and responsibility, nor any hint that they should be available to the public. Still, I see no reason to shift all of the credit to Muskie's corner or to deny Nelson's reported contribution.

In shaping the final language of NEPA, Muskie's contribution was critical. Only Muskie had the standing, the expertise, the stubbornness, and the clout to hold up Jackson's bill for significant revision. I think Muskie's specific contribution was to make environmental impact statements open to interagency scrutiny and challenge; his more general addition was to open up the opportunity that Nelson then took to suggest that the EIS be open to the public. That idea may have been circulating already, as the undated memo from Van Ness would seem to indicate, but it still appears that the idea became concrete in the Jackson-Nelson-Muskie conversation.

Other late changes in the proposed law included mandating that the detailed statement must include analysis of alternatives to the action proposed. Earlier references to alternative courses of action had been general, without a requirement for "written presentation or public review." This was in line with Senator Muskie's view that a serious examination of alternatives would happen only if alternatives were taken up in a public document.[94] This also points to the power of Muskie's intervention.

I belabor the discussion of Section 102's evolution because it is only the publicness of the environmental impact statement that made NEPA action-forcing for executive agencies and therefore action-enabling for environmental law groups and others able to initiate civil suits against the government for failure to write environmental impact statements or for failure to write them sufficiently well to accord with the law. Without that little phrase—"and to the public"—NEPA would have been a notable statement of philosophy and very likely a useful mechanism for more rational sharing of information among executive agencies, but it would not have been the revolutionary opening of the "environmental decade." In retrospect, "and to the public" are the most important words in NEPA, incorporated only at the eleventh hour and having no individual author (except possibly Nelson). Caldwell, Van Ness, and Jackson himself all agreed that the public accountability that emerged from the negotiations between Muskie and Jackson helped to ensure the legislation's effectiveness, even though they acknowledged it as "a major concession on the part of Senator Jackson" to Muskie's views.[95] But, as best as I can judge, the publicness of this review process was not a concession to anything that Muskie specifically advocated so much as it was an addition consistent with the direction in which Muskie was pushing.[96] Environmental protection, not publicness, was the objective for both Jackson and Muskie. Publicness was a means to making an environmentalist objective take concrete and surprisingly effective form.

One other battle over the bill's final language is worthy of note. The draft bill that had passed the Senate included the declaration that "each person has a fundamental and inalienable right to a healthful environment." This was not part of the House version of the bill. In the conference committee, Rep. Wayne Aspinall (D-Colo.), a powerful member of the conference committee, a stalwart opponent of environmental legislation, and a skeptic about NEPA from the outset, vigorously objected to this provision, holding that "it will be seized upon as the basis for numerous lawsuits."[97] Senator Jackson responded that the purpose of the provision was precisely to enable environmental lawsuits, but he agreed with Rep. John Dingell, the sponsor of the legislation in the House, that it was important to defer to Aspinall on this point lest he torpedo the entire bill when the conference report was returned to the House for approval. So, in deference to Aspinall, the conference committee agreed to omit the term "right" and to declare simply that each person "should enjoy a healthful environment." This mollified Representative Aspinall and reduced the size of the legislative billboard announcing to citizens an opportunity to sue.[98] As it would turn out, Aspinall's effort was undercut by "and to the public," and the power of NEPA would be determined in the courts.

Senator Jackson, in defending the language of rights against Representative Aspinall (but losing that skirmish), acknowledged that NEPA was intended to make litigation possible. Still, the authors of NEPA labored to write a law that would most of all influence the culture of the executive agencies; they spent little or no time debating the merits or the mechanisms of involving a broader public. Dan Tarlock, the young colleague of Lynton Caldwell's teaching at the Indiana University School of Law, wrote in 1972 that Caldwell "did not envision that the courts would play a major role—at least in the first years of its administration—in enforcing the Act."[99] Caldwell's writings for Senator Jackson's committee, as Tarlock read them, "focus almost exclusively on the role of administrative agencies in policy formulation and decision making."[100] Jackson, Caldwell, and staff aides Van Ness and Dreyfus focused primarily on establishing environmental objectives as an overriding common goal that would trump "segmental public decision making," in Caldwell's terminology, and instill environmental awareness in every agency.[101]

The White House had no more idea about litigation than Congress did. John Whitaker recalled later,

> I don't remember anybody saying to me when we did the option paper . . . that it had a legal implication, and the government would end up being sued and this would be kind of a cottage industry for the lawyers and this was really going to change the world.
>
> Maybe somebody in OMB [the Office of Management and Budget] knew. I certainly didn't know. The president didn't know. John Ehrlichman didn't know. On the other hand, I'm certainly glad we signed it. I think the National Environmental Policy Act and the exercise of going through and writing environmental impact statements has been a very salutary worthwhile thing.[102]

The Aftermath: Making NEPA Public and Making NEPA Matter

Congress wrote NEPA and so helped give the public a role in making U.S. environmental policy and planning. But Congress did not consummate this transformation of public policy. The executive was about to play a key role; a little later, so would the courts. The first important move after NEPA became law on January 1, 1970, was President Nixon's Executive Order 11514 on March 5, 1970, prepared with the advice of the newly established Council on Environmental Quality, headed by Russell Train. It called on the heads of all federal agencies to comply with NEPA and specifically enjoined them to "develop procedures to ensure the fullest practicable provision of timely public information and understanding of Federal plans and programs with environmental impacts in order to obtain the views of interested parties." This meant instituting, "whenever appropriate, provision for public hearings" and it meant providing the public with "relevant information, including information on alternative courses of action."

The executive order called on the newly established Council on Environmental Quality to issue regulations to the agencies to implement NEPA and, specifically, "to make the environment impact statement process more useful to decisionmakers and the public." Statements should be "concise, clear, and to the point, and supported by evidence that agencies have made the necessary environmental analyses."[103] As Richard Andrews observed, the executive order went further than NEPA itself in specifying the publicness of the environmental impact statement process. The executive order's emphasis on "timely" public information, on hearings, and on securing the views of interested parties "implied a further policy of increased public participation before the process of recommendation, review, and approval was completed."[104]

On April 30 the Council on Environmental Quality promulgated interim guidelines for agencies preparing environmental impact statements. These guidelines remained vague but would themselves be revised a year later, by that time responding both to the early experience of the agencies and to initial decisions in the courts reviewing cases where the adequacy of the statements was challenged.[105] By December 1970, CEQ chairman Train testified before Rep. John Dingell's Subcommittee on Fisheries and Wildlife Conservation, reporting that nineteen executive agencies had established 102(2)(C) procedures (that is, procedures for producing environmental impact statements), that these procedural guidelines had been made public, and that by November statements were coming to CEQ at a rate of about a hundred a month.[106] Overall, by early December, about 300 draft and final statements had been submitted to CEQ.[107]

Train emphasized in his testimony the importance of public disclosure. He highlighted the procedures of the U.S. Army Corps of Engineers that made not only draft environmental statements but also "preliminary draft statements" available to "interested citizen groups." He assured the subcommittee that "our policy is the fullest practicable disclosure to the public of environmental information in advance of decision or action."[108] Much remained undefined at that point, as Train acknowledged. The CEQ could and did comment on environmental impact statements but had no authority to veto them. Still, it is clear from Train's testimony that negative comment from the CEQ sometimes did lead to revision of proposed agency actions. At the time, Train testified, there was much NEPA-generated litigation but only one appeals court decision related to it. The role of the courts had scarcely begun to be defined.

That changed in 1971. The key early judicial decision concerning NEPA was *Calvert Cliffs' Coordinating Committee v. the U.S. Atomic Energy Commission.* It was argued before the District of Columbia Circuit Court in April 1971 and decided on July 23. In the decision, Judge J. Skelly Wright, writing for a unanimous three-judge panel, correctly saw that there would be "a flood of new litigation—litigation seeking judicial assistance in protecting our natural environment." He declared the National Environmental Policy Act of 1969 to be the most important environmental statute to date, and asserted that the challenge before the court "is to see that important legislative purposes, heralded in the hall of Congress, are not lost or misdirected in the vast hallways of the federal bureaucracy." For Judge Wright, NEPA created "judicially enforceable duties" on federal agencies.[109]

The Calvert Cliffs' Coordinating Committee was a Maryland environmental group whose members objected to the Atomic Energy Commission's plan to build a nuclear power plant at Calvert Cliffs, to empty heated water into Chesapeake Bay, and thereby, in their view, to endanger the health and safety of marine life in the bay and the uses of the bay for human recreation. They thus sued the Atomic Energy Commission for failing to demonstrate that the environmental impact of the plant would not be harmful.

Judge Wright left no doubt that he took the case seriously: "Several recently enacted statutes attest to the commitment of the Government to control, at long last, the destructive engine of material 'progress.' But it remains to be seen whether the promise of this legislation will become a reality. Therein lies the judicial role."[110] Had the Atomic Energy Commission lived up to the strictures of NEPA by providing an appropriately detailed statement of the environmental impact of building the nuclear plant at Calvert Cliffs? The court's task was to answer that question. It concluded that the Atomic Energy Commission had fallen short of its legal obligations.

As early as April 1970, courts used NEPA to enjoin construction of a trans-Alaska oil pipeline until an environmental impact statement was completed. The Department of Interior had produced an environmental impact statement March 20 (all of eight pages long) that was immediately challenged in court. Federal district court judge George Hart found that Interior's environmental impact statement did not meet NEPA's requirements.[111] Also in 1970, environmental plaintiffs delayed or halted the construction of highways, a barge canal, and a dam.[112]

Citizen suits against the government concerning adverse environmental impacts multiplied not simply because environmental organizations initiated them. Rather, the membership of environmental organizations grew in part because the possibility of citizen suits provided them a new domain of action. "Citizen suits, in short," legal scholar Barton Thompson writes, "are in part responsible for the acceptance and growth of a sizable environmental nonprofit community."[113] Even so, Thompson argues, lawsuits are just one part of the monitorial function that leads to better enforcement of environmental laws. Yes, citizen groups initiate legal actions, but they also gather information about possible legal violations, and they are in fact encouraged to do so by federal laws that provide financial rewards to individuals who give evidence of violation of federal laws.[114] Not only did NEPA provide the lever with which environmental lawyers could challenge federal projects that might prove harmful to the environment, but the wave of environmental legislation that followed NEPA, by pushing the regulation of pollution from the states to the federal government, both simplified the task of litigation and magnified its consequences.[115]

Ecology and the environment became powerful, popular concerns across the country in the 1960s and 1970s; public opinion and organized popular action came to exert influence on local, state, and national public policy. Yet this does not justify a populist reading of the story of environmentalism in which social change springs up unbidden from the unquenchably humane instincts of the general public. If you go to the Environmental Protection Agency's website and look at the (unsigned) article there on the origins of the EPA, note that it begins, "American environmentalism dawned as a popular movement on a mild spring afternoon in 1970." The reference, of course, is to the first Earth Day.

Why is a "popular movement" the starting point for the essay? Even Earth Day, though spectacularly popular, had been preceded by at least half a dozen environmental teach-ins, but it took U.S. senator Gaylord Nelson, a veteran of promoting environmental legislation for a decade in Washington, D.C.—and before that as governor of Wisconsin—to put together such a remarkable national event.[116] By the first Earth Day, NEPA was already law, its legislative path going back to 1967; NEPA was already in the courts, and the Alaska pipeline was about to be delayed for lack of an environmental impact statement; and the Ash Council report that proposed consolidating various environment-related activities in an independent Environmental Protection Agency was on its way to President Nixon. Environmental legislation had become law in the Clean Air Act (1963), the Wilderness Act (1964), the Water Quality Act (1965), and the Solid Waste Disposal Act (1965). Why should the massive public gatherings of Earth Day occlude these prior developments?[117]

———————

As the National Environmental Policy Act required, the first members of the Council on Environmental Quality were appointed soon after the act became law, but nothing else in the law directed any well-specified action. The law required that every federal agency should take the environment into consideration "to the fullest extent possible" and should prepare a "detailed statement" about the environmental impact of its significant actions. But what should a detailed statement look like? What environmental and ecological elements should it take into account? Who should review it? At what stage or stages in decision making should it circulate? What should citizens who judge the statement inadequate be empowered to do about it, if anything? Answers would take shape only as the Council on Environmental Quality began issuing guidelines and instructions governing how federal agencies should comply with the law, and as the courts made clear that their doors were open.

Nearly two decades after NEPA became law, Lynton Keith Caldwell, looking back, wrote that NEPA's drafting "afforded a rare opportunity to infuse an action-forcing procedure of revolutionary potential into the political processes of public planning and decision making."[118] The term "revolutionary" is not too strong. As environmental law professor A. Dan Tarlock has suggested, the rise of environmental litigation that NEPA invited married "the two parts of the now mythic 1960s. . . . NEPA, the statute, is actually a product of the more optimistic, technocratic, and decidedly non radical early 1960s. NEPA, the practice area, is the product of the more familiar, radical 60s." NEPA came from a wave of reform efforts in the period 1960–1969; Judge Wright's decisive opinion speaks more from the late 1960s and the skepticism of that moment about whether "expert" administrative agencies could be trusted to define the public good without the public itself playing a role.[119] There *is* a popular dimension to the evolution of NEPA, but that was not its starting point.

NEPA helped give rise to environmental impact assessment as a worldwide practice. By the early twenty-first century, more than a hundred countries had followed the United States in establishing environmental impact assessment as a normal part of governmental action; Canada began environmental assessment in 1973, Australia and New Zealand in 1974, France in 1976, Brazil in 1981, Germany in 1985, Japan in 1987, and China in 1989.[120]

With FOIA, openness was the objective. With consumer information reform, there was no doubt that transparency—or at least prohibitions of duplicity, and empowerment of individual citizens with facts—was cardinal. With sunshine reforms in Congress, openness was a means to an end, with the goal of weakening the committee chairs and creating a better climate for passing liberal legislation. With NEPA, public access to the environmental assessment process seems almost but not quite accidental. There was nothing accidental about Caldwell's insistence on finding a mechanism to hold government agencies to account. There was nothing accidental in Senator Jackson's effort to insert environmental assessment into the operation of each agency rather than locating it in an outside agency of review. It was no accident that Senator Muskie rebelled at this and insisted on a mechanism to hold agencies accountable to external review. And Jackson seemed well aware that this might happen through litigation and involvement of the courts.

When the phrase "and to the public" came into the draft legislation in the fall of 1969, it was a phrase legislators were getting used to. Perhaps what is noteworthy about it is that it was so little noted at the time. But an entire domain of federal actions that had long proceeded with little or no public review or public participation, and rarely with any consideration of the environment, was suddenly, by law, said to require public knowledge and public input at formative stages before the government took action. The public was to enter the process not after the fact but in the very formation of proposed public action—even if specifying the stage at which the public was to be invited into the process had to wait for an executive order from President Nixon and guidelines from the newly established Council on Environmental Quality.[121] As David Brower would have wished, the people or their organized representatives in government, public interest law firms, and environmental organizations would be "able to know in time."

However complex and compromised the final formulation of NEPA, however fortunate and unforeseen that the White House and the Council on Environmental Quality followed up with speed and a strong hand, however lucky it was that Judge Wright insisted on construing the intentions of Congress in NEPA in a tough-minded way, and however different the operation of the EIS process has become over time from the way it was originally envisioned, the result has extended the principles of democracy that imply and encompass a right to know.[122]

seven

Transparency in a Transformed Democracy

E arly in 2009, not long before it would become world famous, Wikileaks, a small independent website that was run by charismatic Australian anarchist Julian Assange and several tech-savvy associates and was committed to disseminating information that powerful corporations and governments seek to hide, made public 6,780 "quasi-secret reports" of the U.S. Congress. This was the complete electronic output (older undigitized reports in the same series were not released) of the Congressional Research Service (CRS), an arm of Congress that provides its parent body with analysis of important public policy issues upon request. These works, as Wikileaks noted, are "highly regarded as non-partisan, in-depth, and timely."

In a report on this document dump, the online news organization ProPublica's headline read, "WikiLeaks Publishes CRS Reports; Gov't Still Doesn't." CRS, with an annual budget of about $100 million, is intended to serve the public by helping Congress make better, more information-based decisions. Nonetheless, CRS reports are not shared with the general public. The ProPublica headline, although accurate, is barbed. Its message is unmistakably that the government should have released the information itself.[1]

That ProPublica should run a headline that so casually and caustically comments on the news is emblematic of a new set of digital norms of transparency. Much of the activity of the 1960s and 1970s I have written about here shows people stumbling into an era of disclosure, confession, accounts, and accountability; in contrast, advocates of disclosure in the Internet era practically leap into openness—intentionally, sometimes recklessly, and at warp speed. This is the consequence of remarkable technological achievements and a transformation of the work life, home life, and cultural horizons of most human beings around the world. But it is also indebted to the slower unfolding of a culture of disclosure that dawned more than half a century ago.

That earlier development took part in and extended a transformation of democracy itself. While my focus has been exclusively on the emergence of practices in the United States, changes in the character of democracy have been worldwide. It is not surprising that developments such as the Freedom of Information Act and environmental impact statements have been among the more dazzling American political exports of the late twentieth century. It is also not surprising that some of the most striking accounts of changes in democracy have come from France (Pierre Rosanvallon) and the United Kingdom and Australia (John Keane) as well as the United States. This broad democratic evolution is the best framework I know for redescribing and coming to understand new practices of disclosure.

Making Sense of Contemporary Democracies

Today, the operation of political parties and their central role in elections are vital to democracies, as they have been for nearly two centuries. Even so, since 1945 they have become a smaller element in governance relative to a newly empowered set of alternative institutions for representing voices of the public and for monitoring governmental activity. We have entered into an era that is so different from what has long been known as representative democracy that it might even be called "post-representative democracy," but this would be misleading. Representation has changed, but it has not been diminished, as "post-representative" may imply. Instead, we should now recognize that classical representative democracy offered a form of representation—in legislatures, through parties and elections—but not the supreme form that casts all others as less perfect variants. Party-centered representative democracy has now been substantially supplemented (but not replaced) with multiple forms of representing the public and holding governments accountable. The democracies we live in today are trans-legislative democracies, that is, political systems in which representation may be stronger than ever before, but not so exclusively located in elections and legislatures. We might follow political theorist John Keane, whose work I will describe below, and call it "monitory democracy" or "monitorial democracy."

Versions of this general position have been proposed by several historians, political scientists, and political theorists. In the early republic, as U.S. historians call the period of American history from 1789 to roughly the 1830s, the government was an elitist republican government, what historian Morton Keller calls a "deferential-republican" regime. In that system, ordinary voters—which is to say white males with at least a modest amount of property—were not expected to "be informed" but to defer to established, known, affluent community leaders. In what Keller terms the "party-democratic regime" that followed, from about 1840 to 1945, politics became less a simple reflection of local social hierarchies and more the product of formal organizations, especially political parties, with the franchise extended to all adult white men, and later adult white women, too. The political culture at the same time became more individualist, with information growing relatively more central as a basis for decisions in the voting booth, and affiliation by kinship and social connection relatively less so. To borrow from familiar British fiction, picture a transition from the settled rural lives of a Jane Austen novel to the urban dangers, adventure, and opportunity facing the young protagonists of Charles Dickens. The whole political atmosphere grew more democratic and more complex, with political parties organizing lengthy and entertaining campaigns, with expanding opportunities for protest, dissent, and demonstration, and with participation in civil society spreading rapidly and well beyond parties into movements such as abolitionism and temperance before the Civil War, and into civil service reform, women's suffrage, and organized labor later on.

In the post-1945 period, there has been a politicization of everyday life, a sprawl of rights consciousness, and a new availability of low-cost civic engagement, from 10K runs for breast cancer research, benefit concerts, and blogging to more traditional forms like petitions. In this era, representative institutions constituted through elections have not been superseded, but they are powerfully supplemented in ways notable enough to constitute a new species of democratic governance. Keller terms this the "populist-bureaucratic regime." For Keller, various nonparty forms of popular participation have become prominent at the same time that the weight of governmental operation has shifted from legislature to executive.[2]

The same reality is characterized somewhat differently in *Democracy Transformed? Expanding Political Opportunities in Advanced Industrial Democracies,* where political scientists Bruce Cain, Russell Dalton, Susan Scarrow, and their colleagues discuss the changes of recent decades as the move to "advocacy democracy."[3] "Advocacy democracy" identifies some of the motivations for the public activity of interest groups in recent decades but misses the full originality of postwar developments. "Advocacy" does not correctly characterize the heart of activity such as the emergence and widespread publicity of commercial and noncommercial opinion polling; the establishment and growth of publicly monitored internal government audits and inspections; the growth of budgets and staffs in Congress for the development of more expert legislative oversight of executive agencies; the development of new modes of citizen participation in government advisory committees; the creation of governmental mechanisms such as the Freedom of Information Act to assist individuals and private organizations to ferret out information that government agencies by habit or subterfuge have kept from the public; the judicial expansion of "standing" for groups that represent in litigation the interests of a public or a set of individuals who are unknown to one another but who all are adversely affected in the same way by particular governmental or corporate decisions; and the growth of administrative procedures, such as those requiring the preparation of environmental impact statements, for public comment and review. All of these developments encourage public monitoring of government power, and many of them, in fact, ease the way for "advocacy" and thereby encourage it, but they are not designed specifically for advocacy's sake. If they collectively advocate anything, it is advocacy for procedural democracy that expands representation from legislatures to a wide variety of other forms by which private people and groups can participate in representing themselves.

French political theorist Bernard Manin names the same post-1945 departure another way. He writes of the history of democracy as a move from the eighteenth century's early "parliamentary democracy," where voters were supposed to select a "person of trust" to represent them, a local "notable" who would then vote his own conscience based on his understanding of the public good, to nineteenth-century "party democracy," where representatives were members of parties expected to maintain a large degree of loyalty to the priorities of their party platforms. Then, largely in the post-1945 era, party democracy gave way to "audience democracy," where the hold of parties on candidates loosened and candidates grew better able to respond individually and idiosyncratically to public opinion and to an increasingly wide array of interest groups, experts, movements, and events.[4] This gets closer to the position I want to argue for, but "audience democracy" implies a passivity on the part of citizens that seems wrong for the era of the civil rights movement, the anti–Vietnam War movement, the women's movement, gay liberation, the rise of an energized neopopulist right in both Europe and North America, the pro-life movement, the environmental movement, the growing political influence of think tanks and foundations, and the many initiatives of single individuals or tiny groups that achieve national significance, from the Ralph Nader family of nonprofit advocacy groups to the Innocence Project.

Australian political theorist and media scholar John Keane (long at the University of Westminster in London but in recent years at the University of Sydney) offers the most fully elaborated historical position and the one I find most apt. In his view, democracy has shifted from the "assembly democracy" model of ancient Greek city-states to the "representative democracy" model that emerged in the eighteenth century and which, in its different variants, has to this day been identified with modern democracy. But for Keane, as for Keller, for Cain and his colleagues, and for Manin, social changes since 1945 have altered the conditions of popular government sufficiently to force upon us a new label for today's democratic forms. For Keane, two features stand out in shaping democracy today. First, there is "communicative abundance." If assembly democracy is linked to the spoken word and representative democracy to print culture, today's democracy—what Keane calls "monitory democracy"—emerges with the rise of multimedia societies.[5] The multiple forms of news media give new force to the print-era aspirations of journalism to serve as a watchdog on government. But in monitory democracy, journalism is by no means the only significant force for holding government accountable. As Keane observes, today we have not only a rapidly proliferating array of civil society organizations that scrutinize government but even organizations (he mentions the Democratic Audit Network and the Global Accountability Project) that monitor the monitors, attending to the quality and effectiveness of the power-scrutinizing work of other civil society organizations. "In the era of monitory democracy, the constant public scrutiny of power by hosts of differently sized monitory bodies with footprints large and small makes it the most energetic, most dynamic form of democracy ever," he writes.[6]

Keane's "monitory democracy" may sound like a recipe for governmental paralysis. Indeed, in the concluding chapter of Keane's ambitious 2009 work, *The Life and Death of Democracy,* he includes a drawing of Lemuel Gulliver tied to stakes in the ground by a flock of Lilliputians. But he does not intend this as a dystopian image. In fact, he makes the case that democracy should be understood not as "rule by the people" but as rule by "nobody." He cites C. S. Lewis, who wrote that he is a democrat "because I believe in the Fall of Man. I think most people are democrats for the opposite reason. A great deal of democratic enthusiasm descends from the ideas of people . . . who believed in a democracy because they thought mankind so wise and good that everyone deserved a share in the government. The danger of defending democracy on those grounds is that they're not true." Lewis champions democracy not because human beings can govern themselves but because "mankind is so fallen that no man can be trusted with unchecked power over his fellows."[7] The moral value of democracy is that it is provisional and revisable, not that it always reflects or expresses the will of the people—if such a thing as the "will of the people" were even something that could be practically designated.[8]

This position is consistent with views of democracy Keane articulated as early as 1991. In *The Media and Democracy,* he emphasized that democracy is not simply a participatory form of government or a government where the majority rules. It "comprises procedures for arriving at collective decisions in a way which secures the fullest possible and qualitatively best participation of interested parties. At a minimum . . . democratic procedures include equal and universal adult suffrage; majority rule and guarantees of minority rights, which ensure that collective decisions are approved by a substantial number of those entitled to make them; the rule of law; and constitutional guarantees of freedom of assembly and expression and other liberties, which help ensure that the people expected to decide or to elect those who decide can choose among real alternatives."[9] Keane insists that the Enlightenment hope for "a rational democratic consensus" is simply "obsolete"; I would add that it was never realizable apart from exceptional, passing moments. The best that can be said for a more fully direct, participatory, and humanly satisfying democratic spirit is what Margaret Canovan has proposed—that there is a "politics of faith" as well as a "politics of skepticism" (quoting Michael Oakeshott), which she retitles as a "redemptive" face of democracy, counterposed to its "pragmatic" face. Canovan is wary of populism, this "redemptive" face, but she raises the possibility that "at least some degree of redemptive democracy's promise of salvation is actually necessary to lubricate the machinery of pragmatic democracy, and that if it is not present within the mainstream political system it may well reassert itself in the form of a populist challenge."[10]

Still, Canovan places her own bets with pragmatism. She sees the redemptive face of democracy, although perhaps necessary, to be full of dangers. I think Keane would agree. For him, what democracy provides is not "good decisions" but the opportunity for citizens "to judge (and to reconsider their judgements about) the quality of those decisions."[11] Reconsideration, revision, second thoughts—for Keane, the virtue of democracy is the humility of its operation, not the transport or ecstasy of its rejuvenating popular moments.

What Keane calls "monitory democracy," Pierre Rosanvallon describes as "counter-democracy." Rosanvallon is, if anything, even more insistent than other thinkers that we have today an entirely new species of democracy with new relations of power among elements in society and with novel advantages and disadvantages. It is a kind of bi-democracy, we might say, in which "the episodic democracy of the usual electoral-representative system" is complemented (or, as he writes, "buttressed") by "a durable democracy of distrust."[12] What Rosanvallon calls "liberal distrust" expresses pessimism about "the people" and about democracy itself, but a contemporary "democratic distrust" is skeptical of elected officials and maintains pressure on them to keep their promises.

For Rosanvallon, democratic distrust operates to constrain the actions of elected representatives—to hold them accountable to the common good. Institutions of democratic distrust that gained authority in the latter half of the twentieth century constitute a "counter-democracy" in that they compensate for the limitations of voting. In representative democracy, citizens acted politically primarily or exclusively by voting. In counter-democracy, individuals act politically as "watchdogs," providing oversight; as "veto-wielders," exercising the power of the negative, denunciation, or a "new 'democracy of rejection'"; and as "judges," who grade, evaluate, or judge in an increasingly judicialized polity.[13] In various institutionalized forms of popular control, public oversight is permanent and continuous—unlike voting, which remains episodic. Counter-democratic control differs from voting also in that it is normally targeted and precise in expression. It does not speak only for or against individual office holders but for (or, more commonly, against) specific policies and behaviors.

The result is that under counter-democracy, society increases its influence over government.[14] But where Keane is generally upbeat about the prospects for monitory democracy and Manin is decidedly reserved, Rosanvallon seems schizophrenic, unable to decide if he should be delighted or depressed by the changes he eloquently details. He seems to be most comfortable with an agnostic historicism—that "citizenship has changed in nature rather than declined" in our own era.[15] While he sees value in the various forms of making democracy a daily business rather than one that most people attend to only on election day, he worries that these various incarnations of democratic distrust indulge in a populism "in which the democratic project is totally swallowed up and taken over by counter-democracy: it is an extreme form of anti-politics." Populism, he holds, is "the political pathology characteristic of an era marked by the rise of counter-democratic forms."[16]

Remarkably and regrettably, we have no shared conceptualization of what is going on. Even to attend to the array of developments these thinkers call our attention to makes one uneasy. As political theorists Nadia Urbinati and Mark Warren write, it "risks looking like an ideological refurbishment," one that may serve to rationalize a declining popular enthusiasm for voting and political elites' apparently tightening control over governing.[17] Perhaps. But I want to examine in somewhat greater detail what, in the American instance, citizenship has begun to look like under this new counter-democratic or audience-centered or trans-legislative or advocacy or populist-bureaucratic regime. We lurch ahead into both an informational future and a political future without a map. How can we move from the civics lessons of "there are three branches of government" and "how a bill becomes a law" to a comprehensible perspective on how things actually work?

"If You See Something, Say Something": Citizenship in Monitorial Democracy

If Keller, Cain, Dalton, Scarrow, Manin, Keane, and Rosanvallon are on the right track, we have to conclude that popular understanding of democracy as a political system is lagging some three-quarters of a century behind fundamental changes in how democracies operate. Keane takes note of developments in Australia in recent decades in which government itself has created quasi-independent oversight agencies. There have been similar changes in U.S. government, including the increased authority of the Government Accountability Office (once the General Accounting Office), the Congressional Budget Office, the creation of inspectors general for all of the major federal agencies (beginning with the Inspectors General Act of 1978), and the complicated, sometimes vexing, but nonetheless powerful Freedom of Information Act. For the news media and other civil society organizations to operate as watchdogs on government, they must work in relationship to these self-surveillant bodies, including also the reports filed with the Federal Elections Commission (created on the basis of two pieces of legislation in 1971 and 1974), the issuing of draft and final environmental impact statements authorized by the National Environmental Policy Act (1969), and other legislatively ordered disclosures of public information, be they the corporate disclosure of toxic emissions required by the Emergency Planning and Community Right-to-Know Act of 1986 or the municipal inspection and posted grades of restaurants on their cleanliness and health standards.

Moreover, efforts to make government activity more transparent to the general public have grown rapidly with the Internet; vast quantities of government data are now available online. Increasingly, this information is not only available but searchable—even if it has required the efforts of private citizens, news organizations, nongovernmental organizations, and universities to do the work to make it actually useable. Joshua Tauberer is among the innovators who improved upon the federal government's own information services with the website GovTrack.us, which he started in 2004 while a doctoral student in linguistics and which was used by eight million people in 2013. Relying on government data, it has built tools that track bills in Congress, enabling citizens and interest groups to easily monitor the progress of legislation and the voting records of members of Congress in ways that would be at best cumbersome for people using the government websites directly. GovTrack asserts that its site "has served as a model for legislative transparency websites around the world."[18]

GovTrack and other nonprofit groups have become part of an umbrella association they call the Congressional Data Coalition. In 2014 GovTrack for the first time started to publish a calendar of all congressional committee hearings and markup sessions, updating the calendar daily. Giving credit to the newly launched House of Representatives website docs.house.gov, the Congressional Data Coalition has expressed hope that Congress will go further to make access to its operations more accessible to citizens. Until that happens, the best access to the daily calendar of Congress is GovTrack.[19]

The growth in this kind of government transparency does not mean that democracy gets better and better. That would have to be judged by a comprehensive account of how well a given democracy is working overall. Nor does this suggest that these various new mechanisms (John Keane counts close to a hundred different categories or types of "monitory" innovations around the world) can or should replace parties and elections.[20] Parties still matter—how healthy are they? Elections still matter, down to the details of voter registration laws, and we know very well that election laws in the United States, past and present, have been designed to disenfranchise poor and minority voters. The role of big money in elections is another potent factor corrupting the central institutions of democracy, and even more so in the United States, where about half of the states select judges by election, not by appointment. Economic inequality, never a good thing for the effectiveness of a democratic system, underlies but is distinct from these alterations in basic election-related operations of democracy.

My contention is not that democracy overall is necessarily improving but that the ways we assess democracy need to change. We should recognize transformations in how "representation" happens and incorporate them into reformulated ideals of what democratic representation is and should be. In retrospect, the common understanding of "representative democracy" accepted that the representation of voters in elected legislatures was the whole of representation or at least its essence. But modern democracies have various modes of representation and, especially after 1945, have added new mechanisms of representation that allow continuous, rather than episodic, representation; popularly generated rather than party-controlled representation; and many platforms for entrepreneurial democratic action. Democracies today are not "post-representative"—they are more representative than ever. They are not even post-legislative; they still depend on legislatures, but the legislatures are cinched into a system where they operate with respect to competing and constraining representative forms. Extralegislative forms of representation have arisen—through political parties, through journalism, and, by the middle of the twentieth century, through public opinion polling.

In this newly evolving, publicly monitored democracy, a wide variety of institutions are expected to act in the "if you see something, say something" manner (to quote the civic admonition posted for New York City subway riders). There are more venues for seeing, there are more opportunities for saying.

In democracies today, citizens' access to governance comes not only from electing representatives but also from influencing them, in at least five ways. First, citizens may address elected and unelected government officials through a variety of civil society organizations that monitor governmental behavior. Second, citizens' access to governance may come through litigation; this avenue to participation through the courts rather than the legislature has expanded greatly from the civil rights movement on. Third, the executive has become so vast since 1945 that a kind of veiled system of government accountability has emerged of which the general public is largely unaware—I have in mind the expansion of governmental self-monitoring and self-surveillance, which I will discuss shortly, as well as legislation (FOIA and NEPA are good examples) that directly provide citizens with opportunities to monitor the work of executive agencies.

Fourth, government today, as always, is operated by individuals, and individuals may choose to violate the implicit or explicit terms of their employment to follow the dictates of conscience. Specifically, they may become whistle-blowers who, publicly or through private leaking, reveal to legal authorities or to the news media evidence of government wrongdoing. The very term "whistle-blower" did not become a part of the public lexicon until around 1970. Only in the 1970s did the value of whistle-blowing for public accountability receive legislative recognition in efforts to protect whistle-blowers from retribution by the governmental agencies they embarrassed, although new legal protections rarely save them from a career-wrecking fate when they go public with embarrassing reports.[21] Still, not only did Daniel Ellsberg, in divulging the Pentagon papers to the news media in 1971, become the most prominent whistle-blower in the country (at least until Chelsea Manning in 2010 and Edward Snowden in 2013), but his action consolidated the meaning of the term "whistle-blower" and helped give it the quasi-heroic Robin Hood aura that it has retained to this day.

Finally, individual citizens may—as individuals—engage in political activity that garners media attention or governmental response. It is perhaps remarkable in such a large country as the United States that determined individuals, including those without obvious political resources of position or wealth, can impress themselves upon the general public in challenging power. The most spectacular example over time has no doubt been Ralph Nader, but many others, usually with narrower agendas and less enduring influence, have also made themselves heard—think of Sarah Brady and James Brady's lobbying for the "Brady bill" on gun control after James Brady, President Ronald Reagan's press secretary, was badly wounded in the attempted assassination of Reagan in 1981; or of Cindy Sheehan's lonely but very well-publicized vigil against the war in Iraq conducted outside President George W. Bush's Texas ranch retreat in 2005, in memory of her son, Casey, who was killed in action while serving in the U.S. Army in Iraq. There is also the advocacy of a group of widows of 9/11 victims that helped force a fuller accounting from the Bush administration about security failures.[22]

All of these are features of a trans-legislative or monitory democracy. They are not unique to it, but they have grown more widespread and more influential in the past half century. Several important social changes provide the conditions that have made trans-legislative democracy possible: the rise of the administrative state, the development of mechanisms in civil society for continuous public surveillance of government, the judicialization of politics, the development of internal audits in government and their public report, and the growth of an inquiring public, intermittently attentive and educated in values fit for critical inquiry.

Rise of the Administrative State.   The administrative state is one where power has shifted substantially from the legislature to relatively autonomous executive bureaucracies. It began to emerge in the United States as early as the end of the nineteenth century, but it became central to the operation of the federal government only with the New Deal reforms of the 1930s. Before 1933, there were only two important federal regulatory agencies, the Interstate Commerce Commission and the Federal Trade Commission.[23] Thereafter, the regulatory agency emerged as a powerful new hybrid form in government. James Landis, himself a chief architect of New Deal regulatory agencies, called attention to (and defended) their "quasi-legislative, quasi-executive, quasi-judicial" character.[24] Many Americans not only were unaccustomed to the authority that New Deal agencies exercised but for a long time refused to accept it. Roosevelt was loved but he was also hated, and it would be a generation or more before programs such as social security came to be taken for granted in American life. The Administrative Procedure Act of 1946, as Judge Richard Posner put it, "signified the acceptance of the administrative state as a legitimate component of the federal lawmaking system, but imposed upon it procedural constraints that have made the administrative process a good deal like the judicial."[25]

Policy initiatives of the 1960s and 1970s were influential, too. The federal budget grew enormously between 1960 and 1980, not only with growth in military spending but also with new programs in everything from medical care and medical insurance to anti-poverty programs, urban housing and transportation, and environmental and energy initiatives. While liberals typically have endorsed most of these expansions of the reach of federal power, conservatives normally drag their feet or openly resist.

None of these developments altered civic education or, for that matter, journalism. For Washington journalism, covering elections, covering the presidency, and covering Congress seemed a full plate. Each grew in complexity. The presidential primaries and the "permanent campaign" replaced party conventions for nominations. The president's weight grew as government expanded and as foreign policy became a permanently large feature of presidential responsibility in a leading world power. The operation of Congress, from the late 1960s on, became more publicly visible and more internally democratic, and, as we have seen, less controlled by custom and seniority, more a platform for newer and younger members—and therefore a far more difficult story to report.

But the bureaucracy? Larger and more autonomous than ever, hard for Congress to keep tabs on, as John Moss learned early on, executive agencies did not come into focus for the media or the public. They did not take center stage—they have found cameo roles at most—in schoolbook accounts of history. Nor are they prominent in the press. In the conceptual model of democracy Americans still work with, administrative discretion is noise in the system more than it is government by design. Although every agency operates with an external set of constraints, each is also responsive to an internal culture of its own, and all of them exercise discretion that is not broadly understood.[26]

There is now an entire academic field—public administration—whose primary concern is the legitimacy and effectiveness of government bureaucracies. The field takes as a key problem the relationship of public administration to democracy: how can a form of government dedicated to public participation delegate so much of its daily operation and decision making to a professionalized, generally unelected, and publicly unknown body of officials?[27]

The field of administrative law has generated sophisticated thinking about these issues. Scholars in this field have looked hard at what the rise of an administrative state portends for representative democracy. Yale Law School professor Charles Reich, later to be famous as the author of *The Greening of America* (1970), published "The Law of the Planned Society" in the *Yale Law Journal* in 1966, presenting a sober portrait of the difficulties of democratic participation in an administered society. "The problem of public participation begins with the question of notice," he wrote. "There is rarely any effective notice of governmental decisions in which the public, or some segment of the public, might be interested. Every day decisions are made concerning highways, dams, air safety, navigation, and hundreds of other issues. Few are reported in even the most complete newspaper. Even if there were adequate notice, the public usually lacks enough information to evaluate the kinds of decisions that planners make." How, then, is democracy to function when the growth of administrative agencies makes ours "a new multi-legislative democracy, in which Congress would perform only certain general functions of arbitration and oversight, and the remainder of its work would be carried out by many different specialized legislatures"? These new "legislatures" have a new form of "constituency"—not individuals living in a territory but organized functional bodies that participate in decision making or act as watchdogs on those who do. Of course, this raises all kinds of questions (and Reich floats many of them) about how representative these groups are, what kind of formal authority they might have, and so forth.[28]

From Occasional to Year-Round Political Participation. Americans go to the polls more frequently, and vote for more offices when they get there, than do citizens in other democracies (Switzerland is the exception). Yet voting is an activity of one or a few days a year, and it rarely excites much attention or turnout, except once every other year when national offices are at stake. Even at that, "votes in themselves are information-poor"; more targeted and sometimes more socially and psychologically satisfying forms of political expression have arisen in a variety of modes of "non-electoral democratic representation."[29] But political participation has grown in non-electoral domains. This is a sprawling topic, not easily covered, but it can at least be sketched in.

There has been a proliferation of opportunities for expressive politics. Public opinion polling was originally imagined (by George Gallup) as an alternative to political parties for identifying people's political attitudes and preferences.[30] One should not put too much faith in polls; they do not tap some underlying political essence. But they offer a more continuous and more fine-grained account of where people stand at a given moment on a range of public questions than do elections or the opinions of political party leaders speaking on behalf of "the people." Politicians have become highly cognizant of polling, and—within limits—it is a good thing that they are to some degree responsive to it. Other arenas for political expression have also grown, not only in online communication but also well before the web: improvements in cheap, easily operated printing technologies (the mimeograph machine, the photocopier, retail photocopy stores), in direct mail solicitations (for campaign contributions or for membership in voluntary organizations), in inexpensive long-distance telephone calling, and now in the widely distributed forms of communication that cell phones and smart phones enable.

Moreover, social movements have become more easily launched, and they do not wait for elections. Sociologists have been perhaps too successful in making the term "social movement" seem to be a common and permanent feature of human political life, but historical sociologists, notably Charles Tilly, show that social movements are relatively modern. Only in the early nineteenth century did the social movement become "a distinctive, connected, recognized and widely available form of public politics."[31] Social movements were rare before the 1800s, but democratization and democracies have encouraged them, and the newer communication mechanisms just mentioned have made them easier than in the past to fire up. For Tilly, social movements emerge when people make collective claims on authorities and "frequently form special-purpose associations or named coalitions, hold public meetings, communicate their programs to available media, stage processions, rallies, or demonstrations, and through all these activities make concerted public displays of worthiness, unity, numbers, and commitment."[32] The social movement "has arrived on its own terms," he declares, when their activities take place outside of the context of "electoral campaigns and management-labor struggles."[33]

Rapid and relatively inexpensive means of communication and transportation have made populous demonstrations more and more easy to stage. Telephones, direct mail advertising, cheap and widely distributed printing, broadcasting, and in recent years personal computers, laptop computers, cell phones, and the various software and social media that make them so useful—email, the web, Facebook, Twitter, YouTube, and specific web-based operations, from Wikipedia to PayPal, Craigslist, Amazon.com, and many others—facilitate the formal and informal communications by which social movement mobilization (for good or ill) thrives. Today, advanced industrial societies are "social movement societies" where social protest has become "a perpetual element" of politics rather than sporadic and where movement activity is so well organized that it must be regarded as an instrument within conventional politics.[34]

As we have seen with the Democratic Study Group, small social movements can arise inside organizations. This happens also inside professional associations that accommodate caucuses and sections within them. When accommodation does not work or when the subgroup's intentions are at cross-purposes with the parent association, the subgroup may break off as an association of its own. Both internal accommodation and occasional separations have taken place in associations of doctors, lawyers, and academics, for example, and in nearly every large business, labor, or professional society there have arisen organized women's caucuses, African American groups, gay and lesbian groups, and often regional groups to provide social bonding and social mobilization around specific interests and initiatives.

Organized interest groups have grown more numerous, more powerful, and more focused on directly influencing government. Yes, as long ago as the 1830s Alexis de Tocqueville marveled at the penchant of Americans for gathering together for common purpose in voluntary associations. Still, from the 1960s on, many new private organizations formed specifically to influence public officials in Washington and old associations for the first time established Washington offices to adapt to the changing power structure. When political scientists in the early 1980s examined organizations with offices in Washington, they discovered that 40 percent had been founded after 1960, 25 percent after 1970.[35]

Why? Political scientist Jack Walker's 1983 analysis of this question remains apt. Walker argued that (1) long-term growth in educational attainment provided "a large pool of potential recruits for citizen movements," (2) improved communications made it easier for central offices in Washington to recruit members (initially through direct mail and WATS long-distance calling) and to mobilize them for letter-writing campaigns or other active political expression, and (3) the civil rights movement and the movements that learned from its tactics and its successes raised a general awareness of shortcomings in American society, prompted a broad desire for social change, and bred a sense of crisis that stimulated participation. Walker noted also that with government programs expanding, particularly during the Johnson presidency, government agencies themselves, along with reform-minded private foundations, promoted the formation of voluntary associations among people who benefited from new social programs and among professionals and others who provided the new services, not to mention among business groups that felt threatened by new legislation on the environment, occupational health and safety, and other matters.[36] Government programs do not just respond to pressure groups; they create the opportunities that lead to their formation. With Washington more a part of the lives of all Americans than ever before, more and more groups actively turned toward Washington to gain specific policy outcomes, to protect benefits already obtained, or to monitor government activity on specific policies, unsatisfied to simply affiliate with one or the other of the leading political parties. All of this built a new set of constituencies for public-interest organizations and special-interest organizing, too.[37]

Walker's claim that the expansion of education provided new recruits for citizens' movements needs elaboration. It. sounds like common sense—but why would better-educated people be more likely to join citizens' movements? Unions recruit members through the workplace regardless of education; churches recruit members through neighborhoods and ethnic groups and families, regardless of education; even political parties recruit members regardless of education, in part by demanding so little of them—in the United States, parties really ask only that supporters subjectively identify with them and declare their identification when they register to vote. But the plethora of new civil society groups that now populate the political landscape are different. They require a generalized public orientation in at least some small part of a citizen's consciousness. And that public orientation can be elevated by the broader perspectives that higher education offers many students and by exposure to the mass media that a more sophisticated and comfortable literacy affords.

Judicialization of Politics.   There has been a judicialization of politics, particularly but by no means only in the United States. It has made the courtroom and not just the polling place a potential arena of individual political influence. Between 1850 and 1935, the U.S. Supreme Court heard just 16 cases concerning discrimination on the basis of race, religion, national origin, or sex; the plaintiff prevailed in 9 of the cases. From 1936 to 1945, there were 17 more cases, and the plaintiff won 12 times. From 1946 to 1964 there were 106 discrimination cases, and the plaintiff won 90 times.[38] Marking the change in a different way, one scholar has noted that the Supreme Court took up civil rights or civil liberties in 2 of the 160 cases it decided in 1935, but in 66 out of 132 cases decided in 1989.[39]

Greater use of the legal system for political ends rapidly increased in the 1960s. Often, individual assertions of legal claims are sponsored—that is, organizations such as the American Civil Liberties Union, the NAACP, and conservative public interest legal organizations have actively prospected for plaintiffs in lawsuits designed to advance a political agenda. At the same time, as William Haltom and Michael McCann have demonstrated, conservative advocates of "tort reform" have effectively popularized a highly distorted portrait of litigants in product liability suits as litigious, greedy, whining bad citizens and not, as is far more commonly the case, individuals who reluctantly initiate a lawsuit, usually with no prior experience of having done so. Here, too, as with the case of vote suppression, concerted efforts seek to discourage people from taking their rights as citizens seriously.[40] In fact, law professor Richard Abel has urged that more people, not fewer, should sue—that, after all, "litigation is an important form of political activity."[41] For Abel, "to assert a legal claim is to perform a vital civic obligation."[42]

The Development of Internal Audits and Their Public Report. In the military, there have been inspectors general going back to George Washington's day, but not until the post-Watergate era did the Inspectors General Act of 1978 establish a systematic plan that all cabinet-level departments and most other major federal agencies (including the Department of Defense, the Central Intelligence Agency, and the Department of Justice—and therefore the FBI) should have their own Office of Inspector General, authorized to audit the department on an ongoing basis. There are now more than sixty Offices of Inspector General with 12,000 staff members whose job it is to investigate the agencies to which they are assigned and report to both the president and Congress on their findings, with recommendations for change or even recommendations for prosecution. Usually the inspectors are looking for waste and fraud and other financial mismanagement; sometimes their efforts are far more extensive. The inspectors general (IGs), through semiannual reports on the agencies they monitor, make public an assessment of waste, fraud, and abuse of the public trust. In fiscal 2008, the IGs collectively made recommendations to save over $14 billion, conducted investigations that identified more than $4 billion the IGs were able to recover, and produced more than 6,000 indictments, more than 6,000 successful prosecutions, and nearly 5,000 suspensions and disbarments.[43]

Another development in which the government keeps watch on itself and makes this watchfulness public is the Federal Elections Commission (FEC), which came into being in 1975 after the passage of the Federal Elections Campaign Acts of 1971 and 1974. Most states have similar agencies. The FEC's budget for 2006 was $54.6 million. Campaign finance regulation has or had various components, but important features of the 1974 campaign finance legislation were found unconstitutional in the Supreme Court's 1976 ruling in *Buckley v. Valeo*. In a word, limits on contributions were judged to be a matter that government could legitimately regulate, but limits on expenditures were seen to violate the candidates' First Amendment right to free speech.

Of the various parts of campaign finance regulation, the requirement that candidates disclose the names of their contributors and the amounts of their contributions is, as political scientist Larry Sabato put it, "probably the most universally supported and certainly the most successful provision of the campaign finance law."[44] It also survived the ruling in *Citizens United v. Federal Elections Commission* (2010). The value of the disclosure requirement is limited because, as Sabato observes, the election is over before serious data analysis can take place. "Still," he argues, "disclosure serves many useful purposes, from permitting postelection enforcement of the laws to allowing connections to be made between campaign contributions and votes cast on the floor of Congress. Disclosure itself generates pressure for more reform. When campaign finance was out of sight, it was out of most people's minds; now that the trail of money can be more easily followed, indignation is only a press release away. Disclosure is the single greatest check on the excesses of campaign finance, for it encourages corrective action, whether judicial or political."[45] Congressional historian Julian Zelizer agrees: "There was a revolution in the disclosure of political information. Until the 1960s, there was little public knowledge about contributions. By 1974, that system had ended. The United States imposed some of the most stringent disclosure regulations in the world."[46]

Congress as a lawmaking body is a central institution of government. It serves also as a public debating society, both a part of government and a part of civil society. Congress not only makes laws but watches that the executive enacts them. In its watchdog capacity, Congress has long had difficulty keeping pace with the rapid expansion of administrative capacity in the executive, but it has nonetheless grown in its machinery for oversight. In 1947 there were about 1,400 staff assistants to members of the House and 600 in the Senate. In the early 1960s the comparable figures were 3,000 and 1,500, and by 1977 the number of personal staff members had doubled again.[47] Theorists of "civil society" or the "public sphere" ordinarily place that society or that sphere entirely outside government, but this is an error. Civil society overlaps with government in that the political parties—private associations that contest for government leadership—take on legislative and executive power when they control the legislative or executive branch. The actions of Congress as an investigative agency (with subpoena power) to hold the executive accountable are just as important as or more important than the news media's efforts in that vein. The work of Congress as a debating society that airs criticism of executive behavior is a source of monitorial assistance to the press and the private associations that watch for government wrongdoing. This dimension of congressional work helps to communicate and to constitute public knowledge, form a public agenda, and set a public tone.

How much do the several thousand FOIA officers and several thousand IG employees and other monitors internal to government matter? FOIA officers help journalists, historians, prisoners, corporations, and others who file FOIA requests, although often frustrating them, too. The IGs save taxpayers dollars, occasionally embarrass the departments they inspect, refer many cases to the Department of Justice for prosecution, sometimes hand a scoop to the news media, and twice a year send reports to Congress for its use in overseeing executive agencies. But compared to elections, direct congressional oversight, or public hearings, how much do these public sentinels inside the executive matter?

Clearly, the long-standing role of Congress as a check on the executive plus these innovations in executive self-surveillance do not obviate a democracy's need for journalists who get in the face of power, NGOs whose representatives ply their trade in Washington, and activists who organize mass actions in the streets. But journalists and other public-minded citizens are less alone than they once were in the task of keeping government (and to a lesser extent nongovernmental institutions) accountable. Journalists themselves are, more than ever, aggregators of relatively accessible and relatively reliable information about government and elections. There is a new environment of public information produced by government agencies, university researchers, nonprofit organizations, advocacy groups, bloggers, and many others, all contributing to a sea of information that the well-educated reporter navigates. There is much praise in journalistic circles of the virtues of "shoe-leather" reporting and "feet on the street," and rightly so, but breakthrough reporting now can come also from journalists with their digits on the digital. And today reporters who relay news to the public are themselves the beneficiaries of government investment of hundreds of millions of dollars—probably several billion dollars annually if one adds up local, state, and federal governmental auditors, inspectors, prosecutors, and enforcers of open-records and freedom-of-information statutes. This is all part of the institutionalization of monitory democracy.

Coda

By 1920, journalist and public intellectual Walter Lippmann had concluded that information about the political world "has long since become too complicated even for the most highly trained reporter." The problem, he believed, was not simply the inadequacies of individual reporters or newspapers, but "the intricacy and unwieldiness of the subject-matter."[48] As editor James Pope would complain to John Moss decades later, there was "so damn much news."[49] But already in 1920, Lippmann—thinking just of government, let alone the rest of society—observed that administration had become more important than legislation, even though it was much harder to follow, with its work spread out across time and its impact not visible in a way that reporters could measure (like votes in Congress). Journalists could comprehend the complexity of the modern world only by making use of other agencies where "a more or less expert political intelligence" hands on to the reporter reliable maps of the world. He refers to these agencies, which are located in government bureaus, inside university walls, and in independent nonprofit institutions, as "political observatories," and called for more of them—independent, nonpartisan, scientific organizations committed to an agenda of research about the political and social world they could produce in a form accessible to the competent journalist.[50] Only this would enable newspapers to offer readers a more thorough, complete, objective, and reliable portrait of relevant public life.

Much as Lippmann imagined, political observatories multiplied, and there are plenty of them now. They began in Lippmann's day—the Brookings Institution in 1921 was among the first, and the General Accounting Office (today the Government Accountability Office), also established in 1921, was the sort of government agency of accounting and accountability that Lippmann had in mind. Political observatories are often called "think tanks," a term that did not become common parlance until about 1970.[51] The very terminology of monitory democracy has arisen with its institutionalization—"think tanks," "whistle-blowers" (also coming into general use around 1970), "NGO" (a shorthand that began to gain currency in the 1980s although the term it stands for, "nongovernmental organization," began to be used in the United Nations and its affiliated organizations in the 1940s). Even the general term "civil society," several hundred years old in works of political theory, found wider currency in eastern Europe in the last decade or two before the fall of the Berlin Wall and, at about that time, became popular in Anglo-American political thought, too.

In 2006, in response to a FOIA request from the Associated Press, the Defense Department released 5,000 pages of information concerning detainees at Guantanamo. At about that time, I attended a conference of the American Society of Access Professionals (ASAP, an acronym with a sense of humor). ASAP is itself an NGO, a part of civil society, but one where, interestingly, the large majority of members are government employees—FOIA officers. FOIA activists, journalists who use FOIA, and others also belong. As several people at the conference noted, no one grows up wanting to become a FOIA officer. But the senior officers expressed and tried to pass on to the novices their commitment to the law. "We have a job that matters," ASAP president Fred Sadler insisted. And Doris Lama, a veteran FOIA officer for the Department of the Navy, called attention to the law's wide applicability—it can be used by "any person for any reason," she reminded new FOIA officers in her audience, adding, "That's a pretty good indicator that we're a democracy, isn't it?" She concluded, "I love FOIA."[52]

ASAP is a hybrid institution in the new information ecology, an independent nonprofit that serves primarily government employees. Or consider an initiative from Princeton University's Center for Information Technology Policy that has created a new database called RECAP that improves upon the existing unsearchable database of the federal court system.[53] (The federal database is PACER; RECAP spells it backward.) Princeton is an independent, nonprofit educational institution (although, of course, any major research university, public or private, receives a significant portion of its financing from government). What it did in this case was to voluntarily take on a task that should have been the government's. Similarly, the Sunlight Foundation, a Washington, D.C., "open government" nonprofit advocacy group, established in 2006, worked with ProPublica, a nonprofit online investigative news start-up founded in 2008, to set up a public, accessible, searchable database consisting of all the 2007–2008 required federal filings of foreign agents in the United States. That effort evolved into www.foreign.influenceexplorer.com. Using the U.S. Department of Justice's own data, based on the Federal Agents Registration Act of 1938, which requires foreign agents who seek to influence or lobby the federal government to register with the Justice Department, the database enables reporters—and everybody else, too—to learn which foreign entity (government, tourist bureau, airline, or any other foreign entity seeking to influence U.S. policies) contacted which individuals or offices of the U.S. government.[54]

There is both sunlight and confusion in the proliferation of these cooperative and hybrid efforts and, as I have noted, there is no commonly agreed-upon map of them, nor do I have such a map in my back pocket waiting to be unfolded. In fact, it will not be unfolded but downloaded. Keane, Rosanvallon, and the others I have discussed here are among its co-cartographers. Since this map will be online, it will change continuously over time, displaying the past as well as the present.

eight

Disclosure and Its Discontents

Public life has not become inexorably more transparent. The world is more governed by information kept secure from prying eyes than ever before.[1] Nor is this only a matter of military secrets. Any of the hundreds of millions of people who transact important parts of their lives online may have handfuls or even scores of passwords that allow them to access operations denied to others. As our lives are more interconnected, they are more visible to others in ways that serve us but that also endanger us. In some domains of common experience, society has found benefit in making things less open. For instance, courtrooms are normally open to the public, and in criminal proceedings the Constitution guarantees an accused person "a speedy and public trial." However, not only are there exceptions to this right of publicity (as in the trials of minors), but a growing share of legal proceedings reach settlement without trial, and with the parties agreeing not to disclose the details of the settlement. There is also a growing array of alternative dispute resolution processes that operate informally and without a public record.[2]

Secrecy, in short, is not disappearing. It remains at the heart of democracy, certainly as it has been practiced in the United States since the adoption of the Australian or "secret" ballot in the 1890s. There is a plausible argument—the English political thinker John Stuart Mill presented it in the mid-nineteenth century—that democracy works better if citizens are publicly held accountable for their votes. But this argument lost out to the concern that public voting subjected relatively powerless individuals to threat, arm-twisting, or bribery by the powerful (notably, employees were vulnerable to coercion by their employers). In designing democracy, a realistic assessment of the consequences of unequal power for the independence of individual voters overcame the conceptual appeal of openness.

So the period I have focused on here, which gave birth to so many important transparency-oriented reforms, was the age of secrecy and the age of transparency, the era of spin and of disclosure, a time of both confidences and the overturning of confidence. (It was in these ways a time much like our own.)

A more transparent government and more transparent social relations emerged in the 1960s and 1970s in part because transparency was a useful means to some other end, not so much because advocates sought transparency for its own sake. Key advances had more to do with relations among the branches of government, especially the desire of Congress to monitor the executive, than they did with an ideological commitment to a right to know. FOIA was established to increase congressional power relative to the executive, and to this day it covers the executive agencies, not Congress or the courts. NEPA and environmental impact assessment began as a mechanism for Congress to hold executive feet to the fire; the opening of the impact assessment process to public review was a late addition to the legislation as it evolved in Congress, not its guiding spirit.

Transparency was in the air before, and separate from, advocacy of participatory democracy, the growing sexual openness of the sixties, and the women's movement of the 1960s and 1970s. It was coincident with the civil rights movement, a general wave of reaction against traditional social hierarchies, and the post-1945 expansion of higher education with an increasingly critical and pluralistic ethos at its heart.

Transparency wears the cloak of the natural and spontaneous, but its practical enactment requires rules and procedures. Rules require bureaucracy and enforcement. They could not advance without pricing, measurement, record keeping, data gathering, deadlines, transcripts, filing. And of course transparency does not happen without the personnel to handle its various tasks. Whole new careers and professional identities have emerged—for example, in the area of environmental impact assessment, the rapid expansion of a specialization in environmental law, and new interstitial civil service positions in the federal bureaucracy (FOIA officers after 1966, inspectors general after 1978), with similar developments in the states. In time, transparency became a powerful cultural norm, an almost unquestioned good, gaining nearly constitutional stature.

Although openness became part of American culture through the work of specific authors, advocates, and innovators, it was also stimulated by the glamour and the broad resonance of specific events. The Kennedy-Nixon television debates in 1960, Ralph Nader's 1965 exposé of the automobile industry's wholesale neglect of safety considerations in designing cars (and public denials of it), and Daniel Ellsberg's act of whistle-blowing in releasing the Pentagon papers to the news media in 1971 all had unusual and enduring influence. In consolidating some of the gains of transparency reforms, including the passage of the 1974 amendments that greatly strengthened FOIA, Watergate provided wind behind the sails of openness. Sociologists, including me, are trained to see structures and processes, not events, and to focus on institutions and roles, not individuals, but historians may remind us that events, unpredicted but impossible to ignore, and forceful individual personalities, not just generational cohorts or offices and roles, matter. I see no alternative to blending the sociological and historical in order to understand social change.

How much did any or all of the developments I have discussed in this book have to do with what Ronald Inglehart in 1977 (and in many subsequent works) referred to as the "silent revolution"? Inglehart argued on the basis of survey data that "the values of Western publics have been shifting from an overwhelming emphasis on material well-being and physical security toward greater emphasis on the quality of life."[3] The unprecedented extension of economic security to millions of people in the postwar Western world made it possible for a focus on economic security to recede relative to other values that Inglehart dubbed "postmaterialist." Moreover, he suggested, in the postmaterialist culture, mass publics became more directly involved in "elite-challenging" rather than simply "elite-directed" political actions. The willingness of people to involve themselves in political decision making beyond voting is associated also with "a decline in the legitimacy of hierarchical authority, patriotism, religion, and so on, which leads to declining confidence in institutions."[4]

Inglehart's argument has held up over time. Later surveys showed that the younger people who in 1970 had been much more likely than older people to adopt postmaterialist values continued decades later to hold them still. In other words, Inglehart had located a "generational" or "cohort" effect rather than an "age" effect—those who were postmaterialist in 1970 did not grow more materialist as they aged but tended to stay as postmaterialist over time, or grow even slightly more so.[5] After the 1970s, radical challenges to the deference conventionally granted to the clergy, to medical professionals, and to lawyers would recede and a new stability would set in, but people's attitudes were not reset to 1950 or 1960. People have continued to trust the doctors, lawyers, accountants, therapists, and journalists they turn to, yet they do so in the Ronald Reagan style: "trust but verify." And verification is now made much more possible with online access that links individuals to a wealth of data and advice (including counsel from one another), some of it very good.

The Kennedy-Nixon televised debates were a symbol of a new age, even though it would not be until 1976 that presidential candidates met again before the cameras and only at that point that the practice became well institutionalized. But the Kennedy-Nixon debates and other live broadcasts of political events, to quote Daniel Dayan and Elihu Katz once more, "bred the expectation of openness in politics and diplomacy."[6]

Vital as the great public theater of presidential politics has proved, private events were just as important. In the period from 1960 to 1980, the public and private were intertwined as perhaps never before—or at least public consciousness of their interconnection was greater than ever, except in monarchies, where the family of the king and the fate of the kingdom had long been indistinguishable. In a 1973 end-of-the-year interview, Walter Cronkite tried to explain Watergate in terms of the blend of the personal and the political: "Watergate just happened to come at the same time as the demand for honesty in relations between the sexes, in advertising, in ecology, in almost everything. . . . That's what is forcing the President's hand right now."[7] A culture of honesty and disclosure, Cronkite was suggesting, had become a force in politics.

New linking mechanisms mediated between the personal and the political, newly imbued with a spirit of openness. Prominent among them, as Ellen Herman noted, was "a booming business in psychological expertise" with a powerful influence on American postwar culture. She finds the fingerprints of the humanistic psychology of Carl Rogers and Abraham Maslow on the Port Huron Statement, the long essay-style proclamation of principles drafted at the launching of Students for a Democratic Society. She sees in the women's movement, too—notably in its consciousness-raising groups, which encouraged "personal sharing in a non-judgmental context"—an echo of Rogers's client-centered therapy.[8]

Another key set of mediators were teachers, perhaps especially college teachers in the humanities and social sciences. These teachers and their teachings were changing. Regarding the teaching of American history, Gary Nash describes a sharp move "away from the male-oriented, Eurocentric, and elitist approaches that had dominated for so long," in part because students coming to graduate school to study history were less white, male, Protestant, and upper-class than before. This was cause for lament among some older historians. As late as 1962, Carl Bridenbaugh, then president of the American Historical Association, expressed concern that "many of the younger practitioners of our craft, and those who are still apprentices, are products of lower middle-class or foreign origins, and their emotions not infrequently get in the way of historical reconstructions."[9] Apparently, historians to the manor born did not have emotions to interfere with the scrupulous prosecution of their work, while scholars from lower-class, immigrant, and Jewish backgrounds polluted the pursuit of truth. The newly recruited teachers tended to be alive to or actively involved in the civil rights movement and other reform and protest struggles of the 1960s, and this prompted new questions in history, particularly about race and gender relations and the role of class and working people. The rapidly decolonizing Third

World interested the new, younger generation of historians, as did the colonization of Native Americans (the very term "Native American" began to replace "Indian" in general usage in the 1960s).[10]

One would not want to exaggerate the influence of the classroom on broad social and cultural change, let alone the U.S. history class, less and less frequently required for college students by the 1960s and 1970s. But neither should the classroom be neglected, especially when there was such a rapid expansion of college enrollments, federal research dollars, and the psychic investment of millions of families in the transformative powers of college. Not unrelated is that book publishing skyrocketed in the same years. The number of new titles and new editions increased from 11,000 in 1950 to 36,000 in 1970.[11] Still, the change I am getting at is more than the sum of these figures. It is a cultural shift that has provided new tools for openness and new faith in disclosure, notably among journalists who have taken on the professional value that their ideal job is to get the story behind the story, the information that someone in power would like not to provide. The change is also that there is a receptivity to or a market for critique, dissent, and unmasking—and, in the digital era, many new resources for making the world visible.

Each of the different episodes I have discussed in this book had its own rhetoric, its own purposes, its own consequences. They are cultural cousins, but they are not clones of one another. The rhetoric promoting FOIA emerged from the Cold War; that surrounding unit pricing and other consumer information reforms rested in a mix of backward-looking nostalgia for personal relations, a distrust of mass marketing and mass merchandising, and a faith that accurate information could empower befuddled consumers to become the rational actors that free-market economic theory presumed they should be. The purpose of FOIA was to keep the executive branch of government accountable to Congress. The drive for the Legislative Reorganization Act of 1970 aimed to give the liberal majority of that time legitimate control of the congressional agenda. The purpose of NEPA was to articulate a national environmental policy to "secure the blessings of liberty to ourselves and our posterity" with respect to the wholesomeness of the environment.

The consequences of these various developments have varied. FOIA became an influential force for holding the executive accountable. NEPA produced the environmental impact statement, which for decades, and to this day, has curtailed government activity that did not modify its intentions with the good of the environment in view. The Legislative Reorganization Act helped empower that era's liberal Congress while opening up much legislative activity to critical scrutiny from lobbyists, public interest groups, and citizens. Unit pricing and other supermarket reforms contributed to providing "democracy by disclosure" in the consumer marketplace. And the tougher, less compliant news media blended professionalism with a commitment to holding government accountable that—even in the face of partisan journalism on cable TV and a wide variety of spicier, speedier, or snarkier models online—stands as what reporters young and old take to be journalism's gold standard: original, fact-based, well-sourced, and analytically sophisticated reporting. Together these developments express a declining deference to power and an augmentation of supervisory, monitorial, public, and judicial oversight of government, corporate, professional, and even interpersonal actions.

If, as Chapter 7 suggests, we have entered a new democratic era since 1945—an era of monitory democracy, a plurally accountable democracy not so much better or worse than earlier models of democracy but different—then, through checks and balances, institutions of review, oversight, and monitorship, there is less and less room for arbitrary or unchecked power.[12] This has not produced a utopian political system in the United States or anywhere else. And yet its operation is, or at least should be, a reminder that the system of representative democracy that it replaces was no paragon of transparency or of information-based decisions by either citizens or their representatives. It was not *the* way to democracy; it was one way.

When I began the research for this book, I thought I would find the dawn of openness in "The Sixties," meaning by that the mass-movement sixties, the cultural-revolution sixties. That sixties is certainly part of the story, but when I learned that the effort to pass a Freedom of Information Act went back to 1955, that FOIA was enacted as an amendment and revision of the Administrative Procedure Act of 1946, and that it found support in national journalism associations that had already expressed concern about government secrecy, I had to acknowledge that my original expectations were mistaken. Complications multiplied when I learned that a key agent of making Congress a more open institution was the Democratic Study Group, founded in 1959, and when it became clear to me that policies to make the pricing, ingredients, and freshness of supermarket products more visible to consumers had been under discussion among some leaders in Congress as early as 1961. All this was under way before American ground troops went to Vietnam, before an antiwar movement existed, before Students for a Democratic Society was founded, before a modern women's movement took off.

A mass base for environmentalism emerged not later than the first Earth Day on April 22, 1970, but the legislation that brought environmental impact statements into existence was signed into law months earlier, based in part on the work of Lynton Keith Caldwell, a public policy professor who had written on the topic as early as 1963, and in part on legislative efforts in Congress in the late 1950s and early

1960s. Earth Day's inventor, U.S. senator Gaylord Nelson, had been sponsoring environmentalist legislation for more than a decade, as he sought to kick-start a broad educational effort to highlight environmental issues. There were environmental activists a decade earlier, including opponents of DDT spraying who helped inspire Rachel Carson's 1962 book *Silent Spring.* A great deal happened in this "liberal hour," as G. Calvin MacKenzie and Robert Weisbrot called the early 1960s, before mass public support rallied to the cause.[13]

General public support proved less crucial in the thrust toward openness than I expected, while leadership in Washington, sometimes presidential leadership, was more important. Among consumer advocates, the resonance of President Kennedy's rhetoric about a consumer "bill of rights," although not matched by his actions, was powerful and enduring. President Johnson was no enthusiast of the Freedom of Information Act, but he signed it. Nor was President Nixon very interested in environmental policy, but he signed the National Environmental Policy Act and appointed people of firm environmental convictions to the new Council on Environmental Quality. Presidents matter.

Even so, most of the attention in this book has focused on members of history's supporting cast, not its marquee players. There is no monument to Esther Peterson and no biography; one biography of John Moss, albeit written by a friend and protégé and not a professional historian; one biography of Henry "Scoop" Jackson, one of Philip Hart, one of Gaylord Nelson, none of DSG staff director Richard Conlon, one (just published in 2014) of Lynton Keith Caldwell. Few reporters who make a difference become celebrities, let alone the whistle-blowers they sometimes depend on—reporters Edie Lederer and Jean Heller and whistle-blower Peter Buxtun are not household names even though the Tuskegee Experiment they revealed is relatively well known. And yet all of these people took initiative, took risks, and played a significant role in making a more open society. Yes, the public mattered, presidents mattered, but social change in this case was powerfully shaped not just by the foot soldiers and the generals but by the second lieutenants I have focused on here. All of these people, in one fashion or another, contributed to the formation of a monitory democracy. All of them were in touch with a critical consciousness whose sources and whose mechanisms of influence lie behind or, to put it more strongly, underlie, the headline persons and events that both journalists and historians usually consider.

The rise of cultural support and institutional mechanisms for a right to know need not be a permanent social transformation. There are shifts to and fro. When documents become more routinely made public, politicians and bureaucrats find ways around using documents. Still, will doctors start deciding they were right not to communicate honestly with their patients? Will gays and lesbians return to the closet? Will "sell by" dates again be coded? Will the Freedom of Information Act be repealed? None of these things is impossible, but neither is any of them easy to imagine. Sometimes the human spirit shifts. When it does, and when it does in a way that enhances human capacities, we should recognize it and accord it the honor it deserves.

There could have been many more chapters in this book as well as extensions of the chapters already here. The whole history of FOIA since 1966 deserves more attention, including not only the changes in the law and its uses but the record of an organization such as the American Society of Access Professionals, an independent, nongovernmental organization founded in 1980 that provides FOIA officers with professional educational training for their work and brings them into contact with the "requester community" of journalists, lawyers, and others who make use of the Freedom of Information Act. The early efforts at truth in packaging and labeling that I have chronicled here went much further later, culminating in the Nutritional Labeling and Education Act of 1990. The landmark efforts that required warning labels on cigarettes were part of what is likely the most consequential public health campaign in American history.

Other chapters could include the history of public reporting requirements for physicians, trespassing on what is otherwise the strongly protected confidentiality of doctor-patient relationships. Also of great interest would be the politics and the cultural shifts that led to Megan's Law, passed in New Jersey in 1994, and similar laws in all other states, as required by a federal act of 1994. Megan's Law was named in memory of seven-year-old Megan Kanka, who was raped and murdered by a released sex offender living in her neighborhood. The public registries of convicted sex offenders who have served their time are controversial; the sentiment in their favor is strong, but so is the concern that they violate civil liberties and institutionalize a kind of vigilante justice.

There are significant journalistic accounts of the crisis in the Catholic church over the disclosure of sexual abuse by members of the Catholic clergy—the *Boston Globe*'s reporting on the topic won the 2003 Pulitzer Prize for public service journalism. There is a valuable study of the role of litigation in forcing these disclosures, but there is much more research to do on the responses of the church, on the groups of victims of the sexual abuse and their families who have organized to keep pressure on the church, and on the wider repercussions for Catholic life and for other religious organizations.[14] For decades, when abuses were reported, the church and other authorities quietly set the matter aside. What was hushed into embarrassed silence in the 1960s and 1970s became devastatingly visible by 2000, even forcing a number of dioceses to declare bankruptcy in the face of lawsuits over sexual crimes.[15] Other religion-related topics deserve study for a more comprehensive history of openness—this would certainly include examination of the impact of the Vatican II reforms and such changes as the shift of the Catholic mass from Latin to the vernacular. And it would need to be understood in relation to the growing conviction of Americans, regardless of what church they affiliate with, that their church is not the only arbiter of morality. In 1955, only 4 percent of adults reported that they had moved from the religion in which they were raised to another; by 1985 it was 33 percent.[16] When there is no fail-safe authority even for moral truths, people become open to openness itself.

Think also of the important (and much censored) writing of Judy Blume. Her fiction for preteens and teens takes up questions that are of great concern to children but were almost entirely absent from children's literature before her—menstruation, masturbation, wet dreams, unwanted erections, breasts too large or too small or too early or too late, and other embarrassments of puberty. A divorced mother of two whom *Newsweek* described, tongue in cheek, as "a suburban flop . . . and a failure at golf, tennis and cooking," Judy Blume turned out to be a success at clear, engaging, affecting fiction. By 2004 she had published twenty-four books, almost all for the juvenile market, and they had sold 75 million copies with translations in more than twenty languages.[17]

The 1970s saw the emergence of a strong pedagogy of open and guilt-free communication. In 1969, in the early stages of the self-conscious women's movement, Nancy Hawley organized a study group at Emmanuel College in Boston to explore issues of women's health and sexuality. At the time, she later recalled, "there wasn't a single text written by women about women's health and sexuality." The study group constituted itself as the Boston Women's Health Collective and produced a 138-page course booklet that the New England Free Press published in 1970. Without advertising, the thirty-cent booklet quickly sold 150,000 copies. In 1973 the collective, now with Simon & Schuster as its publisher, authored *Our Bodies, Ourselves* and became a multimedia, multibook organization. *Our Bodies, Ourselves* has been translated into seventeen languages and Braille and has sold over four million copies.[18] It has gone through multiple editions, the latest of them published in 2011.

As with Judy Blume's work, entertainment television came increasingly to be self-consciously pedagogical. This was most famously the case with Norman Lear's pathbreaking situation comedies: *All in the Family* (CBS, 1971–1979), *Maude* (CBS, 1972–1978), *Sanford and Son* (NBC, 1972–1977), and others. These shows talked out loud about deeply uncomfortable conflicts in American life—between the sexes, between the generations, and, perhaps most shocking of all, between blacks and whites.

Other relevant topics would include the rapid publication as paperback books for general consumption of significant government reports soon after their release and later the huge development of "e-government" publications; the growing prominence of public confessions and apologies by governments, heads of state, individual politicians, and universities (Brown and Yale, for example, spoke frankly about the slave-owning and slavery-supporting views of their founders); the increasing publicness of once forbidden topics, from homosexuality to death and dying; and the open adoption movement, through which adoptive parents could communicate with birth mothers and sometimes birth fathers in a system that had once operated with complete impersonality through social service agencies.

This is only a sampling. Most of these topics are separately familiar. Listing them together in a few pages, however, makes one wonder why, in the midst of so much that has gone so wrong in our own times, we have done so little to recognize these considerable achievements as an important, far-reaching cultural change.

This is not to assume that openness is a supreme good. In a number of ways, nontransparency is a requirement of human survival, of political democracy, of the protection of vulnerable populations, of civility in social interaction, and of human dignity. To make good on this claim would take a book in itself, but I can list the largest reasons quickly:

- *Human survival.* While governments protect all sorts of things in the name of "national security" that have nothing to do with national security, there is nonetheless information that would actually endanger national security and even human survival if made public. No one should want to see information on how to build nuclear weapons or how to steal them published on a website or in a newspaper. The same pertains to biological and chemical weapons. The world will always have its share of fanatics, practical jokers, and mentally or emotionally unstable people, one or more of whom might use that information, for a cause or a whim or a delusion, to murder tens of thousands, or possibly many, many more.

- *Supporting political democracy.* The secret ballot is a hallmark of democracy, enabling citizens who could face intimidation at the polls if their intended vote was known and could likewise face retribution after voting from others who objected to how they voted. In the nineteenth century, employees could lose their jobs if it was known that they voted contrary to the wishes of their employers. Second, secrecy protects government employees who leak information to the news media; these whistle-blowers sometimes take a grave risk when leaking information. Even with whistle-blower protection statutes, the best protection for those who leak is not to become known as leakers. Third, secrecy or confidentiality of deliberation in meetings inside the government enables full and fair deliberation that would be curbed or chilled by ongoing publicity. This is true in the executive branch (where such deliberations are protected from FOIA disclosure), and it is a serious concern that members of Congress and congressional staffers express in resisting the opening of markup sessions and some other committee and subcommittee deliberations to the press and the public.

- *Protecting vulnerable populations.* A case in point would be the Supreme Court decision (*NAACP v. Alabama,* 1958) that found the Alabama chapter of the NAACP to be within its rights to withhold its membership lists from the state of Alabama. In the 1950s, for a black person to be a member of this leading group of civil rights activists was asking for trouble—harassment, threats, bullying, firing from a job, physical violence, even murder. To a significant degree, Alabama sheltered white terrorist organizations; forcing the NAACP to be transparent about its membership rolls would have exposed its members to dangerous white citizens. To take a much simpler example, parents withhold information from children that would upset, confuse, or traumatize them. This is the classic meaning of paternalism (or what we might better call "parentalism"). All parents learn or instinctively adopt some version of it—not everything the parent knows can be or should be communicated to their children.

- *Maintaining civility in social interaction.* People learn not to casually say to others everything that is on their minds. Avoiding insult, avoiding embarrassment, and avoiding making someone ill at ease in everyday life are important and humane goals that are frequently more important than speaking every inch of the truth. Such everyday uses of nontransparency lubricate all the small encounters of life that make society function; in that context, total honesty would be almost freakish. There is such a thing as tact, and it helps smooth social life in ways that make achieving larger goals more possible.

- *Enabling human dignity.* Nontransparency is important to the full flourishing of human individuals in two ways. First, it protects privacy—the shielding of personal information from the public. Second, it protects intimacy, the sharing of information with a small set of selected others, usually spouses, lovers, very close friends, and trusted authority figures (clergy, physicians, therapists, attorneys).

There is much more conceptual work to be done to think through when transparency should be vigorously pursued and when it would weaken other institutions, relationships, and values we cherish. But while there is no way to quantify what the new culture of disclosure has done to improve the lot of human beings, and then to balance that against what harm disclosure has done, it seems to me important to acknowledge and honor the good. My mother once told me that her favorite song was "The Inch Worm," the plaintive Frank Loesser melody from the 1952 movie *Hans Christian Andersen*. Danny Kaye, playing Andersen, watches an inchworm and sings to it, "Inch worm, inch worm, measuring the marigolds / You and your arithmetic, you'll probably go far / Inch Worm, inch Worm, measuring the marigolds / Seems to me you'd stop and see how beautiful they are." A fuller history may find that the beauty of openness is more sullied than it looks to me now, but there is a lot of beauty in what has been achieved through openness in the past half century. Millions of people have been unchained from exclusion, silence, and ignorance and are now able to enjoy the world in ways once possible only for the privileged, and their liberation has enriched all of us. Others have taken advantage of new possibilities in the Freedom of Information Act or in environmental impact statements in ways that have brought to light governmental travesty and crime, in the former case, or have sidetracked or modified or simply stopped initiatives that would have done significant damage to our common environment, in the latter. These are not small things; it seems to me we'd stop and see how beautiful they are.

Notes

1. A Cultural Right to Know

1. The website for the Thomas Jefferson Foundation, the private foundation that operates Jefferson's home, Monticello, and compiles the online *Thomas Jefferson Encyclopedia,* lists in one part of the website thirty-eight famous Jefferson quotations—and forty-eight spurious ones. To read more about "information is the currency of democracy," see www.monticello.org/site /jefferson/information-currency-democracy-quotation. The earliest mention the Thomas Jefferson Foundation has located that attributes this quotation to Jefferson is 1987. Various websites attribute the quote to Jefferson—for instance, ThinkExist.com with its motto "Finding Quotations Was Never This Easy!" or BookBrowse.com (both accessed July 14, 2014). That Jefferson never said or wrote this is further confirmed in email to the author from Anna Berkeles, research librarian, Thomas Jefferson Foundation, June 7, 2013.

2. Ralph Nader, *The Ralph Nader Reader* (New York: Seven Stories Press, 2000). "Information is the currency of democracy" appears in both Nader's January 10, 1986, article from the *New Statesman,* "Knowledge Helps Citizens, Secrecy Helps Bureaucrats" (51) and his December 2, 1996, article from *Forbes,* "Digital Democracy in Action" (403). In an important early critique of the Freedom of Information Act ("Freedom from Information: The Act and the Agencies"), Nader wrote: "A well informed citizenry is the lifeblood of democracy; and in all arenas of government, information, particularly timely

information, is the currency of power." See "Freedom from Information: The Act and the Agencies," *Harvard Civil Rights–Civil Liberties Law Review* 5 (1970): 1–15, at 1.

3. Gerald Markowitz and David Rosner, *Deceit and Denial: The Deadly Politics of Industrial Pollution* (Berkeley: University of California Press, 2002), 3.

4. David M. O'Brien, *The Public's Right to Know* (New York: Praeger, 1981), 32.

5. Hugh Heclo, "The Sixties' False Dawn: Awakenings, Movements, and Postmodern Policy-making," in Brian Balogh, ed., *Integrating the Sixties* (University Park: Pennsylvania State University Press, 1996), 34–63, at 57.

6. Interview with Sarah Cohen, September 24, 2009, former *Washington Post* reporter, in 2009 professor of public policy at Duke University, and now a reporter and editor at the *New York Times*.

7. James Wilson, cited in O'Brien, *The Public's Right to Know,* 38.

8. "Draft Structural Amendments to the Constitution, ante-27 June," in John P. Kaminski, Gaspare J. Saladino, Charles H. Schoenleber, and Margaret A. Hogan, eds., *The Documentary History of the Ratification of the Constitution Digital Edition* (Charlottesville: University of Virginia Press, 2009), 10:1548–1549.

9. Patrick Henry and George Mason, cited in O'Brien, *The Public's Right to Know,* 39.

10. Cooper's remarks (from a speech at Temple Emanu-El in New York) are cited in an editorial, "The Right to Know," *New York Times,* January 23, 1945. The Times calls it "a good new phrase for an old freedom."

11. Simon Hoggart, "Once Again, Bafflement Abroad," *New York Times,* March 23, 1994. Hoggart had served as Washington correspondent for the *Observer* and was a political reporter for the *Guardian* at the time.

12. Amy Farrell, "Attentive to Difference: *Ms.* Magazine, Coalition Building and Sisterhood," in Stephanie Gilmore, ed., *Feminist Coalitions: Historical Perspectives on Second-Wave Feminism in the United States* (Urbana: University of Illinois Press, 2008), 48–62.

13. John B. Thompson, "The New Visibility," *Theory, Culture and Society* 22 (2005): 31–51, at 38.

14. Dominique Mehl, "The Public on the Television Screen: Towards a Public Sphere of Exhibition," in Sonia Livingstone, ed., *Audiences and Publics* (Bristol, UK: Intellect Books, 2005), 77–96, at 90.

15. On Johnson's gall bladder operation, see Robert E. Gilbert, "The Political Effects of Presidential Illness: The Case of Lyndon B. Johnson," *Political Psychology* 16, no. 4 (December 1995): 761–776. On the Eisenhower-Johnson meeting, see Jack Valenti, "Memorandum of Presidential Visit with General Eisenhower," October 13, 1965, entered into the President's daily diary, Lyndon B. Johnson Presidential Library, Austin, Texas. The phrase "abdominal showman" became a popular joke as George Dixon reported in his "Washington Scene" column in the *Washington Post*, November 6, 1965.

16. Rick Perlstein, "Betty Ford, Pioneer," *New York Times,* July 12, 2011.

17. Betty Ford, "Betty Ford Today: Still Speaking Out" (interview by Gloria Steinem), *Ms.,* April 1984, 41–42, 94–95, at 42. See also John Robert Greene, *Betty Ford* (Lawrence: University Press of Kansas, 2004), 45–51, and Ron Nessen, *It Sure Looks Different from the Inside* (Chicago: Play Press, 1978), 19–28. A valuable discussion of changing doctor-patient relations is Jonathan Imber, "Doctor No Longer Knows Best," in Alan Wolfe, ed., *America at Century's End* (Berkeley: University of California Press, 1991), 298–317.

18. Donald Oken, "What to Tell Cancer Patients," *Journal of the American Medical Association* 175, no. 13 (April 1, 1961): 86–94.

19. Dennis H. Novack, Robin Plumer, Raymond L. Smith, Herbert Ochitill, Gary R. Morrow, and John M. Bennett, "Changes in Physicians' Attitudes toward Telling the Cancer Patient," *Journal of the American Medical Association* 241, no. 9 (March 2, 1979): 897–899.

20. Elisabeth Kübler-Ross, *On Death and Dying* (New York: Macmillan, 1969).

21. David J. Rothman, *Strangers at the Bedside* (New York: Basic Books, 1991).

22. Ibid., 89.

23. Joshua Gamson, *Freaks Talk Back* (Chicago: University of Chicago Press, 1991), 68.

24. Ibid., 70.

25. Ibid., 100.

26. Ibid., 118.

27. Ibid., 167.

28. Thomas Nagel, "Concealment and Exposure," *Philosophy and Public Affairs* 27 (1998): 3–30. On civil inattention, see Erving Goffman, *Relations in Public* (New York: Basic Books, 1971). Goffman uses the term many times in

this book, defining it as "persons circumspectly treating one another with polite and glancing concern while each goes about his own separate business" (331–332). On the decision legitimating the privacy from government of the NAACP's membership lists, see *N.A.A.C.P. v. Alabama*, 357 U.S. 449 (1958).

29. Ann Douglas, *Terrible Honesty: Mongrel Manhattan in the 1920s* (New York: Farrar, Straus and Giroux, 1995), 33–34.

30. Cas Wouters, *Informalization: Manners and Emotion since 1890* (London: Sage, 2007).

31. In *Grand Expectations: The United States, 1945–1974* (New York: Oxford University Press, 1996), prominent historian James Patterson offers a sentence on the Freedom of Information Act and a couple of pages on campaign finance reform with but a single sentence on disclosure, no mention of informed consent in medicine, and half a dozen mentions of Gerald Ford but none of Betty Ford. In a popular history of the 1970s with the striking title *It Seemed like Nothing Happened: The Tragedy and Promise of America in the 1970s* (New York: Holt, Rinehart and Winston, 1982), Peter Carroll mentions campaign finance reform, but without noting that disclosure was among its provisions. He does not mention informed consent in medicine or medical research, nor the Freedom of Information Act (passed in 1966 but made into a significant force only when it was strengthened in 1974). Carroll mentions the National Environmental Policy Act and environmental impact statements (125), the 1974 campaign finance reform (186), and Betty Ford's appearance on *60 Minutes* (198) when she said she expected her daughter might one day have an affair, that premarital sex might reduce the divorce rate, and that she applauded the Supreme Court's *Roe v. Wade* decision. In a more recent volume on the 1970s, its title a wry comment on Carroll's work, Edward D. Berkowitz's *Something Happened: A Political and Cultural Overview of the Seventies* (New York: Columbia University Press, 2006), there is no mention of FOIA, campaign finance legislation, or informed consent in medicine, and although Gerald Ford turns up about thirty times, Betty Ford appears just once—for her remark on *60 Minutes*. Few of these topics turn up in Bruce J. Schulman's *The Seventies: The Great Shift in American Culture, Society, and Politics* (New York: Free Press, 2001), where the Gerald-to-Betty score is 13–0.

32. *Cohen v. California*, 403 U.S. 15 (1971).

33. Mary Graham, *Democracy by Disclosure: The Rise of Technopopulism* (Washington, DC: Brookings Institution, 2002); Archon Fung, Mary Graham, and David Weil, *Full Disclosure: The Perils and Promise of Transparency* (Cam-

bridge: Cambridge University Press, 2007); James T. Hamilton, "Pollution as News: Media and Stock Market Reactions to the Toxics Release Inventory Data," *Journal of Environmental Economics and Management* 28, no. 1 (1995): 98–113; and James T. Hamilton, *Regulation through Revelation: The Origin, Politics, and Impacts of the Toxics Release Inventory Program* (New York: Cambridge University Press, 2005).

34. Alasdair MacIntyre, *Secularization and Moral Change* (London: Oxford University Press, 1967), 24.

35. Dennis Thompson, "Democratic Secrecy," *Political Science Quarterly* 114 (Summer 1999): 181–193.

2. Origins of the Freedom of Information Act

1. James Madison to W. T. Barry, August 4, 1822, in *The Writings of James Madison,* ed. Gaillard Hunt (New York: G. P. Putnam's Sons, 1900–1910), 9:103–109.

2. Harold L. Cross, *The People's Right to Know: Legal Access to Public Records and Proceedings* (New York: Columbia University Press, 1953), 129.

3. See Subcommittee on Administrative Practice and Procedure of the Committee on the Judiciary, U.S. Senate, "Freedom of Information Act Source Book: Legislative Materials, Cases, Articles," 93rd Cong., 2nd sess. (Washington, DC: Government Printing Office, 1974). This useful compendium reprints statements from the *Congressional Record,* including remarks using the Madison quotation presented by Reps. David S. King (D-Utah), Cornelius Gallagher (D-N.J.), and Donald Rumsfeld (R-Ill.), and by Sen. Edward Long (D-Mo.), on 54, 81, 72, and 93.

4. For instance, in a 2012 Congressional Research Service report, Wendy Ginsberg, Maeve Carey, L. Elaine Halchin, and Natalie Keegan, "Government Transparency and Secrecy: An Examination of Meaning and Its Use in the Executive Branch," Congressional Research Service, Report R42817, November 8, 2012, 1.

5. Kate Doyle, "The End of Secrecy: U.S. National Security and the Imperative for Openness," *World Policy Journal,* Spring 1999, 34–51, at 37.

6. Clark Hoyt, "Information That Doesn't Come Freely," *New York Times,* May 11, 2008. See also Nina Bernstein, "Few Details on Immigrants Who Died in Custody," *New York Times,* May 5, 2008.

7. U.S. Department of Justice, Office of Information Policy, *FOIA Post,* "Summary of Annual FOIA Reports for Fiscal Year 2008," www.justice.gov/oip /foiapost/2009foiapost16.htm, accessed August 3, 2013.

8. National Security Archive, "FOIA in the News—2004–2006," www.gwu .edu/~nsarchiv/nsa/foia/stories.htm, accessed March 16, 2011.

9. Sarah Cohen, testimony on behalf of the Sunshine in Government Initiative, Senate Judiciary Committee, March 15, 2011.

10. Ibid.

11. Philip H. Melanson, *Secrecy Wars: National Security, Privacy, and the Public's Right to Know* (Washington, DC: Brassey's, 2001), 31. On Marks, see John Marks, *The Search for the "Manchurian Candidate": The CIA and Mind Control* (New York: Times Books, 1979). On Garrow, see David J. Garrow, *Bearing the Cross: Martin Luther King, Jr., and the Southern Christian Leadership Conference* (New York: Random House, 1986), 627–628. The seventeen-year figure is one Garrow mentioned in a National Public Radio interview; see Shannon E. Martin, *Freedom of Information: The News the Media Use* (New York: Peter Lang, 2008), 92, 228. Garrow did not remember this precisely when queried by email (April 4, 2013) but wrote that this seemed about right.

12. Jon Wiener, "'National Security' and Freedom of Information: The John Lennon FBI Files," in Athan Theoharis, ed., *A Culture of Secrecy: The Government versus the People's Right to Know* (Lawrence: University Press of Kansas, 1998), 83–96, at 84. See also Henry Weinstein, "FBI to Release Last of Its John Lennon Files," *Los Angeles Times,* December 20, 2006.

13. 5 U.S.C. 552 (a) (4) (A) (iii). This language comes from the 1986 amendments to FOIA that mandated fee reductions or fee waivers for requests in the public interest.

14. On "predecisional deliberation" or the "deliberative process privilege," see Dianna G. Goldenson, "FOIA Exemption Five: Will It Protect Government Scientists from Unfair Intrusion?," *Boston College Environmental Affairs Law Review* 29 (2001–2002): 311–342.

15. See Tim Francisco, Alyssa Lenhoff, and Michael Schudson, "The Classroom as Newsroom," *International Journal of Communication* 6 (2012): 2677–2697, at 2694.

16. *New York Times,* July 5, 1966. The bill cleared Congress on June 20 with a 307–0 vote in the House (the Senate bill had passed on October 13, 1965). In the news story in the *Times* by William M. Blair on June 21, the headline reads,

"Information Bill Sent to Johnson," and in the story the bill is not named, only described as "a bill to grant Americans the right of access to Federal records" and "designed to insure the public's right to know about Government affairs."

17. Telephone interview, Rep. Lionel Van Deerlin (D-Calif.), May 18, 2004.

18. Benny Kass, personal interview, Washington, DC, May 5, 2004.

19. There is one biography of John Moss: Michael R. Lemov, *People's Warrior: John Moss and the Fight for Freedom of Information and Consumer Rights* (Madison, NJ: Fairleigh Dickinson University Press, 2011). Lemov served as a staff attorney to Moss, joining him in 1970 as special counsel in his position as chair of the Commerce and Finance Subcommittee of the House Commerce Committee. Since Lemov came to his biography many years after Moss died, he could not interview him, and though he knew Moss well, his direct knowledge dates to the 1970s; his account of how Moss came to the topic of freedom of information and became the leading champion of freedom of information in the Congress relies on earlier works. The most useful works on the history of FOIA from the beginnings of the Moss Committee and the right-to-know efforts in national journalism organizations until the 1966 passage of FOIA are three dissertations: Robert O. Blanchard, "The Moss Committee and a Federal Public Records Law (1955–1965)," Ph.D. dissertation, Syracuse University, 1966; George P. Kennedy, "Advocates of Openness: The Freedom of Information Movement," Ph.D. dissertation, University of Missouri, 1978; and Paul E. Kostyu, "The Moss Connection: The Freedom of Information Movement, Influence and John E. Moss, Jr.," Ph.D. dissertation, Bowling Green State University, 1990.

20. *New York Times,* November 16, 1956.

21. Nancy L. Rosenblum, "Navigating Pluralism: The Democracy of Everyday Life (and Where It Is Learned)," in Stephen L. Elkin and Karol E. Soltan, eds., *Citizen Competence and Democratic Institutions* (University Park: Pennsylvania State University Press, 1999), 67–92.

22. Michael R. Lemov, personal interview, May 2004, Washington, DC.

23. Blanchard's account of Moss's life, "The Moss Committee," is based on working with the committee for several months in 1965; Kennedy, "Advocates of Openness," is based on interviews with Moss in the late 1970s; Kostyu, "The Moss Connection," relies on interviews done in 1990. The discrepancies between these accounts seem to arise from somewhat different memories Moss passed on at different times. Here I am following in particular the account in Kostyu,

"The Moss Connection," 25–30. The Kostyu dissertation is summarized in Paul E. Kostyu, "Partners in the Freedom of Information Movement: The Press and John E. Moss Jr.," paper presented at the AEJMC national convention, Boston, MA, 1991. Kostyu's position is similar to that of Kennedy in "Advocates of Openness." Kennedy presents a brief version of the dissertation in "How Americans Got Their Right to Know," *American Editor,* October 1996, 11–13. For Kennedy, the effort to open up government information through the work of the Moss subcommittee implicated media leaders in "a story of high-minded principle and aggressive lobbying, of selfless and selfish interests in uneasy alliance, and of a handful of heroes—most of them newspaper editors who put aside any pretense of detachment to lead a movement that many of their most influential colleagues regarded with skepticism and apathy" ("How American Got Their Right to Know," 11). For the fullest account of the Moss Committee's efforts between 1955 and 1966 to draft and to enact federal freedom of information legislation, the Kennedy and Kostyu dissertations are the best accounts, along with Blanchard's.

24. Moss to Walter Kelley, March 26, 1953, John E. Moss Papers, California State University, Sacramento, Box 244, Folder 2.

25. Paul Leake to Moss, June 8, 1953, Moss Papers, Box 244, Folder 7.

26. George R. Berdes, *Friendly Adversaries: The Press and Government* (Milwaukee, WI: Center for the Study of the American Press, College of Journalism, Marquette University, 1969), 61. This interview took place April 13, 1965, although not published by Marquette until 1969. Cited in Blanchard, "The Moss Committee," 53–54. Kostyu reports that Moss requested from the Civil Service Commission a breakdown of the 2,200 loyalty-security firings in the Truman administration—he asked especially about postal employee dismissals. Philip Young, chair of the Civil Service Commission, responded that the commission had "neither the responsibility nor the authority" to release this information. This is from an article in the *Washington Evening Star,* January 26, 1954, that Kostyu found in the Moss Papers without author, title, or page number indicated. See Kostyu, "Partners," 33.

27. Dawson to Moss, June 9, 1955, quoted in Herbert N. Foerstel, *Freedom of Information and the Right to Know* (Westport, CT: Greenwood Press, 1999), 22.

28. Berdes, *Friendly Adversaries,* 61. When Paul Kostyu interviewed Moss on March 20, 1990, the latter seemed at a loss to explain how his special interest in freedom of information had developed: "It is one of those things that

is very difficult to say how or where. It was a matter of interest at the time." See Kostyu, "The Moss Connection," 49.

29. See Kostyu, "The Moss Connection," Appendix D, 317–319, for the full slate of committee members.

30. Ibid., 34–47. See Kennedy, "Advocates of Openness," 67.

31. Kennedy, "Advocates of Openness," 64.

32. Kennedy, "Advocates of Openness," remains the best source on the journalists' freedom of information movement but I do not know of a good work on how the movement developed at the state level. At the national level, see also Alice Fox Pitts, *Read All About It! 50 Years of ASNE* (Easton, PA: American Society of Newspaper Editors, 1974).

33. Kennedy, "Advocates of Openness," 67. Kennedy quotes here a 1978 letter to him from Pope.

34. Blanchard, "The Moss Committee," 62.

35. Address to the Upper Midwest News Executives Conference, Minneapolis, Minnesota, May 3, 1957, Moss Papers, Box 427, Folder 3.

36. See Kennedy, "Advocates of Openness," 20–30. Kennedy's information comes largely from contemporaneous ASNE and Sigma Delta Chi publications.

37. Ibid.

38. Cross, *The People's Right to Know,* xiii.

39. Ibid., xvi.

40. Blanchard, "The Moss Committee," 69.

41. In a letter to the Freedom of Information Committee of the ASNE, May 2, 1966—after the full Government Operations Committee unanimously endorsed S. 1160, which had already been passed by the Senate, and before the full House took it up—John Moss wrote, "In conversation with the late Dr. Harold Cross 12 years ago, the idea of amending Section 3 of the Administrative Procedures Act was first discussed." I think this means that on that occasion Cross made it clear to Moss that amending APA would be the precise strategy for achieving more ample freedom of information. See the report of the ASNE's Committee on Freedom of Information, *Problems of Journalism: Proceedings of the American Society of Newspaper Editors Convention,* 1966, 213–14.

42. A footnote added that school boards barred the public from meetings in Chicago, Illinois; Columbia, Missouri; Denver, Colorado; Roanoake, Virginia; Providence, Rhode Island; Evansville, Indiana; Flint, Michigan; Baltimore,

Maryland; and elsewhere as well. "Access to Official Information: A Neglected Constitutional Right," *Indiana Law Journal* 27 (1951–1952): 209–230.

43. Jacob Scher, "Access to Information: Recent Legal Problems," *Journalism Quarterly* 37 (1960): 41–52. David O'Brien reported that every state except Mississippi had by that time open-records laws, open-meeting laws, or both. Laws in California, Montana, Wisconsin, Massachusetts, and Michigan date to the nineteenth century. The greatest number of such laws were enacted between 1945 and 1960; eighteen states passed open-meeting or open-records laws in that period. See David O'Brien, *The Public's Right to Know: The Supreme Court and the First Amendment* (New York: Praeger, 1981), 179–182.

44. Cited in Kennedy, "Advocates of Openness," 42.

45. Kennedy, "Advocates of Openness," 45, quoting ASNE Committee for Freedom of Information, "Report," 1953, 7.

46. Kennedy, "Advocates of Openness," 54–56.

47. Robert O. Blanchard, "A Watchdog in Decline," *Columbia Journalism Review,* Summer 1966, 17–21, at 18. See the next several issues of the *Review* for letters objecting.

48. Foerstel, *Freedom of Information and the Right to Know,* 22.

49. Moss Papers, Box MP 372. Newton's letter is December 15, 1959, and Archibald's is December 22, 1959.

50. Speech of May 5, 1958, Moss Papers, Box 427.

51. On the impact of foreign policy considerations in bringing the State Department and a variety of forces, including some conservative Republicans, to support civil rights legislation, see Mary L. Dudziak, *Cold War Civil Rights* (Princeton, NJ: Princeton University Press, 2000); Paul Lauren, *Power and Prejudice: The Politics and Diplomacy of Racial Discrimination* (Boulder, CO: Westview Press, 1988); and John Skrentny, *The Minority Rights Revolution* (Cambridge, MA: Harvard University Press, 2002).

52. Edward A. Shils, "America's Paper Curtain," *Bulletin of the Atomic Scientists* 8, no. 7 (October 1952): 210–217. See also Victor F. Weisskopf, "Visas for Foreign Scientists," *Bulletin of the Atomic Scientists* 10, no. 3 (March 1954): 68.

53. House Committee on Government Operations, Availability of Information from Federal Departments and Agencies: Hearings before a Subcommittee of the Committee on Government Operations, November 7, 1955, 84th Cong., 1st sess. (Washington, DC: Government Printing Office, 1956), 14.

54. Ibid., 15. None of the other journalists who spoke to the committee on this first day of hearings was nearly so adversarial; none of the others came close to suggesting that executive secrecy was a Soviet-like practice. Still, the "paper curtain" metaphor was catchy. See also John B. Oakes, "The Paper Curtain in Washington," *Nieman Reports,* October 1958, 3–5, in Moss Papers, Box 426, Folder 1.

55. Blanchard, "The Moss Committee," 73. The speech was published under that title in the *Congressional Record,* 84th Cong., 2nd sess., August 25, 1965, A6213–A6214.

56. Speech before American Society of Newspaper Editors convention, April 20, 1956, Moss Papers, Box 334, Folder 16.

57. Speech to Associated Press Managing Editors Association Convention, New Orleans, November 20, 1957, Moss Papers, Box 427, Folder 9.

58. Convocation Speech, Syracuse University School of Journalism, February 21, 1958, Moss Papers, Box 427, Folder 15.

59. *New York Times,* January 11, 1959, cited in Miles Beardsley Johnson, *The Government Secrecy Controversy* (New York: Vantage Press, 1967), 39.

60. Associated Press in the *Washington Star,* January 11, 1959, Moss Papers, Box 428, Folder 10.

61. Article prepared for Weekly Service, Inc. in September 1960, Moss Papers, Box 429, Folder 3.

62. John E. Moss, *Bulletin of the Atomic Scientists* 17 (January 1961): 35. See Moss Papers, Box 429, Folder 7.

63. Excerpt from a speech at Western Reserve University, Cleveland, Ohio, November 11, 1961, 13, Moss Papers, Box 429, Folder 13.

64. "Excerpts from an Address by Congressman John E. Moss, Chairman, Special Subcommittee on Government Information, at the California Press Association Conference, San Francisco, November 30, 1962," 15, Moss Papers, Box 429, Folder 19. In the archived copy of this speech there is a page added that is headed, "Add Following Asterisks on Page 19, if Desired." Moss may or may not have used it, but it is very striking at such an early point in U.S. involvement in Vietnam. The text says that foreign aid is in trouble "in part because the American people have not had enough information about it to have full confidence in its necessity." It then continues: "The same thing can be said about Viet Nam, where we have a serious involvement of men and equipment with little information given the people about our activities. There comes a time

when a free nation refuses to accept leadership that is unwilling to back up its promises and assurances with the facts. We must make sure that the stress of the Cold War does not lead us to impose more and more secrecy until— inevitably—the people no longer trust nor believe in the programs of our elected leaders." In June 1962, Moss had insisted that a much larger share of complaints his subcommittee pursued in the first year of the Kennedy administration, compared to the final half year of Eisenhower's presidency, were initiated by the subcommittee rather than following up on complaints from others. See Kennedy, "Advocates of Openness," 102, citing a Moss address to the New Mexico Press Association, June 29, 1962.

65. See discussion in Chapter 1.

66. Kent Cooper, *The Right to Know: An Exposition of the Evils of News Suppression and Propaganda* (New York: Farrar, Straus and Cudahy, 1956), xiii.

67. This is what I infer from the *Columbia Journalism Review* article and from the concluding page of Blanchard's Ph.D. dissertation, in which he mourns the Moss Committee's shift from a set of methods that included "changes in statutes" to a focus on "legislation." I do not see the distinction—after all, FOIA as it passed in 1966 was, in fact, a change in a statute. See Blanchard, "The Moss Committee," 266.

68. American Society of Newspaper Editors Freedom of Information and Press-Bar Committee, 1966–1967 Annual Report, April 20, 1967, available at Freedom of Information Center, University of Missouri.

69. Kenneth Culp Davis, "The Information Act: A Preliminary Analysis," *University of Chicago Law Review 34* (1967): 761–816, at 803, 804, 807.

70. Blanchard, "The Moss Committee," 140.

71. Kennedy, "Advocates of Openness," 117–131.

72. Robert O. Blanchard, "A Watchdog in Decline," *Columbia Journalism Review,* Summer 1966, 17–21, at 20.

73. Ibid., 21.

74. John E. Moss, "The Moss Committee," *Columbia Journalism Review,* Fall 1966, 57–58.

75. Paul Kostyu found a decline in articles in the *New York Times* that mentioned the Moss Committee, from a high of thirty-nine in 1957 to a low of nine in 1963. But the decline was significant even while Eisenhower remained in office—just ten stories in 1960. This does not provide support for Blanchard.

See Kostyu, "Partners in the Freedom of Information Movement." Donald Rumsfeld, before he took a post in the Nixon White House in 1969, was a Republican congressman from Illinois, a minority member of Moss's subcommittee, and a co-sponsor of the Freedom of Information Act. In his 2011 memoirs he foreshortened FOIA's history, remembering the act as "crafted in reaction to the Johnson administration's behavior." He deletes from his account the fact that Moss began his efforts when Eisenhower was president and continued them for six years. He recognized that Moss was in a difficult position, promoting "a bill that went against the express wishes of the President," and so he helped Moss move the bill through the House. "For me, support of the bill came down to one long-held belief: Good judgments require accurate information," he noted. In his glance backward, Rumsfeld wrote that he still supported FOIA but found, from the vantage of the executive branch, that it had very costly unintended consequences. Donald Rumsfeld, *Known and Unknown: A Memoir* (New York: Penguin Sentinel, 2011), 100–101.

76. See O'Brien, *The Public's Right to Know,* 29, citing a Hennings article from 1959.

77. Richard R. John, *Spreading the News: The American Postal System from Franklin to Morse* (Cambridge, MA: Harvard University Press, 1996). See also Paul Starr, *The Creation of the Media: Political Origins of Modern Communications* (New York: Basic Books, 2004), 83–92, which adds useful cross-national data showing just how extensive, and how unusual, the federally subsidized postal system was, particularly for the circulation of newspapers.

78. See Thomas Jefferson, "A Bill for the More General Diffusion of Knowledge" (1778), in *The Papers of Thomas Jefferson,* ed. Julian P. Boyd (Princeton, NJ: Princeton University Press, 1950), 2:526–27. For further discussion of Jefferson's education bill and its significance, see Michael Schudson, *The Good Citizen: A History of American Civic Life* (New York: Free Press, 1998), 69–73.

79. George Washington to Burges Ball, September 25, 1794, in *George Washington: Writings,* ed. John Rhodehamel (New York: Library of America, 1997), 885. See also Washington to Edmund Randolph, October 16, 1794, in ibid., 887. A fuller discussion of the founders' skepticism about popular participation in government can be found in Schudson, *The Good Citizen,* 55–64.

80. Moss said, in a March 20, 1990, interview with Paul Kostyu, that Article I of the Constitution mentions secrecy as something that Congress might

sometimes legitimately require. "But they did not make a similar exception in Article Two. I think it is a persuasive example. Construction is giving an indication of the intent." See Kostyu, "The Moss Connection," 96.

81. James S. Pope to Rep. John E. Moss Jr., August 12, 1955, reprinted as Appendix E in Kostyu, "The Moss Connection," 320–322.

82. Lotte E. Feinberg, "Mr. Justice Brandeis and the Creation of the Federal Register," *Public Administration Review* 61 (May–June 2001): 359–370.

83. On legislative precedents to FOIA, see Lotte E. Feinberg, "Managing the Freedom of Information Act and Federal Information Policy," *Public Administration Review* 46 (1986): 615–621.

84. Joanna L. Grisinger, *The Unwieldy American State: Administrative Politics since the New Deal* (Cambridge, UK: Cambridge University Press, 2012), 10, 11.

85. Harold L. Cross to Samuel J. Archibald, September 16, 1958, in Blanchard, "The Moss Committee," 21. Archibald was a journalist who had covered the California statehouse for the *Sacramento Bee* and who became an administrative assistant to Moss after his 1952 election. See Blanchard, "The Moss Connection," 89–90.

86. Foerstel, *Freedom of Information and the Right to Know,* 33–35.

87. Speech to the Pennsylvania Society of Newspaper Editors, University Park, May 15, 1959, 4, Moss Papers, Box 428, Folder 17. See also Address to the International Labor Press Association (AFL-CIO), San Francisco, September 14, 1959, Moss Papers, Box 428, Folder 20.

88. Remarks for Freedom of Information Symposium, Aviation Writers Association annual meeting, Washington, DC, May 12, 1959, Moss Papers, Box 428, Folder 16.

89. Cited in Foerstel, *Freedom of Information and the Right to Know,* 48. See also *Congressional Quarterly, Congress and the Nation* (Washington, DC: Congressional Quarterly, 1977), 4:805–806. For a detailed account of this and subsequent amendments to FOIA, see James T. O'Reilly, *Federal Information Disclosure,* 3rd ed. (St. Paul, MN: West Group, 2000): 43–49.

90. On the importance of these 1974 post-Watergate amendments, see Fred H. Cate, D. Annette Fields, and James K. McBain, "The Right to Privacy and the Public's Right to Know: The 'Central Purpose' of the Freedom of Information Act," *Administrative Law Review* 46 (1994): 41–74, and Patricia M. Wald (who as judge in the U.S. Court of Appeals for the District of Columbia

heard many FOIA cases), "The Freedom of Information Act: A Short Case Study in the Perils and Paybacks of Legislating Democratic Values," *Emory Law Journal* 33 (1984): 649–683.

91. Bob Taylor, "It's an Abrupt Change in John Moss' Lifestyle," *Sacramento Bee,* January 7, 1979.

92. Kennedy, "Advocates of Openness," 135, citing his interview with Moss in 1977. Harold Cross, in 1957, objected to any and all exemptions except when Congress wrote laws that specifically exempted some body of materials from disclosure. See Kennedy, "Advocates of Openness," 95.

93. "Clarifying and Protecting the Right of the Public to Information, and for Other Purposes," Senate Report No. 813, 89th Congress, October 4, 1965, 3.

94. Thomas S. Blanton, "The Openness Revolution: The Rise of a Global Movement for Freedom of Information," *Development Dialogue* 1 (2002): 7–21. On Sweden, see Gustaf Pedren, "Access to Government-Held Information in Sweden," in Norman S. Marsh, ed., *Public Access to Government-Held Information* (London: Stevens & Sons, 1987), 35–54, and Sigvard Holstad, "Sweden," in Donald C. Rowat, ed., *Administrative Secrecy in Developed Countries* (New York: Columbia University Press, 1979), 29–50.

95. John Moss in 112 *Congressional Record* 13007, House of Representatives, June 20, 1966.

96. Benny Kass did not remember any discussion about the phrase "any person." It just seemed the obvious phrase to use. There was discussion at the time of the 1974 amendments, when at least one member of Congress expressed concern that foreigners, even foreign nationals serving in governments hostile to the United States, might by the terms of the law make use of FOIA in ways to harm U.S. interests, but this was fairly quickly waved aside (by Moss among others). Benny Kass, personal interview, Washington, DC, May 5, 2004.

3. The Consumer's Right to Be Informed

1. John F. Kennedy, "Remarks of Senator John F. Kennedy, Concourse Plaza Hotel, Bronx, N.Y., November 5, 1960," American Presidency Project, www.presidency.ucsb.edu/ws/?pid=60430.

2. John F. Kennedy, "Special Message to the Congress on Protecting the Consumer Interest," March 15, 1962, American Presidency Project, www.presidency.ucsb.edu/ws/?pid=9108.

3. Esther Peterson, "Oral History Interview," John F. Kennedy Presidential Library, Ann W. Campbell, interviewer, February 11, 1970. Peterson recalled that White House aide Ralph Dungan asked her on President Kennedy's behalf to take on the job of consumer representative. She was vague on the details but remembers discussing the matter with Secretary of Labor William Wirtz at the time. "And then all the other tragic events happened. That it first originated with Kennedy, that's the thing I think is important" (83).

4. Important historical studies of consumer issues in America include Lizabeth Cohen, *Making a New Deal: Industrial Workers in Chicago, 1919–1939* (New York: Cambridge University Press, 1990); Lizabeth Cohen, *A Consumers' Republic: The Politics of Mass Consumption in Postwar America* (New York: Knopf, 2003); Gary Cross, *An All-Consuming Century: Why Commercialism Won in Modern America* (New York: Columbia University Press, 2000); Daniel Horowitz, *The Anxieties of Affluence: Critiques of Consumer Culture 1939–1979* (Amherst: University of Massachusetts Press, 2004); and Meg Jacobs, *Pocketbook Politics: Economic Citizenship in Twentieth-Century America* (Princeton, NJ: Princeton University Press, 2005). A book that takes up consumer culture in both Europe and the United States is Martin Daunton and Matthew Hilton, eds., *The Politics of Consumption* (Oxford, UK: Berg, 2001). The U.S. contributors are Lizabeth Cohen, "Citizens and Consumers in the United States in the Century of Mass Consumption" (203–222); Meg Jacobs, "The Politics of Plenty: Consumerism in the Twentieth-Century United States" (223–239); and Gary Cross, "Corralling Consumer Culture: Shifting Rationales for American State Intervention in Free Markets" (283–299).

5. See Eric C. Wall, "A Comprehensive Look at the Fair Packaging and Labeling Act of 1966 and the FDA Regulation of Deceptive Labeling and Packaging Practices: 1906 to Today," Harvard Law School, May 2002, http://leda.law.harvard.edu/leda/data/444/Wall.html, accessed November 30, 2010.

6. Kennedy, "Special Message to the Congress on Protecting the Consumer Interest."

7. David M. Potter, *People of Plenty: Economic Abundance and the American Character* (Chicago: University of Chicago Press, 1954), 173. On this intellectual history, see Horowitz, *The Anxieties of Affluence*.

8. Jerry Cohen, "Consumer Fraud and Protection Inquiry—Proposed Program," memorandum, April 20, 1961, Philip A. Hart Papers, Bentley Historical

Library, University of Michigan, Box 76, Folder "Staff Files, Consumer Legislation."

9. Philip A. Hart, "Truth in Packaging," *The Nation,* June 29, 1963, 542–543. The idea that the package is a salesman, regularly repeated by Senator Hart, seems to have come from the food industry itself. Hart's aide Jerry S. Cohen wrote to him: "It has been stated by industry spokesmen that the package has replaced the pound as a unit of measure; that the package has become the salesman of the product. Our task then is to determine to what extent does the package function as an honest salesman." "Market Pricing Practices," memorandum, May 2, 1961, Hart Papers, Box 76. In "Truth in Packaging," Hart cites economist Irston Barnes, who wrote that supermarkets do very little selling at all—they essentially rent shelf space to manufacturers.

10. Personal interview with Monroe P. Friedman, February 5, 2011, Santa Monica, CA, and email from Friedman, May 19, 2012.

11. Monroe Peter Friedman, "Consumer Confusion in the Selection of Supermarket Products," *Journal of Applied Psychology* 50 (1965): 529–534. Friedman wrote about his research in an interesting paper much later, "Consumer Research Enters the 1960s Legislative Arena: A Participant-Observer Report on the Role of Behavioral Research in the U.S. Congressional Hearings on the 'Truth Bills,'" in Klaus G. Grunert and John Thogersen, eds., *Consumers, Policy and the Environment: A Tribute to Folke Olander* (New York: Springer Science & Business Media, 2005), 115–126.

12. Margaret M. Merchant, ed., *The American Council on Consumer Interests: An Oral History 1954–1984* (Columbia, MO: American Council on Consumer Interests, 1987). A copy of this volume is in the Morse Papers, Kansas State University. This material is from the interview with Richard Morse conducted by Norman Silber, 77–113, at 100.

13. Typescript of Senator Hart's remarks, with a handwritten note: "Property of Richard L. D. Morse—given to him by Senator Philip A. Hart following his address to the Council on Consumer Information in St. Louis April 7, 1961," Morse Papers, Box 82, Folder 8.

14. "A Special Report from Senator Hart: Truth in Packaging," letter to constituents, September 22, 1965, Hart Papers, Box 131, Folder "Truth in Packaging."

15. Sarah H. Newman, "Lobbying for the Fair Packaging and Labeling Act," in Erma Angevine, ed., *Consumer Activists: They Made a Difference: A History*

of Consumer Action Related by Leaders in the Consumer Movement (Mt. Vernon, NY: Consumers Union Foundation, 1982), 328.

16. For an overview of the rise of a consumer economy, see Richard S. Tedlow, *New and Improved: The Story of Mass Marketing in America* (New York: Basic Books, 1990), 3–4. There Tedlow observes how rapid economic growth in the twentieth century benefited the American consumer: "A higher percentage of the population has been able to purchase a greater variety of goods and services than even the most visionary dreamer in the mid-nineteenth century would have imagined possible."

17. Henry Fairlie, "Frozen Foods Become Soul of Supermarkets," *Pittsburgh Press,* April 17, 1980. Fairlie recalls this introduction to Washington, but without the comment about Chartres, in "Why I Love America," a column for the *New Republic,* July 4, 1983, reprinted as "My America!" in Henry Fairlie, *Bite the Hand That Feeds You,* ed. Jeremy McCarter (New Haven, CT: Yale University Press, 2009), 162–179.

18. Newman, "Lobbying for the Fair Packaging and Labeling Act," 328. Newman cites the speech by Grocery Manufacturers Association president Paul Willis.

19. See Gary S. Cross, *All-Consuming Century: Why Commercialism Won in Modern America* (New York: Columbia University Press, 2000), 155. My list of important legislation follows the list Cross offers and which he judges "breathtaking."

20. Roger Biles, *Crusading Liberal: Paul H. Douglas of Illinois* (DeKalb: Northern Illinois University Press, 1971), 145.

21. See ibid., 145–146, 161–162, 183–185, 202–203, and Douglas's own account in his *In the Fullness of Time* (New York: Harcourt Brace Jovanovich, 1972), 523–535.

22. Peterson herself observes that she became widely known as "the Giant Food Lady." See Esther Peterson with Winifred Conkling, *Restless: The Memoirs of Labor and Consumer Activist Esther Peterson* (Washington, DC: Caring Publishing, 1995), 143.

23. Hart Papers, Box 64, Folder "Antitrust Subcommittee Consumer Frauds—Packaging and Labeling." This file includes "Senator Hart's Happy Landing," an editorial from the *St. Louis Post-Dispatch,* June 17, 1963, that Hart inserted in the *Congressional Record.*

24. Dorothy Sue Cobble, *The Other Women's Movement: Workplace Justice and Social Rights in Modern America* (Princeton, NJ: Princeton University Press, 2004), 34–35.

25. The report of the President's Commission on the Status of Women (PCSW), originally published as a government document, was republished with an introduction by Margaret Mead in 1965. See Margaret Mead and Frances Balgley Kaplan, eds., *American Women: The Report of the President's Commission on the Status of Women and Other Publications of the Commission* (New York: Charles Scribner's Sons, 1965). Discussion of the PCSW can be found in Cobble, *The Other Women's Movement;* Esther Peterson, "The Kennedy Commission," in Irene Tinker, ed., *Women in Washington: Advocates for Public Policy* (Beverly Hills, CA: Sage, 1983), 21–34; Leila J. Rupp and Verta Taylor, *Survival in the Doldrums: The American Women's Rights Movement, 1945 to the 1960s* (New York: Oxford University Press, 1987), 166–174; Janet M. Martin, *The Presidency and Women: Promise, Performance, and Illusion* (College Station: Texas A&M University Press, 2003); and Cynthia E. Harrison, "A 'New Frontier' for Women: The Public Policy of the Kennedy Administration," *Journal of American History* 67 (December 1980): 630–646.

26. Esther Peterson, "Consumer Representation in the White House," in Emma Angevine, ed., *Consumer Activists: They Made a Difference, A History of Consumer Action Related by Leaders in the Consumer Movement* (Mt. Vernon, NY: Consumers Union Foundation, 1982), 198–212, at 201. See also Peterson, "Oral History Interview." Kennedy's asking Peterson to be consumer adviser is not mentioned in her memoir, *Restless.*

27. Philip A. Hart, "Remarks before a Meeting of the Cooperative League of the USA," Washington, DC, April 13, 1964, Hart Papers, Box 110, File "Speeches, 1964 (2)."

28. Peterson, "Consumer Representation in the White House," 202.

29. Ibid., 203.

30. Peterson, "Oral History Interview," 86.

31. Peterson, "Consumer Representation in the White House," 204. Peterson tells a somewhat different story here than in her 1995 memoir. For the latter, put together a decade later, see Peterson, *Restless,* 120.

32. Lyndon B. Johnson, Annual Message to the Congress on the State of the Union, January 12, 1966, American Presidency Project, www.presidency.ucsb .edu/ws/index.php?pid=28015.

33. Peterson, "Consumer Representation in the White House," 205.

34. Ibid., 206.

35. Peterson, *Restless,* 131–136.

36. See Giant Food, "Fifty Years of Caring" (1986), 59, in Esther Peterson Papers, Schlesinger Library, Radcliffe Institute for Advanced Study, Harvard University, Cambridge, MA, Box 74, Folder 1466.

37. Martin, *The Presidency and Women,* 103, citing a March 30, 1966, Moyers memorandum, and 105, citing a February 9, 1967, memorandum.

38. Giant Food, "Fifty Years of Caring."

39. Paul Forbes to Esther Peterson, January 22, 1965, Peterson Papers, Box 74, Folder 1471.

40. Joseph Danzansky to Esther Peterson, April 24, 1970, Peterson Papers, Box 74, Folder 1471.

41. Peterson, *Restless,* 140.

42. Peterson Papers, Box 75, Folder 1472.

43. Martin Weil, "2 Chains to Start Per-Unit Pricing: Safeway and Giant Adopt Plan," *Washington Post,* October 31, 1970.

44. Peterson, "Consumer Participation in Business," 251.

45. Monroe Friedman, email to author, May 26, 2012.

46. Monroe Friedman, email to author, August 30, 2013.

47. Weil, "2 Chains to Start Per-Unit Pricing."

48. "Safeway Stores to Price by Unit," *Baltimore Sun,* October 31, 1970.

49. Peterson, "Consumer Participation in Business," 252. See also Peterson, *Restless,* 147.

50. Jean Mayer, "Toward a National Nutrition Policy," *Science* 176 (April 21, 1972): 237.

51. Was it the first? The *Washington Post* praised Giant in an editorial in 1971, "Learning the Nutritional Truth," for beginning "the first nutritional labeling of food in the nation." The editorial—I do not know its exact date—was reprinted in a photo collage in Giant's 1971 Annual Report, 8, Peterson Papers, Box 74, Folder 1467. And Jean Mayer seemed to agree in his 1972 article, alluding to "various attempts" to arrive at a way to present nutritional information on product labels but then singling out Giant Food's adoption of "an experimental scheme" that put nutritional labeling into practice. See Mayer, "Toward a National Nutrition Policy," 240.

52. Peterson Papers, Box 75, Folder 1473.

53. Peterson, "Consumer Participation in Business," 253.

54. Giant Food, 1971 Annual Report, Peterson Papers, Box 74, Folder 1467.

55. Peterson Papers, Box 77, Folder 1529.

56. Paul Forbes to Esther Peterson, memorandum, September 21, 1970, 3, Peterson Papers, Box 75, Folder 1472.

57. Letter to Charles Percy, October 11, 1971, Peterson Papers, Box 77, Folder 1521.

58. Comptroller General of the United States, *Food Labeling: Goals, Shortcomings, and Proposed Changes* (Washington, DC: U.S. General Accounting Office, 1975), 72.

59. Peterson, *Restless*, 150.

60. John D. Morris, "Unit Pricing Grows Fast, but Use by Buyers Lags," *New York Times*, June 13, 1972.

61. Ibid., 31.

62. "Consumer Policy on Food Labeling: Highlights and Policy Statement of a National Seminar," ed. Helen E. Nelson, Center for Consumer Affairs, University of Wisconsin Extension, Milwaukee, January 17, 1972, Roy Kiesling Papers, Kansas State University, Box 6, Folder 5. This fifteen-page document was based on the December 8–10, 1971, conference in Milwaukee.

63. Notes taken by Roy Kiesling, Kiesling Papers, Box 6, Folder 5. Kiesling wrote the notes on his program from the national conference at the Center for Consumer Affairs, University of Wisconsin Extension, Milwaukee, December 9, 1971.

64. Esther Peterson to Joseph Danzansky, memorandum, December 28, 1973, Peterson Papers, Box 150, Folder 3518.

65. Susan Seliger, "Her Last Big Battle," *National Observer*, June 13, 1977.

66. Monroe Friedman, email to author, May 26, 2012. Safeway announced its system-wide adoption of unit-pricing labels at a press conference at the Rayburn House Office Building with a Safeway executive, Representative Rosenthal, and Professor Friedman all participating. The *Washington Post* ran a story on the front page of its business section and included a photo of the three. The second chain was Giant, and the story cited Esther Peterson, who said that Giant would be introducing unit pricing by Thanksgiving—and denied that this was a response to the Safeway announcement. On the contrary, she insisted, Giant had been working on the change since the spring and that Peterson had "requested unit pricing as a condition of her employment with Giant." See Weil,

"2 Chains to Start Per-Unit Pricing." The *Baltimore Sun* covered the story, too: "Safeway Stores to Price by Unit," October 31, 1970.

67. Michael Pertschuk, *Revolt against Regulation: The Rise and Pause of the Consumer Movement* (Berkeley: University of California Press, 1982), 32. Uncomfortable with the intensity of Nader's passion, Pertschuk interestingly offers as an epigraph for his memoir a quotation from Nikos Kazantzakis: "One of man's greatest obligations is anger."

68. Horowitz, *The Anxieties of Affluence,* 166–176, offers a brief and illuminating sketch of Nader's education, with the instructive information about H. H. Wilson.

69. Ibid., 174.

70. On auto safety, see Jerry L. Mashaw and David L. Harfst, *The Struggle for Auto Safety* (Cambridge, MA: Harvard University Press, 1990), 50–58.

71. Hearings before the Committee on Commerce, U.S. Senate, 89th Cong., on S. 985, "Fair Packaging and Labeling," Serial 89-28, Washington, DC, 1965, hearings of April 28, 1965, 20–22.

72. Ibid., 22.

73. Undated column, Peterson Papers, Box 78, Folder 1541.

74. Comptroller General, *Food Labeling,* 36–42. This report takes up some labeling issues that I do not cover here, notably U.S. Department of Agriculture quality grading standards that began as early as 1917 (for potatoes). Grading standards originated to help the wholesale trade in agricultural products, but food processors began to label products by grade at the retail level as early as 1924 (butter was the first product so labeled). Grading developed product by product, however, and the GAO found that it became very confusing. There were ten different "top quality" grades for different products—"AA" for eggs, "A" for apple juice or fresh carrots, "extra fancy" for apples but "fancy" for canteloupes, "No. 1" for beets but "extra No. 1" for celery, and so forth. See ibid., 36–37.

75. Ibid., 1.

76. Ibid., 6.

77. See Wallace F. Janssen and Enoc P. Waters, "What Some Food Labels Don't Tell," *FDA Consumer,* July-August 1972, 13–17. Janssen was historian for the Food and Drug Administration, and Waters was the FDA's information specialist on food. See also "HEW News," March 29, 1972, a news release of the Department of Health, Education and Welfare. Both documents are in Hart Papers, Box 200, "Subject Files, 1972, Commerce, Truth in Labeling."

78. Comptroller General, *Food Labeling,* 18.

79. Ibid., 46.

80. Ibid., 52.

81. Ibid., 57.

82. Ibid., 59.

83. Ibid., 58.

84. Emma Angevine, "Lobbying and Consumer Federation of America," in Erma Angevine, ed., *Consumer Activists: They Made a Difference: A History of Consumer Action Related by Leaders in the Consumer Movement* (Mt. Vernon, NY: Consumers Union Foundation, 1982), 331–342, at 336.

85. Transcript of Westinghouse Broadcasting Company, "Washington Viewpoint," November 22, 1965, Hart Papers, Box 131, Folder "Radio-TV."

86. Cohen, *A Consumers' Republic,* 348–353. On changes in Congress, specifically in the Senate, see Michael Foley, *The New Senate: Liberal Influence on a Conservative Institution 1959–1972* (New Haven, CT: Yale University Press, 1980). Changes in the House were just as important and are discussed more fully in Chapter 4.

87. Cohen, *A Consumers' Republic,* 357.

88. David A. Hollinger, *Science, Jews, and Secular Culture* (Princeton, NJ: Princeton University Press, 1996), 4. William J. Rorabaugh makes the same point in *Kennedy and the Promise of the Sixties* (Cambridge, UK: Cambridge University Press, 2002), organizing the whole book on the premise that these first few years of the decade constitute an era of their own, what he calls an "in-between time" (xix).

89. Hart Papers, Box 1, Folder "Biographical."

4. Opening Up Congress

1. Jerome R. Waldie, "Newsletter No. 1," January 1970, James G. O'Hara Papers, Bentley Historical Library, University of Michigan, Ann Arbor, Box 12.

2. In 1971, just a few years after FOIA became law, when confidential proceedings in the House and Senate were being challenged, the Committee on Government Operations—the parent committee of Moss's subcommittee—voted to hold its organizational meeting in executive session. But by then the Legislative Reorganization Act of 1970—the chief subject of this chapter—had become law, and its provisions enabled reporters to get the recorded roll call vote on that decision. John Moss, as well as his successor as chair of the

Subcommittee on Government Information, William Moorhead, both had joined the majority of Democrats in voting to keep the organizational meeting closed. The annual report of Sigma Delta Chi's Advancement of Freedom of Information Committee was not reluctant to point this out. "Report of the 1971 Sigma Delta Chi Advancement of Freedom of Information Committee," 20, available at Freedom of Information Center, University of Missouri, Columbia, MO.

3. James L. Sundquist, *Politics and Policy: The Eisenhower, Kennedy, and Johnson Years* (Washington, DC: Brookings Institution, 1968), 513.

4. Nelson Polsby, *How Congress Evolves* (New York: Oxford University Press, 2004), 16.

5. Ibid., 19–20, citing Jeffrey R. Biggs with Thomas Foley, *Honor in the House: Speaker Tom Foley* (Pullman: Washington State University Press, 1999), 37–38. This would have taken place in 1965, at the beginning of Foley's first term. See also Steven S. Smith, *Call to Order: Floor Politics in the House and Senate* (Washington, DC: Brookings Institution, 1989), 132–135, on norms of "apprenticeship" in the Congress.

6. See Polsby, *How Congress Evolves,* 73–75, for the analysis I follow here. The specific importance of the 1958 elections in bolstering the contingent of liberals in the Congress and paving the way for legislative reform is also identified in Barbara Sinclair, "Congressional Reform," in Julian E. Zelizer, ed., *The American Congress* (Boston: Houghton Mifflin, 2004), 628.

7. Democratic Study Group, "The Proposal for Recording Teller Votes," Special Report, July 7, 1970, 3, O'Hara Papers, Box 12, Folder "Congressional Reorganization 1." This is where I first ran across it, but it was also read into the *Congressional Record* and can be found in the DSG Papers at the Library of Congress as well.

8. See Norman J. Ornstein and David W. Rohde, "The Strategy of Reform: Recorded Teller Voting in the U.S. House of Representatives," paper prepared for the 1974 Midwest Political Science Association convention, Chicago, April 25–27, 1; see also Smith, *Call to Order,* 256. On procedural reform in the Congress, see Sinclair, "Congressional Reform," 625–637. Thanks to David Rohde for unearthing the unpublished Ornstein and Rohde paper for my use.

9. See "First Congressional Reform Bill Enacted since 1946," *CQ Almanac* 1970, 26th ed., 05-117-05-119 (Washington, DC: Congressional Quarterly, 1971).

10. Julian E. Zelizer, "Without Restraint: Scandal and Politics in America," in Mark C. Carnes, ed., *The Columbia History of Post–World War II America* (New York: Columbia University Press, 2007), 226–254.

11. See David P. Brady, *The Schooled Society* (Stanford, CA: Stanford University Press, 2014). Brady develops the idea of an "educational revolution" (but he traces the phrase to Talcott Parsons, "Higher Education as a Theoretical Focus," in Herman Turk and Richard L. Simpson, eds., *Institutions and Social Exchange* [Indianapolis, IN: Bobbs-Merrill, 1971], 233–252).

12. This is not the same categorization offered by Leroy Rieselbach, "Assessing Congressional Change, or What Hath Reform Wrought (or Wreaked)?," in Dennis Hale, ed., *The United States Congress* (New Brunswick, NJ: Transaction Books, 1983), 167–207, but I have relied heavily on his account here.

13. Smith, *Call to Order,* 27.

14. Public Law 91-510, Section 116b.

15. Quoted in John F. Bibby and Roger H. Davidson, *On Capitol Hill: Studies in the Legislative Process,* 2nd ed. (Hinsdale, IL: Dryden Press, 1972), 259. This is part of a chapter, "Inertia and Change: The Legislative Reorganization Act of 1970," 252–280, added for the book's second edition.

16. Frank Thompson Papers, Seeley Mudd Library, Princeton University, Box 82, Folder "Democratic Study Group 91st Congress."

17. Susan Webb Hammond, *Congressional Caucuses in National Policy Making* (Baltimore: Johns Hopkins University Press, 1998), 39.

18. Robert Jay Dilger and Matthew E. Glassman, "Congressional Member Organizations: Their Purpose and Activities, History, and Formation," Congressional Research Service, Washington, DC, August 14, 2014, 1.

19. Hammond, *Congressional Caucuses,* 45, 42 (Table 3-1).

20. Dilger and Glassman, "Congressional Member Organizations," 18, 27.

21. See Hammond, *Congressional Caucuses,* 43, 49, 50.

22. Ibid., 47.

23. Ibid., 49.

24. Ibid., 54.

25. That something comparable to a social movement in a nation-state can arise inside an organization is enough of a novelty that it took some time for sociologists to recognize it. The key essay on the topic (which, among other things, gathers together prior works that hint at the same phenomenon) was a

1978 paper by Mayer Zald and Michael Berger, "Social Movements in Organizations: Coup d'Etat, Bureaucratic Insurgency, and Movement," in Mayer N. Zald and John D. McCarthy, eds., *Social Movements in an Organizational Society* (New Brunswick, NJ: Transaction Books, 1987), 185–222; it originally appeared in *American Journal of Sociology* 83, no. 4 (January 1978): 823–861.

26. See Abigail McCarthy, *Private Faces/Public Places* (Garden City, NY: Doubleday, 1972), 216–217, and Kenneth Kofmehl, "The Institutionalization of a Voting Bloc," *Western Political Quarterly* 17 (June 1964): 256–272, at 261.

27. Kofmehl, "The Institutionalization of a Voting Bloc," 259.

28. Ibid., 261–262.

29. Bruce R. Hopkins to Richard P. Conlon, "Opinion Letter," February 26, 1981, DSG Papers, Library of Congress, Box II-36, Folder 16.

30. See Mark F. Ferber, "The Formation of the Democratic Study Group," in Nelson W. Polsby, ed., *Congressional Behavior* (New York: Random House, 1971), 249–269.

31. Interview with Richard Conlon, 1974, DSG Papers, Box II-2, Folder 13.

32. Richard Conlon, interview by Thomas Mann, 1971, DSG Papers, Box II-2, Folder 13.

33. Linda Heller Kamm, personal interview, July 16, 2013.

34. "Campaign Workshop No. 1, News Coverage," 1968 Democratic National Convention, Chicago, August 26, 1968, 13, DSG Papers, Box I-4, Folder 1.

35. Marti Conlon, telephone interview, August 7, 2013.

36. "Campaign Workshop No. 1, News Coverage," 13.

37. DSG Papers, Box II-2, Folder 13. This is part of a handwritten transcript of an interview that Mann had conducted with Conlon, very likely for the paper he co-authored with Arthur H. Miller and Arthur G. Stevens Jr. and delivered at the American Political Science Association annual meeting in September 1971.

38. Norman C. Miller, "House Liberals: A Frustrated Majority," *Wall Street Journal,* September 4, 1969, 8.

39. There are substantial numbers of DSG publications not only in the DSG Papers at the Library of Congress but also in the Frank Thompson Papers at the Seeley Mudd Library at Princeton University. In the Frank Thompson Papers, see, for instance, Box 162 for Conlon-era publications and Box 386 for many publications from 1962. Marti Conlon's remarks are from a phone interview with her and with her son Charles Conlon, August 7, 2013.

40. Roy Dye, telephone interview, September 2013.

41. Telephone interview with Marti Conlon and Charles Conlon, August 7, 2013.

42. Burton D. Sheppard, *Rethinking Congressional Reform* (Cambridge, MA: Schenkman Books, 1985), 40. Sheppard's detailed study is strongly informed by a set of interviews in 1975 with Richard Conlon; Rep. James O'Hara (D-Mich.), a key DSG leader; Rep. Richard Bolling (D-Mo.), a leading voice for procedural reform; and Rep. Wayne Hays (D-Ohio), a powerful House committee chairman.

43. My interpretation here is informed by Sheppard, *Rethinking Congressional Reform;* Zelizer, *On Capitol Hill;* and the other works cited above.

44. Ornstein and Rohde, "The Strategy of Reform," 3.

45. From undated interview, quoted in Ornstein and Rohde, "The Strategy of Reform," 2.

46. Unidentified liberal House member, quoted in Ornstein and Rohde, "The Strategy of Reform," 3.

47. Interview with unidentified Executive Committee member, quoted in Ornstein and Rohde, "The Strategy of Reform," 4.

48. Democratic Study Group, "Secrecy in the House of Representatives," June 24, 1970, 7, O'Hara Papers, Box 12, Folder "Congressional Reorganization 1."

49. Ibid., 8.

50. This account follows the narrative in Sheppard, *Rethinking Congressional Reform,* 37–49. See also Donald Rumsfeld, *Known and Unknown: A Memoir* (New York: Penguin Sentinel, 2011), 95.

51. Ornstein and Rohde, "The Strategy of Reform," 5.

52. Roy Dye, telephone interview with author, September 2013.

53. Cited in Sheppard, *Rethinking Congressional Reform,* 52.

54. "Edited Version of 7/5/74 Interview with Richard Conlon, Staff Director, DSG," 19–20, DSG Papers, Box II-2, Folder 13.

55. Richard Conlon to Frank Eleazar, July 12, 1979, DSG Papers, Box II-162, Folder 5. Conlon may have exaggerated Eleazar's role in this letter. In his 1974 interview, all he said is that Eleazar observed that he couldn't get his editor's attention on the topic of procedural reforms in Congress.

56. Tom Wicker, "In the Nation: Democracy in Action," *New York Times,* July 12, 1970; *Los Angeles Times,* "Congress, Heal Thyself," July 14, 1970; *New*

York Post, "Ending Secrecy in the House," July 10, 1970; *Washington Evening Star,* "On the Record," July 13, 1970; and *Washington Post,* "Striking at Secrecy in the House." These and many other press clippings can be found in DSG Papers, Box II-129, Folder 2.

57. DSG Papers, Box II-162, Folder 4.

58. "Special Report: Secrecy in the House of Representatives," June 24, 1970, DSG Papers, Box I-4, Folder 7.

59. Email from Roy Dye, November 24, 2014.

60. Richard Conlon, interview, July 5, 1974. This is a typed transcript of an interview with Conlon in DSG Papers, Box II-2, Folder 13. There is no indication of who conducted the interview or for what purpose.

61. Ornstein and Rohde, "The Strategy of Reform," 8. Many editorials and other news clippings the DSG generated are collected in the DSG Papers, Box II-129, Folder 2.

62. Ornstein and Rohde, "The Strategy of Reform," 12.

63. In 1985 Rep. Bill Frenzel (R-Minn.), who described himself as having been earlier an "open meeting freak," had come around to finding closed meetings "less flawed" and building "much stronger" consensuses. "I think it's the only way to fly." Cited in Leroy N. Rieselbach, *Congressional Reform: The Changing Modern Congress* (Washington, DC: Congressional Quarterly Press, 1994), 107.

64. Rieselbach, *Congressional Reform,* 48, 49.

65. Ibid., 50.

66. Richard P. Conlon, "Response by Richard P. Conlon," in Dennis Hale, ed., *The United States Congress* (New Brunswick, NJ: Transaction Books, 1983), 240.

67. Ibid., 243–244.

68. Rep. David Obey, telephone interview, June 3, 2013.

69. Thomas Mann, personal interview, Washington, DC, April 10, 2013.

70. Rep. David Obey, telephone interview, June 3, 2013.

5. The Media's Presence

1. Henry Fairlie, "How Journalists Get Rich," in *Bite the Hand That Feeds You: Essays and Provocations,* ed. Jeremy McCarter (New Haven, CT: Yale Uni-

versity Press, 2009), 293–304, at 296. This essay originally appeared in *Washingtonian,* August 1983.

2. Ibid., 294–295.

3. Ibid., 303.

4. William Safire, *Before the Fall: An Inside View of the Pre-Watergate White House* (New York: Da Capo Press, 1975), 351.

5. Ibid., 342.

6. Fairlie, "How Journalists Get Rich," 294.

7. Ibid., 296. Fairlie asks, "How does the transformation of Washington into a media city debilitate the profession? How does it debilitate the political life of the capital? How does it debilitate the public?"

8. Telephone interview with Jean Heller, October 18, 2005.

9. James H. Jones, *Bad Blood: The Tuskegee Syphilis Experiment,* rev. ed. (New York: Free Press, 1993), 2. This is the classic account of the Tuskegee syphilis experiment.

10. Telephone interview with Jean Heller, October 18, 2005; Jean Heller, "The Legacy of Tuskegee," *St. Petersburg Times,* July 20, 1997.

11. David Halberstam, *The Powers That Be* (New York: Knopf, 1979), 611.

12. For a listing of these and other investigative teams in the late 1960s and early 1970s, see Michael Schudson, *Discovering the News* (New York: Basic Books, 1978), 189–191.

13. Bernard C. Cohen, *The Press and Foreign Policy* (Princeton, NJ: Princeton University Press, 1963), 20.

14. Roger Mudd, lecture, February 15, 2000, cited in Donald Ritchie, *Reporting from Washington: The History of the Washington Press Corps* (New York: Oxford University Press, 2005), 220.

15. Daniel Dayan and Elihu Katz, *Media Events: The Live Broadcasting of History* (Cambridge, MA: Harvard University Press, 1992), 203, 214.

16. Cynthia Harrison, *On Account of Sex: The Politics of Women's Issues 1945–1968* (Berkeley: University of California Press, 1988), 70.

17. On Washington, see Michael Schudson, *The Good Citizen: A History of American Civic Life* (New York: Free Press, 1998), 70; on Jefferson, see Leonard W. Levy, *Freedom of the Press from Zenger to Jefferson* (Indianapolis: Bobbs-Merrill, 1966; reprint, Durham, NC: Carolina Academic Press, 1996), 362–371. The term "press-ocracy" is used by a character in James Fenimore Cooper's 1838 novel,

Homeward Bound, and it is clear from Cooper's other writings of that era that he shared his character's contempt for the press and fear of its influence; see Schudson, *Discovering the News,* 12–14. On Theodore Roosevelt's "muckraker" speech, see Doris Kearns Goodwin, *The Bully Pulpit* (New York: Simon & Schuster, 2013), 467–496.

18. David Greenberg, *Republic of Spin* (New York: W. W. Norton, forthcoming).

19. Katherine Fink and Michael Schudson, "The Rise of Contextual Reporting, 1950s–2000s," *Journalism: Theory, Practice, Criticism* 15, no. 1 (January 2014): 3–20. I am indebted to Kate Fink for her research, ideas, and editorial collaboration in the original article and for permitting me to incorporate our jointly created work in this new setting.

20. Michael J. Robinson, "Three Faces of Congressional Media," in Thomas Mann and Norman Ornstein, eds., *The New Congress* (Washington, DC: American Enterprise Institute, 1981), 55.

21. Potter Stewart, " 'Or of the Press,' " *Hastings Law Journal* 26 (1974–1975): 631.

22. Donald R. Matthews, *U.S. Senators and Their World* (New York: Vintage Books, 1960), 207.

23. Ibid., 214.

24. Joe S. Foote, "Rayburn, the Workhorse," in Everette E. Dennis and Robert W. Snyder, eds., *Covering Congress* (New Brunswick, NJ: Transaction Publishers, 1998), 139–146.

25. See the somewhat different accounts in Ronald Steel, *Walter Lippmann and the American Century* (Boston: Atlantic Monthly Press, 1980), 418–419, and James Reston, *Deadline* (New York: Random House, 1991), 156–161.

26. For examples, see Michael Schudson, "Persistence of Vision: Partisan Journalism in the Mainstream Press," in Carl F. Kaestle and Janice A. Radway, eds., *Print in Motion,* vol. 4 of *A History of the Book in America* (Chapel Hill, NC: University of North Carolina Press, 2009), 140–150.

27. Julian E. Zelizer, "Without Restraint: Scandal and Politics in America," in M. C. Carnes, ed., *The Columbia History of Post–World War II America* (New York: Columbia University Press, 2007), 230.

28. Ibid., 236.

29. Kathy R. Forde, "Discovering the Explanatory Report in American Newspapers," *Journalism Practice* 1 (2007): 230.

30. Stephen Hess, "Washington Reporters," *Society* 18, no. 4 (1981): 57.

31. Carl Sessions Stepp, "Then and Now." *American Journalism Review* 21 (1999): 60–75, at 65.

32. Thomas R. Patterson, *Out of Order* (New York: Knopf, 1993), 20.

33. Jeffrey E. Cohen, *The Presidency in the Era of 24-Hour News* (Princeton, NJ: Princeton University Press, 2008), 91. Cohen's figures summarize a study by Lynn Ragsdale.

34. Patterson, *Out of Order,* 11–12, 68–77.

35. Timothy Crouse, *The Boys on the Bus* (New York: Ballantine, 1973), 36–38.

36. Steven E. Clayman, Marc N. Elliott, John Heritage, and Megan K. Beckett, "A Watershed in White House Journalism: Explaining the Post-1968 Rise of Aggressive Presidential News," *Political Communication* 27 (2010): 229–247. See also Steven E. Clayman, Marc N. Elliott, John Heritage, and Laurie L. McDonald, "When Does the Watchdog Bark? Conditions of Aggressive Questioning in Presidential News Conferences," *American Sociological Review* 72 (February 2007): 23–41; Steven E. Clayman, Marc N. Elliott, John Heritage, and Laurie L. McDonald, "Historical Trends in Questioning Presidents 1953–2000," *Presidential Studies Quarterly* 36 (2006): 561–583; and Steven E. Clayman and John Heritage, *The News Interview: Journalists and Public Figures on the Air* (Cambridge, UK: Cambridge University Press, 2002).

37. Erving Goffman, *The Presentation of Self in Everyday Life* (Garden City, NY: Doubleday Anchor, 1959), 35.

38. Kevin G. Barnhurst and Diana Mutz, "American Journalism and the Decline in Event-Centered Reporting." *Journal of Communication* 47, no. 4 (1997): 27–52, at 32; see also Kevin G. Barnhurst, "The Great American Newspaper," *American Scholar* (Winter 1991): 110. Barnhurst's research is consistent with Stepp's findings. Stepp found a large reduction between 1964 and 1999 in the number of very short stories (under six inches long) in the ten metropolitan dailies he examined and a substantial increase in very long stories (more than twenty inches). See Stepp, "Then and Now," 62.

39. Stepp, "Then and Now," 62.

40. Patterson, *Out of Order,* 82–83.

41. Ibid., 79.

42. Ibid., 81.

43. Peter Benjaminson, *Death in the Afternoon: America's Newspaper Giants Struggle for Survival* (Kansas City: Andrews, McMeel & Parker, 1984), viii–x.

44. Kevin G. Barnhurst, "The Problem of Modern Time in American Journalism," *KronoScope* 11 (2011): 100–101, 114.

45. Lucas Graves, unpublished interview with Max Frankel, February 24, 2009, transcript in my possession.

46. A small group of "other" stories did not fit any of our four categories. For a discussion, see Fink and Schudson, "The Rise of Contextual Reporting."

47. Katherine Fink did the coding. Fink and Schudson discussed the coding on several occasions, going over individual stories to arrive at a common understanding of what the categories mean and how to categorize borderline cases. And there are borderline cases. No doubt we would be better off to have used two or more coders, but we see no reason to doubt that other sensitive coders would have come up with similar results. Of the 1,891 stories coded, the vast majority were easy calls.

48. Clayman, Elliott, Heritage, and Beckett, "A Watershed," 229.

49. Meg Greenfield, *Washington* (New York: Public Affairs, 2001), 83.

50. Ibid., 85.

51. Larry Sabato, *Feeding Frenzy: How Attack Journalism Has Transformed American Politics* (New York: Free Press, 1983), 31.

52. Ibid.

53. Douglass Cater, *The Fourth Branch of Government* (Boston: Houghton Mifflin, 1959), 107, 111.

54. Barnhurst and Mutz, "American Journalism and the Decline in Event-Centered Reporting," 45–50.

55. Donald Ritchie, U.S. Senate Historical Office, telephone interview, January 9, 1991.

56. David H. Weaver et al., *The American Journalist in the 21st Century* (Mahwah, NJ: Lawrence Erlbaum, 2007), 36.

57. Kevin G. Barnhurst, "News Ideology in the Twentieth Century," in Svennik Hoyer and Horst Pöttker, eds., *Diffusion of the News Paradigm 1850–2000* (Göteborg: Nordicom, 2005), 253.

58. Forde, "Discovering the Explanatory Report in American Newspapers," 229.

59. Monika Djerf-Pierre and Lennert Weibull, "From Public Educator to Interpreting Ombudsman: Regimes of Political Journalism in Swedish Public

Service Broadcasting 1925–2005," in Jesper Strömbäck, Mark Ørsten, and Toril Aalberg, eds., *Communicating Politics: Political Communication in the Nordic Countries* (Göteborg: Nordicom, 2008), 195–214; Susana Salgado and Jesper Strömbäck, "Interpretive Journalism: A Review of Concepts, Operationalizations and Key Findings," *Journalism: Theory, Practice, Criticism* 13 (2012): 144–161.

60. Frank Esser and Andrea Umbricht, "The Evolution of Objective and Interpretative Journalism in the Western Press: Comparing Six News Systems since the 1960s," *Journalism and Mass Communication Quarterly* 9, no. 2 (2014): 229–249, at 240.

61. Svennik Hoyer and Hedda A. Nossen, "Revisions of the News Paradigm: Changes in Stylistic Features between 1950 and 2008 in the Journalism of Norway's Largest Newspaper," *Journalism: Theory, Practice, Criticism,* published online March 24, 2014, 1–18, at 15.

62. Clark Kerr, *The Uses of the University,* 5th ed. (Cambridge, MA: Harvard University Press, 2001), 142–143.

63. David John Frank and John W. Meyer, "University Expansion and the Knowledge Society," *Theory and Society* 36 (2007): 287–311.

64. "The nationalization of higher education tended to establish a single standard for excellence—the model of the major research university." Thomas Bender, "Politics, Intellect, and the American University, 1945–1995," in Thomas Bender and Carl E. Schorske, eds., *American Academic Culture in Transformation: Fifty Years, Four Disciplines* (Princeton, NJ: Princeton University Press, 1997), 17–54, 21.

65. Christopher Jencks and David Riesman, *The Academic Revolution* (New York: Doubleday, 1968).

66. Jamie Cohen-Cole, *The Open Mind: Cold War Politics and the Sciences of Human Nature* (Chicago: University of Chicago Press, 2014), 23.

67. Bender, "Politics, Intellect, and the American University," 22.

68. Ibid., 33.

69. Cohen-Cole, *The Open Mind,* 4.

70. Ibid., 22.

71. See Joshua Gamson, *Freaks Talk Back* (Chicago: University of Chicago Press, 1991).

72. A stimulating effort at articulating the problem is Todd Gitlin, *Media Unlimited* (New York: Henry Holt, 2007).

6. "To Let People Know in Time"

1. Richard Nixon, "Remarks on Signing the National Environmental Policy Act of 1969," January 1, 1970, American Presidency Project, www.presidency .ucsb.edu/ws/?pid=2446. For one instance of the sense that there was a public demand for dealing with the environment, see Lynton Keith Caldwell, *Science and the National Environmental Policy Act* (University: University of Alabama Press, 1982), 52, where he recalls a "public demand during the 1960s that 'something be done about the environment'" but notes that this was rarely linked to specific legislative proposals.

2. Council on Environmental Quality Interim Guidelines, April 30, 1970. See Richard A. Liroff, *A National Policy for the Environment: NEPA and Its Aftermath* (Bloomington: Indiana University Press, 1976), 38.

3. Robert V. Bartlett, "Impact Assessment as a Policy Strategy," in Robert V. Bartlett, ed., *Policy through Impact Assessment* (Westport, CT: Greenwood Press, 1989), 1–16, at 16. Richard J. Lazarus, *The Making of Environmental Law* (Chicago: University of Chicago Press, 2004), 185, refers to "NEPA's legal revolution" and writes that NEPA "marks the commencement of the modern environmental law era." Bradley C. Karkkainen refers to NEPA as "the most widely emulated environmental policy innovation of the twentieth century"; see his "NEPA and the Curious Evolution of Environmental Impact Assessment in the United States," in Jane Holder and Donald McGillivray, eds., *Taking Stock of Environmental Assessment* (London: Routledge-Cavendish, 2007), 45–63, at 45.

4. Sec. 102 of the National Environment Policy Act of 1969 (42 U.S.C. 4321).

5. Wendy Espeland, *The Struggle for Water: Politics, Rationality, and Identity in the American Southwest* (Chicago: University of Chicago Press, 1998), 135, 142.

6. September 1, 1969, speech to the International Botanical Congress, Seattle, WA, Henry Jackson Papers, Allen Library Special Collections, University of Washington, Box 233, Folder 18; speech to King County Bar Association, April 8, 1969, Box 233, Folder 22; speech to National Soft Drink Association, San Francisco, April 18, 1969, Box 233, Folder 23; and speech to the annual meeting of the National Audubon Society, April 26, 1969, St. Louis, Box 233, Folder 45.

7. Address in Seattle, April 3, 1970, Jackson Papers, Box 234, Folder 30.

8. Richard N. L. Andrews, *Managing the Environment, Managing Ourselves: A History of American Environmental Policy,* 2nd ed. (New Haven, CT: Yale University Press, 2006), 314.

9. James Patterson, in *Grand Expectations: The United States, 1945–1974* (New York: Oxford University Press, 1996), 782, writes that NEPA established the EPA, which "was empowered to require" federal agencies to prepare environmental impact statements. This is not correct, however; NEPA established not the Environmental Protection Agency but the Council on Environmental Quality, which advised the president on the model of the Council of Economic Advisers. President Richard Nixon created the EPA by executive order in July 1970 as part of a government reorganization plan. During hearings Congress held on the EPA later that summer, it approved legislation that sanctioned the new agency. The EPA became a full-fledged, legislatively established federal agency in December 1970, many months after executive agencies had started preparing environmental impact statements. Kirkpatrick Sale, *The Green Revolution: The American Environmental Movement, 1962–1992* (New York: Hill and Wang, 1993), 26, makes the same mistake as Patterson.

10. In practice, the EPA has come to assume responsibility for reviewing environmental impact statements. See Charles H. Eccleston, *The NEPA Planning Process: A Comprehensive Guide with Emphasis on Efficiency* (New York: John Wiley, 1999). Specific provisions have been established by the Council on Environmental Policy in its Section 1502, "Regulations for Implementing the Provisions of the National Environmental Policy Act." See U.S. Environmental Protection Agency, "Submitting Environmental Impact Statements," www.epa.gov/compliance/nepa/submiteis, accessed July 2, 2014.

11. Karkkainen, "NEPA and the Curious Evolution," 45.

12. William N. Eskridge Jr. and John Ferejohn, "Super-Statutes," *Duke Law Journal* 50 (2001): 1215–1276, at 1215. Thanks to David Pozen for alerting me to the concept of super-statutes.

13. Eva H. Hanks and John L. Hanks, "An Environmental Bill of Rights: The Citizen Suit and the National Environmental Policy Act of 1969," *Rutgers Law Review* 24 (1970): 230–272, at 245.

14. For instance, Peter N. Carroll, in *It Seemed Like Nothing Happened: The Tragedy and Promise of America in the 1970s* (New York: Holt, Rinehart and Winston, 1982), 125, writes, "Responding to public opinion Congress enacted the National Environmental Policy Act of 1969." This is, at the least, disputable. Lynton Keith Caldwell, a key figure in the formulation of NEPA, denies that public opinion or environmental organizations influenced its development, sponsorship, or passage. Members of Congress "recognized an inchoate but

persistent public demand for national action" on the environment, he wrote. But NEPA was not a response to specific pressures. "In this respect, the National Environmental Policy Act was a political anomaly. It was not promoted by lobbyists, and although supported by the mainline conservation organizations, was not a product of their draftsmen. It developed its constituency after rather than before enactment, although in its drafting congressional committee staffs consulted extensively with groups interested in environmental legislation." See Caldwell, *Science and the National Environmental Policy Act,* 51–52. NEPA has had other, related effects—it had real consequences for the internal culture of executive agencies, just as Senator Jackson had hoped. Sociologist Wendy Espeland has closely studied the Bureau of Reclamation, a key federal agency of the Department of Interior that regularly makes decisions with enormous impact on the environment. The bureau is responsible for building dams and other projects that by providing drinking and irrigation waters and hydroelectric power have done much to enable the economic development of the West. Espeland was particularly impressed about this agency that in the 1970s "it changed. Furthermore, it changed in ways that most people would not have predicted, becoming more open and inclusive in its decision making." Espeland acknowledges that social movements that favored citizen involvement in public policy making, the writings of academics and law professors seeking reform, and improved mechanisms for citizen participation all contributed to these changes. But in her view, the single most important factor was "the passage of NEPA, which opened up agency decision making for judicial review." See Wendy Nelson Espeland, "Bureaucratizing Democracy, Democratizing Bureaucracy," *Law and Social Inquiry* 25 (2000): 1087 n. 10.

15. J. Brooks Flippen, *Nixon and the Environment* (Albuquerque: University of New Mexico Press, 2010), 1.

16. For the 20 million figure and the 1,500 figure, see Adam Rome, "'Give Earth a Chance': The Environmental Movement and the Sixties," *Journal of American History* 90, no. 2 (September 2003): 525–554, at 550. See also Adam Rome, *The Genius of Earth Day* (New York: Hill and Wang, 2013).

17. Lazarus, *The Making of Environmental Law,* xi, xiv.

18. Anthony Downs, "Up and Down with Ecology—The 'Issue-Attention Cycle,'" *Public Interest,* 1972, 38–50. Shep Melnick made exactly this point in a 1999 essay that criticizes Downs. Melnick offers a long list of prominent envi-

ronmental issues that have surfaced in the news, keeping the general issue of the environment alive for decades along with a consistently growing investment of the country's public and private resources in environmental protection. See R. Shep Melnick, "Risky Business: Government and the Environment after Earth Day," in Morton Keller and R. Shep Melnick, eds., *Taking Stock: American Government in the Twentieth Century* (Washington, DC: Woodrow Wilson Center Press, 1999), 156–184.

19. Downs, "Up and Down with Ecology," 49, 50.

20. Michael E. Kraft, Mark Stephan, and Troy D. Abel, *Coming Clean: Information Disclosure and Environmental Performance* (Cambridge, MA: MIT Press, 2011), 3.

21. Lazarus, *The Making of Environmental Law,* xi, xiv. Many others have also assessed NEPA as the keystone of environmental policy progress. For instance, political scientists H. Paul Friesema and Paul J. Culhane in 1976 wrote that it is "generally regarded as the single most important piece of federal legislation on the environment." See Friesema and Culhane, "Social Impacts, Politics, and the Environmental Impact Statement Process," *Natural Resources Journal* 16 (1976): 339–356, at 340.

22. Philip Shabecoff, *A Fierce Green Fire* (New York: Hill and Wang, 1993), 134, citing an estimate by J. William Futrell, president of the Environmental Law Institute.

23. Richard Lazarus, "The National Environmental Policy Act in the U.S. Supreme Court: A Reappraisal and a Peek behind the Curtains," *Georgetown Law Journal* 100, no. 5 (June 2012): 1507–1586, at 1510.

24. Lettie M. Wenner, *The Environmental Decade in Court* (Bloomington: Indiana University Press, 1982), 5–7, gathers the data on the frequency of litigation under different laws. The history of the Clean Water Act and its increasingly potent revisions is summarized in Claudia Copeland, "Clean Water Act: A Summary of the Law," Congressional Research Service Report for Congress, April 23, 2010. A very brief "History of the Clean Air Act" from the Air Pollution Control Act of 1955 on can be found at the EPA website, http://epa .gov/air/caa/caa_history.html, accessed September 21, 2012.

25. Wenner, *The Environmental Decade in Court,* 28–29.

26. Karl Boyd Brooks, *Before Earth Day: The Origins of American Environmental Law, 1945–1970* (Lawrence: University Press of Kansas, 2009).

27. Editors of *Ramparts,* "Editorial," in *Eco-Catastrophe* (San Francisco: Canfield Press, 1970), vii.

28. David Brower, *For Earth's Sake: The Life and Times of David Brower* (Salt Lake City: Peregrine Smith Books, 1990), 349. Eliot Porter's book itself preserved this theme of the importance of knowledge in its title: *The Place No One Knew* (1963). The trauma of the Glen Canyon Dam for environmentalists is indicated in the obituary for Martin Litton (Paul Vitello, "Martin Litton, 97, Fighter for Environment, Is Dead," *New York Times,* December 7, 2014). Litton, in his later years, "would speak more of his disappointments" than of his achievements, and "the one that seemed to haunt him most" was the compromise that allowed the Glen Canyon Dam to be built.

29. Cited in Rachel Carson, *Silent Spring* (Boston: Houghton Mifflin, 1962), 13. The Rostand line comes from a short essay he wrote, "Popularization of Science," *Science* 131, no. 3412 (May 20, 1960): 1491.

30. Carson, *Silent Spring,* 174.

31. Ibid., 177.

32. Lyndon B. Johnson, October 20, 1965, *Public Papers of the Presidents,* 1965, 1067, cited in James L. Sundquist, *Politics and Policy: The Eisenhower, Kennedy, and Johnson Years* (Washington, DC: Brookings Institution, 1968), 371. Priscilla Coit Murphy, *What a Book Can Do: The Publication and Reception of Silent Spring* (Amherst: University of Massachusetts Press, 2005) is a rich and fascinating account of the publication history of the book and its impact. There are nonetheless good grounds for some skepticism about the unique influence often ascribed to Carson's book on environmentalism, Ralph Nader's book on consumer safety, Michael Harrington's book on the "discovery" of poverty, and Betty Friedan's book on the women's movement. See David S. Meyer and Deana A. Rohlinger, "Big Books and Social Movements: A Myth of Ideas and Social Change," *Social Problems* 59 (2012): 136–153.

33. Brooks, *Before Earth Day,* esp. chapter 6, "Across the New Frontier: Nationalizing Environmental Law," 123–143.

34. 115 *Congressional Record* 29087 (1969), cited in Daniel A. Dreyfus and Helen M. Ingram, "The National Environmental Policy Act: A View of Intent and Practice," *Natural Resources Journal* 16 (1976): 243–262, at 246.

35. Robert Cameron Mitchell, "From Conservation to Environmental Movement: The Development of the Modern Environmental Lobbies," in Michael J.

Lacey, ed., *Government and Environmental Politics* (Baltimore: Johns Hopkins University Press, 1991), 81–113, at 97.

36. "Van Ness, Bill," in Don Schmeckel, Oral History Interviews, Allen Library, Special Collections, University of Washington, Seattle, Box 2, Folder 14. (A note from Van Ness to Karyl Winn of the University of Washington's Manuscripts and University Archives division reports that he reviewed Schmeckel's notes from the 1987 interview and found them difficult to comprehend. He rewrote them and had them typed up in 1994, and that's the typed transcript in the archives.)

37. The paper was published in *Public Administration Review.* It is also reprinted in Lynton K. Caldwell, *Environment as a Focus for Public Policy,* ed. Robert V. Bartlett and James N. Gladden (College Station: Texas A&M University Press, 1995), 27–41, at 36.

38. Russell E. Train, *Politics, Pollution, and Pandas: An Environmental Memoir* (Washington, DC: Island Press/Shearwater Books, 2003), 52. See also the oral history interview with Train on the EPA website, www.epa.gov/history/publications/train/04.htm, accessed August 24, 2004.

39. A. Dan Tarlock, personal interview, Chicago, August 10, 2012.

40. A. Dan Tarlock, "The Story of *Calvert Cliffs:* A Court Construes the National Environmental Policy Act to Create a Powerful Cause of Action," in Richard J. Lazarus and Oliver A. Houck, eds., *Environmental Law Stories* (New York: Foundation Press, 2005), 77–107, at 86 n. 29.

41. Lynton K. Caldwell, "Epilogue: Comprehending the Environmental Problem: A Personal Retrospective on the Evolution of a Concept" (1994), in Caldwell, *Environment as a Focus for Public Policy,* 326.

42. Wendy Read Wertz, *Lynton Keith Caldwell: An Environmental Visionary and the National Environmental Policy Act* (Bloomington: Indiana University Press, 2014), 76.

43. From Caldwell's unpublished notes, cited in Wertz, *Lynton Keith Caldwell,* 76.

44. Wertz, *Lynton Keith Caldwell,* 77. Two of Caldwell's former doctoral students would later write that Caldwell was about to "propose the wholly new field of inquiry now known as environmental policy studies," in which he would promote the previously unheard of need for a holistically oriented, interdisciplinary, and interdepartmental approach to resolving complex environmental

issues. See Robert Bartlett and James Gladden, "Lynton K. Caldwell and Environmental Policy: What Have We Learned?," in Caldwell, *Environment as a Focus for Public Policy,* 3.

45. Gifford Pinchot, cited in Stewart Udall, *The Quiet Crisis* (New York: Holt, Rinehart, and Winston, 1963), 105.

46. The Leopold story, which he reported in his *Sand County Almanac,* provides the title for *New York Times* environmental reporter Philip Shabecoff's book *A Fierce Green Fire* and is retold in that book on 89. Shabecoff also notes the moments of transformation of Pinchot (66) and Muir (70).

47. Dwight D. Eisenhower, "Veto of Bill to Amend the Federal Water Pollution Control Act," February 22, 1960, www.presidency.ucsb.edu/ws/?pid=12103.

48. John F. Kennedy, "Introduction," in Udall, *The Quiet Crisis,* xiii.

49. Lyndon B. Johnson, Special Message to the Congress on Conservation and Restoration of Natural Beauty, February 8, 1965, www.presidency.ucsb.edu/ws/index.php?pid=27285.

50. Sundquist, *Politics and Policy,* 323.

51. "Beyond NEPA," 203, cited in Matthew J. Lindstrom and Zachary A. Smith, *The National Environmental Policy Act: Judicial Misconstruction, Legislative Indifference, and Executive Neglect* (College Station: Texas A&M University Press, 2001), 17.

52. Gaylord Nelson, oral history interview by Don Nicoll, December 5, 2000, Edmund S. Muskie Archives and Special Collections Library, Bates College, Lewiston, Maine, available online at http://digilib.bates.edu/collect/muskieor/index/assoc/HASH01dd/1a484ba6.dir/doc.pdf.

53. Ibid.

54. John C. Whitaker, *Striking a Balance: Environment and Natural Resources Policy in the Nixon-Ford Years* (Washington, DC: American Enterprise Institute, 1976), 264.

55. A. Clay Schoenfeld, "The Press and NEPA: The Case of the Missing Agenda," *Journalism Quarterly,* 1979, 577–585, at 581. See also A. Clay Schoenfeld, Robert F. Meier, and Robert J. Griffin, "Constructing a Social Problem: The Press and the Environment," *Social Problems* 27, no. 1 (October 1979): 38–61.

56. Schoenfeld, "The Press and NEPA," 581.

57. Philip Shabecoff, "The Environment Beat's Rocky Terrain," *Nieman Reports,* December 15, 2002, available at http://niemanreports.org/articles/the-environment-beats-rocky-terrain.

58. William Van Ness, interview with Terence Finn, May 20, 1971, in Terence T. Finn, "Conflict and Compromise: Congress Makes a Law: The Passage of the National Environmental Protection Act," Ph.D. diss., Georgetown University, 1972, 422.

59. Finn, "Conflict and Compromise," 422. Short of a detailed study of media coverage, I cannot say with confidence that the media did or did not give ample coverage to the environment. Some contemporaries thought there was too much media interest in the environment; others judged the media to be indifferent to the whole topic. In the end, actual media interest is less important than the perception in Washington about whether the media coverage was substantial or not. Finn cites a June 19, 1969, memo from Tom Jorling, a key staff aide for Senator Muskie's Public Works committee, in which Jorling wrote that "the Jackson proposal has momentum in the press, in the public and the conservation organizations. This momentum should not be underestimated."

60. Shabecoff, "The Environment Beat's Rocky Terrain."

61. Lynton K. Caldwell, "Administrative Possibilities for Environmental Control," in F. Fraser Darling and John P. Milton, eds., *Future Environments of North America* (Garden City, NY: Natural History Press, 1966), cited in Wertz, *Lynton Keith Caldwell,* 115.

62. Jackson, speech in the Senate, July 10, 1969, *Congressional Record* 115, pt. 14, 19009, cited in Wertz, *Lynton Keith Caldwell,* 180. On the emergence of federal authority over the economy, see Bartholomew H. Sparrow, *From the Outside In: World War II and the American State* (Princeton, NJ: Princeton University Press, 1996).

63. Senator Henry Jackson, *Congressional Record,* 91st Cong., 1st sess., 1969, CXV, Part 3, 3700, cited in Finn, "Conflict and Compromise," 396.

64. Congressional White Paper on a National Policy for the Environment, under the auspices of the Committee on Interior and Insular Affairs, U.S. Senate, and Committee on Science and Astronautics, U.S. House of Representatives, 90th Cong., 2nd sess. (Washington, DC: Government Printing Office, 1968), 9.

65. Ibid.

66. Caldwell provides a useful account of the evolution of his own thinking about an "action-forcing mechanism" in "The Environmental Impact Statement: A Misused Tool," in Ravinder K. Jain and Bruce L. Hutchings, eds., *Environmental Impact Analysis: Emerging Issues in Planning* (Urbana: University of Illinois Press, 1978), 11–26; on the checklist, see 12.

67. Lynton Keith Caldwell, "Problems of Applied Ecology: Perceptions, Institutions, Methods, and Operational Tools," *BioScience* 16 (1966): 524–527, reprinted in Caldwell, *Environment as a Focus for Public Policy*, 127–138, at 134.

68. Testimony of Lynton K. Caldwell before the Committee on Interior and Insular Affairs, U.S. Senate, 91st Cong., 1st sess., on S. 1075, S. 237, and S. 1752, April 16, 1969, 116. Caldwell acknowledges that it was at the suggestion of Van Ness that he introduced the idea of an action-forcing mechanism in his April 16, 1969 testimony and that the specific language detailing the EIS in NEPA was "worked out by William J. Van Ness and Daniel A. Dreyfus in consultation with me and others." See Caldwell, "The Environmental Impact Statement," 15.

69. Testimony of Lynton K. Caldwell before the Committee on Interior and Insular Affairs, U.S. Senate, 91st Cong., 1st sess., on S. 1075, S. 237, and S. 1752, April 16, 1969, 116. This paragraph is also reproduced in Lynton K. Caldwell, "The National Environmental Policy Act: Retrospect and Prospect," part of Workshop on the National Environmental Policy Act, *A Report,* 94th Cong., 2nd sess., Serial 94-E (Washington, DC: Government Printing Office, 1976), 69–86, at 74. In addition, this section draws on Finn, "Conflict and Compromise," 394–413, and on Caldwell, "The Environmental Impact Statement."

70. Whitaker, *Striking a Balance,* 27.

71. Helen M. Ingram, David H. Colnic, and Dean E. Mann, "Interest Groups and Environmental Policy," in James P. Lester, ed., *Environmental Politics and Policy: Theories and Evidence,* 2nd ed. (Durham, NC: Duke University Press, 1995), 115–145, at 128, 134.

72. Ibid., 125.

73. This is not unique to environmentalism. On government's influence in engendering the women's movement, see Georgia Duerst-Lahti, "The Government's Role in Building the Women's Movement," *Political Science Quarterly* 104, no. 2 (1989): 249–268.

74. Ingram, Colnic, and Mann, "Interest Groups and Environmental Policy," 125.

75. Ibid. For a detailed and lucid exposition, see Mitchell, "From Conservation to Environmental Movement."

76. Finn, "Conflict and Compromise," 465.

77. Ibid.

78. *Congressional Record,* 91st Cong., 1st sess., 1969, CXV, Part 21, 29053.

79. Ibid.

80. Finn, "Conflict and Compromise," 470.

81. Ibid.

82. Ibid., based on an interview with Charles Cook, May 7, 1971.

83. Ibid., 471.

84. Ibid., 471–472.

85. Daniel Dreyfus, telephone interview with Wertz, June 2006, quoted in Wertz, *Lynton Keith Caldwell,* 171.

86. Finn, "Conflict and Compromise," 490.

87. Richard N. L. Andrews, *Environmental Policy and Administrative Change* (Lexington, MA: Lexington Books, 1976), 13.

88. Finn, "Conflict and Compromise," 503.

89. Ibid., 504. Finn reports (from a May 20, 1971, interview with Van Ness) that Van Ness agreed that all the Muskie amendments to Section 102 were constructive (505).

90. Ibid., 503–504.

91. Rome, *The Genius of Earth Day,* 57.

92. This includes Lynton Caldwell, who called it "the most complete and comprehensive legislative history of NEPA." See Caldwell, *Science and the National Environmental Policy Act,* 169.

93. Personal conversation with Leon Billings and Tom Jorling, New York, October 28, 2014.

94. Finn, "Conflict and Compromise," 506.

95. Ibid., 504.

96. Ibid., 493, for the Van Ness memo, and 503–504 for Nelson's role. I had scheduled a telephone interview with Terence Finn for June 30, 2014, hoping to confirm (as much as the passage of more than forty years might allow) several matters with him, including this one. Sadly, Finn died unexpectedly on June 27, 2014.

97. Quoted in Finn, "Conflict and Compromise," 528.

98. Ibid., 547.

99. A. Dan Tarlock, "Balancing Environmental Considerations and Energy Demands: A Comment on *Calvert Cliffs' Coordinating Committee Inc. v. AEC,*" *Indiana Law Journal* 47, no. 4 (1972): 645–679, at 660.

100. Ibid., 660.

101. Lynton Caldwell, "Environment: A New Focus for Public Policy," in Caldwell, *Environment as a Focus for Public Policy,* 27–41, at 31, 38. This is the

essay originally published as "Environment: A New Focus for Public Policy?" in *Public Administration Review* 23 (1963): 132–39. See also Tarlock, "Balancing Environmental Considerations and Energy Demands," 660–661.

102. "Inside Interior: John C. Whitaker," 7, an interview with John C. Whitaker conducted by Charles Wilkinson and Patty Limerick, Center of the American West, University of Colorado, Boulder, November 19, 2003, available at http://centerwest.org/wp-content/uploads/2011/01/whitaker.pdf, accessed August 27, 2013.

103. Richard Nixon, "Executive Order 11514—Protection and Enhancement of Environmental Quality," March 5, 1970, American Presidency Project, www.presidency.ucsb.edu/ws/?pid=59077.

104. Andrews, *Environmental Policy and Administrative Change,* 28.

105. See Richard A. Liroff, *A National Policy for the Environment: NEPA and Its Aftermath* (Bloomington: Indiana University Press, 1976), 38–43.

106. Ibid., 4–5.

107. Russell Train, Testimony in Hearings before the Subcommittee on Fisheries and Wildlife Conservation of the Committee on Merchant Marine and Fisheries, December 7, 1970, "Administration of the National Environmental Policy Act, Part 1," 91st Cong., 2nd sess., Series 91–41 (Washington, DC: Government Printing Office, 1971), 3.

108. Ibid., 4–5.

109. *Calvert Cliffs' Coordinating Committee v. U.S. Atomic Energy Commission,* U.S. Court of Appeals for the District of Columbia, 449 F. 2d 1109, July 23, 1971, 1111.

110. Ibid.

111. On the journey of the Trans-Alaska pipeline, see a summary in Lindstrom and Smith, *The National Environmental Policy Act,* 86–90.

112. Karkkainen, "NEPA and the Curious Evolution," 55.

113. Barton H. Thompson Jr., "The Continuing Innovation of Citizen Enforcement," *University of Illinois Law Review,* 2000, 185–236 at 211.

114. Ibid., 186.

115. Mitchell, "From Conservation to Environmental Movement," 100–101. See also Ingram, Colnic, and Mann, "Interest Groups and Environmental Policy," 125.

116. Thomas Jundt, *Greening the Red, White, and Blue: The Bomb, Big Business, and Consumer Resistance in Postwar America* (New York: Oxford Univer-

sity Press, 2014), 201–203, documents the earlier teach-ins to make the point that Nelson should get less credit for the originality of Earth Day. I think Jundt's evidence should suggest a different conclusion: that Nelson had the political authority and visibility to put an environmental teach-in on the national map. Nelson, as Wisconsin governor, appeared on the national stage as an environmental advocate as early as January 1960. See Finn, "Conflict and Compromise," 17.

117. "The Guardian: Origins of the EPA," EPA Historical Publication 1, Spring 1992, available at www2.epa.gov/aboutepa/guardian-origins-epa, accessed August 3, 2013.

118. Lynton Keith Caldwell, "Understanding Impact Analysis: Technical Process, Administrative Reform, Policy Principle," in Robert V. Bartlett, ed., *Policy through Impact Assessment* (Westport, CT: Greenwood Press, 1989), 7–16, at 16.

119. Tarlock, "The Story of *Calvert Cliffs*."

120. Brian F. Noble, *Introduction to Environmental Impact Analysis* (Don Mills, ON: Oxford University Press, 2006), 10–11.

121. On the role of President Nixon's Executive Order 11514 (March 5, 1970) and the CEQ's first "interim guidelines" (April 1970), see Andrews, *Environmental Policy and Administrative Change*, 27–30.

122. One of the first changes in the EIS process from what NEPA drafters had in mind was that the statements became volumes long, not statements the length of a graduate-school term paper, and they became technically sophisticated, not summary statements that any member of Congress could easily follow. A second major change is that agencies moved toward preparing "environmental assessments" rather than "environmental impact statements"—much shorter and designed to support a "finding of no significant impact" (FONSI) so that the agency would not be obliged to prepare a full-scale EIS. By the mid-1990s, federal agencies prepared about 50,000 environmental assessments that led to FONSIs and, by comparison, only 500 EISes. Does that disproportion mean that the government has evaded the intent of NEPA? Not necessarily. To be awarded a FONSI, the agencies often have to modify their intended actions; in mitigating the anticipated environmental impact to reach a FONSI, they in fact accomplish exactly what NEPA hoped for. See Bradley C. Karkkainen, "Whither NEPA?," *New York University Environmental Law Journal* 12 (2004): 347–363, at 348. See also Karkkainen, "NEPA and the Curious Evolution," 58.

7. Transparency in a Transformed Democracy

1. Jennifer LaFleur, "WikiLeaks Publishes CRS Reports; Gov't Still Doesn't," ProPublica, February 10, 2009.

2. Morton Keller, *America's Three Regimes: A New Political History* (New York: Oxford University Press, 2007).

3. Bruce E. Cain, Russell J. Dalton, and Susan E. Scarrow, eds., *Democracy Transformed? Expanding Political Opportunities in Advanced Democracies* (New York: Oxford University Press, 2003), 10.

4. Bernard Manin, *The Principles of Representative Democracy* (Cambridge, UK: Cambridge University Press, 1997).

5. John Keane, *The Life and Death of Democracy* (New York: Simon & Schuster, 2009), 737.

6. Ibid., 743.

7. Ibid., 865.

8. George Kateb, "The Moral Distinctiveness of Representative Democracy," in *The Inner Ocean: Individualism and Democratic Culture* (Ithaca, NY: Cornell University Press, 1992), 36–56, is a brilliant account of what makes representative democracy a moral improvement over "assembly democracy" or participatory democracy.

9. John Keane, *The Media and Democracy* (Oxford, UK: Polity Press, 1991), 168–169.

10. Margaret Canovan, "Trust the People! Populism and the Two Faces of Democracy," *Political Studies* 47 (1999): 2–16, at 11.

11. Keane, *Media and Democracy,* 190.

12. Pierre Rosanvallon, *Counter-Democracy: Politics in an Age of Distrust,* trans. Arthur Goldhammer (Cambridge, UK: Cambridge University Press, 2006), 8.

13. Ibid., 15–17.

14. Ibid., 14.

15. Ibid., 19.

16. Ibid., 273.

17. Nadia Urbinati and Mark Warren, "The Concept of Representation in Contemporary Democratic Theory," *Annual Review of Politial Science* 11 (2008): 387–412, at 407. See also the papers in Sonia Alonso, John Keane, and Wolfgang Merkel, eds., *The Future of Representative Democracy* (Cambridge, UK: Cambridge University Press, 2011).

18. "About GovTrack.us," www.govtrack.us/about, accessed July 12, 2014.

19. "Congress at a Glance," Congressional Data Coalition, http://congressional data.org/congress-at-a-glance, accessed June 25, 2014. The Congressional Data Coalition was formed in March 2014, according to a March 8, 2014 post by Joshua Tauberer on his GovTrack.us blog: "The Congressional Data Coalition Writes to House Appropriators," www.govtrack.us/blog/2014/03, accessed June 25, 2014.

20. John Keane, "Monitory Democracy?," in Sonia Alonso, John Keane, and Wolfgang Merkel, eds., *The Future of Representative Democracy* (Cambridge, UK: Cambridge University Press, 2011), 212–235, at 213.

21. A book that early on recognized the term is Charles Peters and Taylor Branch, eds., *Blowing the Whistle: Dissent in the Public Interest* (New York: Praeger, 1972). On the damage that whistle-blowing does to many whistle-blowers psychologically, socially, and occupationally, see C. Fred Alford, *Whistleblowers: Broken Lives and Organizational Power* (Ithaca, NY: Cornell University Press, 2001).

22. On the 9/11 widows, see the account of one of them, Kristen Breitweiser, *Wake-up Call: The Political Education of a 9/11 Widow* (New York: Grand Central Publishing, 2006).

23. Thomas K. McCraw, *Prophets of Regulation* (Cambridge, MA: Harvard University Press, 1984), 210.

24. Ibid., 213.

25. Richard A. Posner, "The Rise and Fall of Administrative Law," *Chicago-Kent Law Review* 72 (1996): 953–963, at 954.

26. For an illuminating essay on the role of administrative cultures, see James Q. Wilson, *Bureaucracy* (New York: Basic Books, 1989), 90–110.

27. Richard C. Box, ed., *Democracy and Public Administration* (Armonk, NY: M. E. Sharpe, 2007).

28. Charles Reich, "The Law of the Planned Society," *Yale Law Journal* 75 (July 1966): 1227–1270, at 1244, 1259–1260.

29. Nadia Urbinati and Mark E. Warren, "The Concept of Representation in Contemporary Democratic Theory," *Annual Review of Political Science* 11 (2008): 387–412, at 402.

30. George Gallup and Saul Forbes Rae, *The Pulse of Democracy: The Public Opinion Poll and How It Works* (New York: Simon & Schuster, 1940). On Gallup and the argument he and Rae present in this book, see also Michael Schudson,

The Good Citizen: A History of American Civic Life (New York: Free Press, 1998), 223–228.

31. Charles Tilly, *Social Movements, 1768–2004* (Boulder, CO: Paradigm, 2004), 29.

32. Ibid.

33. Ibid.

34. David S. Meyer and Sidney Tarrow, *The Social Movement Society: Contentious Politics for a New Century* (Lanham, MD: Rowman and Littlefield, 1998), 4.

35. Kay Lehman Schlozman and John T. Tierney, *Organized Interests and American Democracy* (New York: Harper & Row, 1986), 75.

36. Jack Walker, "The Origins and Maintenance of Interest Groups in America," *American Political Science Review* 77, no. 2 (1983): 390–406, at 397; Burdett A. Loomis and Allan J. Cigler, "Introduction: The Changing Nature of Interest Group Politics," in Allan J. Cigler and Burdett A. Loomis, eds., *Interest Group Politics*, 5th ed. (Washington, DC: CQ Press, 1998), 1–32, at 20.

37. Here I follow in part the account in G. Calvin Mackenzie, *Irony of Reform: Roots of American Political Disenchantment* (Boulder, CO: Westview Press, 1996), 59–60.

38. Paul Burstein, *Discrimination, Jobs, and Politics* (Chicago: University of Chicago Press, 1985), 17.

39. William Leuchtenberg, *The Supreme Court Reborn* (New York: Oxford University Press, 1995), 235.

40. William Haltom and Michael McCann, *Distort-ing the Law: Politics, Media, and the Litigation Crisis* (Chicago: University of Chicago Press, 2004).

41. Richard Abel, "The Real Tort Crisis—Too Few Claims," *Ohio State Law Journal* 48 (1987): 450.

42. Ibid., 454.

43. Council of the Inspectors General on Integrity and Efficiency, *A Progress Report to the President, Fiscal Year 2008,* September 8, 2009, https://www.ignet.gov/sites/default/files/files/fy08apr.pdf.

44. Larry Sabato, *Elections American Style* (Washington, DC: Brookings Institution, 1987), 155–179, at 171.

45. Ibid., 171–172.

46. Julian E. Zelizer, "Seeds of Cynicism: The Struggle over Campaign Finance, 1956–1974," *Journal of Policy History* 14, no. 1 (2002): 73–111, at 105.

47. S. Patterson, "The Semi-Sovereign Congress," in Anthony King, ed., *The New American Political System* (Washington, DC: American Enterprise Institute, 1978), 165.

48. Walter Lippmann, *Liberty and the News* (1920; repr., Princeton, NJ: Princeton University Press, 2008), 53.

49. James S. Pope to Rep. John E. Moss Jr., August 12, 1955, reprinted as Appendix E in Paul E. Kostyu, "The Moss Connection: The Freedom of Information Movement, Influence and John E. Moss, Jr.," Ph.D. dissertation, Bowling Green State University, 1990, 320–322.

50. Lippmann, *Liberty and the News* 55–56.

51. Thomas Medvetz, *Think Tanks in America* (Chicago: University of Chicago Press, 2012), 50.

52. I attended the ASAP workshop in San Jose, California, in 2006. These remarks come from my notes on the conference.

53. Katherine Mangu-Ward, "Transparency Chic," *Wall Street Journal,* August 21, 2009.

54. See Al Kamen, "Who's Lobbying Whom, Cross-Border Edition," *Washington Post,* August 21, 2009, for the beginnings of the Sunlight Foundation/ProPublica collaboration. For its current status, see www.foreign.influenceexplorer.com.

8. Disclosure and Its Discontents

1. Peter Galison, "Removing Knowledge," *Critical Inquiry* 31 (2004): 229–243.

2. See, for instance, Judith Resnik, "Uncovering, Disclosing, and Discovering How the Public Dimensions of Court-Based Processes Are at Risk," *Chicago-Kent Law Review* 81 (2006): 101–151. See also Joseph F. Anderson Jr., "Hidden from the Public by Order of the Court: The Case against Government-Enforced Secrecy," *South Carolina Law Review* 55 (2004): 711; Judith Resnik, "Due Process: A Public Dimension," *University of Florida Law Review* 39 (1987): 405–426, at 405; Emily Bazelon, "Public Access to Juvenile and Family Court: Should the Courtroom Doors Be Open or Closed?," *Yale Law and Policy Review* 155 (1999): 18; Jonathan Simon, "Parrhesiastic Accountability: Investigatory Commissions and Executive Power in an Age of Terror," *Yale Law Journal* 114 (2005): 1419; Arthur R. Miller, "Confidentiality, Protective Orders

and Public Access to the Courts," *Harvard Law Review* 105 (1991): 427–502; Richard L. Marcus, "The Discovery Confidentiality Controversy," *University of Illinois Law Review,* 1991, 457–506.

3. Ronald Inglehart, *The Silent Revolution: Changing Values and Political Styles among Western Publics* (Princeton, NJ: Princeton University Press, 1977), 3.

4. Ibid., 4.

5. Ronald Inglehart and Christian Welzel, *Modernization, Cultural Change, and Democracy: The Human Development Sequence* (Cambridge, UK: Cambridge University Press, 2005), 101. The 1970 data were collected by the European Union and included six EU member nations. The United States and several other countries were added, as were additional questions, in work that Inglehart undertook in 1973, and many subsequent surveys with the same and similar questions have been undertaken by Inglehart and colleagues since.

6. Daniel Dayan and Elihu Katz, *Media Events* (Cambridge, MA: Harvard University Press, 1992), 203.

7. Quoted in Keith W. Olson, *Watergate: The Presidential Scandal That Shook America* (Lawrence: University Press of Kansas, 2003), 129. The quote is from a *Christian Science Monitor* interview, December 26, 1973.

8. Ellen Herman, "Being and Doing: Humanistic Psychology and the Spirit of the 1960s," in Barbara L. Tischler, ed., *Sights on the Sixties* (New Brunswick, NJ: Rutgers University Press, 1992), 87–101, at 98.

9. Carl Bridenbaugh, "The Great Mutation," *American Historical Review* 68 (1963), cited and discussed in Peter Novick, *That Noble Dream: The "Objectivity Question" and the American Historical Profession* (New York: Cambridge University Press, 1988), 339.

10. Gary B. Nash, "American History Reconsidered: Asking New Questions about the Past," in Diane Ravitch and Maris Vinovskis, eds., *Learning from the Past: What History Teaches Us about School Reform* (Baltimore: Johns Hopkins University Press, 1995), 135–163, at 140–142. The quotation from Bridenbaugh is from his "The Great Mutation," quoted in Novick, *That Noble Dream,* 173.

11. Laura J. Miller and David Paul Nord, "Reading the Data on Books, Newspapers, and Magazines: A Statistical Appendix," in David Paul Nord, Joan Shelley Rubin, and Michael Schudson, eds., *The Enduring Book,* vol. 5 of *A History of the Book in America* (Chapel Hill: University of North Carolina Press, 2009), 511.

12. I borrow the language suggesting that contemporary democracy is "different," rather than better or worse, from Michael Saward, "Making Repre-

sentations: Modes and Strategies of Political Parties," *European Review* 16, no. 3 (July 2008): 271–286, at 272, 283–284.

13. G. Calvin MacKenzie and Robert Weisbrot, *The Liberal Hour* (New York: Penguin Books, 2008).

14. Timothy D. Lytton, *Holding Bishops Accountable: How Lawsuits Helped the Catholic Church Confront Clergy Sexual Abuse* (Cambridge, MA: Harvard University Press, 2008).

15. Cathy Lynn Grossman, "Wash. Diocese to File for Bankruptcy," *USA Today,* November 11, 2004. The Spokane, Portland, and Tucson dioceses all announced bankruptcy filings in 2004.

16. Robert Wuthnow, *The Restructuring of American Religion* (Princeton, NJ: Princeton University Press, 1988), 88–89.

17. See Linda Bird Francke with Lisa Whitman, "Growing up with Judy," *Newsweek,* October 9, 1978, 99; Julie Salmon, "Judy Blume, Girls' Friend, Makes a Move to the Movies," *New York Times,* April 8, 2004; Annie Gottlieb, "A New Cycle in 'YA' Books," *New York Times Book Review,* June 17, 1984.

18. Molly M. Ginty, "Our Bodies, Ourselves Turns 35 Today," *Women's Enews,* August 12, 2004, www.womensenews.org/article/cfm/dyn/aid/1820/context/archive. See Kathy Davis, *The Making of "Our Bodies, Ourselves": How Feminism Travels across Borders* (Durham, NC: Duke University Press, 2007) for an interesting study of the book's international influence.

Acknowledgments

This book follows up my 1998 book, *The Good Citizen,* where I made the argument that contemporary American democracy is not a fulfillment of the dreams of the founding fathers but the reconstruction of them for a world very different from the one the founders imagined—one that accepts at the voting booth people without property as well as the propertied class, blacks as well as whites, women as well as men. None of this was anticipated in 1776 or 1787. At the voting booth, citizens would (finally, in 1914) vote directly for representatives to the U.S. Senate as well as the House and might sometimes, in some states, also vote directly on legislative proposals. In the post-1945 era, citizens who once focused their political action primarily on elections and related affairs of political parties moved in large numbers to join policy-oriented civic organizations, to participate in social movements, and even to become litigants in rights-oriented lawsuits. Political theorists have been searching for several decades now for a vocabulary to describe and help assess this new incarnation of democracy the founders did not foresee.

Once you accept that today there's much, much more to educating ourselves in self-governance than deciding who to vote for or learning "how a bill becomes a law," you begin to notice developments that do not have an assigned seat in the conceptual world of "there are three branches of government." We don't know how to place the news media. We don't talk at all about newly created institutions that straddle the separate branches of government, such as the

Freedom of Information Act (1966) or the Ethics in Government Act (1978), which has placed inspectors inside the various executive agencies with primary responsibility to report to the Congress and to the public.

This is just to say that I kept stumbling upon topics I knew little about or topics I had never heard of (such as the Legislative Reorganization Act of 1970). I knew of the Freedom of Information Act of 1966, but I did not know where it came from or who sponsored it, and not because I am unusually ignorant. The three most complete accounts of FOIA's origins, all of them Ph.D. dissertations, were never published as books and led to only brief published articles. Similarly, the only full-scale account of the legislative history of the National Environmental Policy Act of 1970, which gave us the environmental impact statement, is an extraordinary unpublished 1972 Ph.D. dissertation.

So it is no wonder that this book has depended greatly on interviews, unpublished materials, and historical archives. It would not have been possible without the John E. Moss Papers at Special Collections, California State University, Sacramento, and curator Julie Thomas; the Democratic Study Group Papers at the Library of Congress; the Philip A. Hart Papers, Clare Hoffman Papers, and James O'Hara Papers at the Bentley Historical Library, University of Michigan; the Esther Peterson Papers at the Arthur and Elizabeth Schlesinger Library on the History of Women in America, Radcliffe Institute for Advanced Study, Harvard University; the Consumer Movement Archives at the Richard L. D. and Marjorie J. Morse Department of Special Collections, Hale Library, Kansas State University, and curator Anthony R. Crawford; the Oral History Collection, Butler Library, Columbia University; the Frank Thompson Papers at the Seeley G. Mudd Manuscript Library, Princeton University; the Senator Henry Jackson Papers at Special Collections, Allen Library, University of Washington, Seattle; the Benjamin S. Rosenthal Papers at the Benjamin S. Rosenthal Library, Queens College, City University of New York; the Freedom of Information Center archives at the University of Missouri School of Journalism; and materials made available online or through correspondence with the John F. Kennedy Presidential Library and the Lyndon Baines Johnson Presidential Library. Sambhari Cheemalapati at *Consumer Reports* sent me several relevant articles.

I had the great privilege of interviewing, in person or by telephone or by email correspondence, Peter Buxtun and Jean Heller concerning the revelations of the Tuskegee syphilis experiment; Marti Conlon, Charles Conlon, Linda

Heller Kamm, Roy Dye, Rep. David Obey, Thomas Mann, and David Rohde on the Legislative Reorganization Act of 1970; Kassy Benson, Benny Kass, Mike Lemov, Thomas Susman, the late Rep. Lionel Van Deerlin, and members of the John E. Moss family for the Freedom of Information Act; Leon Billings, Daniel Dreyfus, Thomas Jorling, A. Dan Tarlock, and William Van Ness on the National Environmental Policy Act; and Monroe Friedman on unit pricing and consumer information reforms. A special thanks goes to Wendy Read Wertz, who spent several hours with me at her home in Bloomington, Indiana, when I learned she was writing a biography of Lynton Keith Caldwell, who played such a key role in developing the conceptual rationale for the environmental impact statement. Wendy made available to me drafts of her book (which has since been published) as well as some of Caldwell's papers just as I was getting my bearings on the origins of the environmental impact statement.

I am grateful to more people than I will be able to remember who have read parts of the book and saved me from errors, although I have no doubt that errors remain. My helpful readers of various chapters include Charles Conlon, Marti Conlon, Roy Dye, Herbert Gans, Lawrence Glickman, David Greenberg, James T. Hamilton, Marjorie Heins, Richard Lazarus, Thomas Mann, David Pozen, Ellen Wartella, Wendy Read Wertz, and Julian Zelizer, not to mention doctoral students at Columbia University in two different seminars on transparency and society and doctoral students in one such seminar at the Annenberg School for Communication, University of Pennsylvania, who suffered through draft chapters as required reading.

Very special thank-yous go to Todd Gitlin and Nicholas Lemann. These friends, both of them thinkers I have learned much from and colleagues at Columbia Journalism School, bravely waded through the entire manuscript when I thought it was nearly ready—about a year before anyone should have had to read through it.

I have had great help from research assistants including Burcu Baykurt, Charles Berret, Aaron Freedman, Reno Gorman, Hyun Tae (Calvin) Kim, Nancy Lee, David Noell, Ben Peters, and Soomin Seo. Katherine Fink, while a graduate student at Columbia, worked with me on what became a coauthored journal article and the backbone of Chapter 5, as so indicated in that chapter. Others provided valuable counsel or guidance in conversation or the occasional email, more than I can name, but let me at least mention Chris W. Anderson, Brian Balogh, Robert V. Bartlett, Nancy Bekavac, Tom Blanton, Howard Brick,

Margaret Capron, Sarah Cohen, Sheila Coronel, Wendy Espeland, Archon Fung, Mary Graham, D. Lucas Graves, Robert Horwitz, Richard John, James H. Jones, John Keane, Paul Kostyu, Bernard Manin, Robert Manoff, Greg Michener, Dana Neacsu, Rasmus Kleis Nielsen, Barbara Osborn, Julie Reuben, Bob Snow, Paul Starr, Andie Tucher, Fred Turner, Charlie Varano, and Bob Woodward.

I have benefited from questions, comments, and criticism when I have presented parts of the book publicly. Thanks to audiences at the University of Colorado, Indiana University, the Medill School at Northwestern University, Pennsylvania State University, Princeton University, Stanford University, the College of New Jersey, the University of Michigan, the University of Southern California, the University of Wisconsin–Milwaukee, and the Center for Cultural Studies at Yale University.

I am grateful to MPL Music Publishing for permission to quote from "The Inch Worm" by Frank Loesser. Copyright © 1951, 1952 (Renewed) Frank Music Corp. All rights reserved.

What a work like this needs most of all is time. I am grateful to Columbia University for sabbatical leave in spring 2015, enabling me to complete the book. I am grateful also to Columbia for permitting me to accept a fellowship at the Annenberg Public Policy Center, University of Pennsylvania, in the spring semester of 2012, and to my sponsor there, Kathleen Hall Jamieson. Likewise, I am indebted to the Annenberg School for Communication for a fellowship in the spring semester of 2013, and especially to Barbie Zelizer, director of the Annenberg Scholars Program.

Twenty years ago Michael Aronson expertly helped shape some of my published essays into a book, *The Power of News,* for Harvard University Press. He has again proved caring and deft in shepherding this project, and I have felt myself in good hands throughout with him and the staff at Harvard University Press.

Julia Sonnevend has come into my life too recently for me to say that she has had a major role in crafting this book, but she has bravely taken on the task of editing *me*. A good editor, I think, finds something to love in the material before her but holds it to the best that it could be. I have always appreciated a good editor; I am very grateful to this one, the love of my life, and a joy beyond words.

Index